A Community of
Individuals

The **Routledge American Philosophy Series** presents original philosophical work advancing traditions of American thought so as to address new intellectual issues and global problems, as well as historical and theoretical studies of pragmatism, classical American philosophy, and related developments in American thought and culture.

Series editor
John J. Stuhr

Series advisors
Susan Bordo
Vincent Colapietro
John Lachs
Lucius Outlaw
Cheyney Ryan
Richard Shusterman

Books in the Series
A Community of Individuals
Pragmatism, Postmodernism, and the Future of Philosophy
Published in 2003 by

A Community of
Individuals

JOHN LACHS

Routledge
New York   London

Published in 2003 by
Routledge
29 West 35th Street
New York, NY 10001
www.routledge-ny.com

Published in Great Britain by
Routledge
11 New Fetter Lane
London EC4P 4EE
www.routledge.co.uk

"Education in the Twenty-first Century" originally appeared in *A Pedagogy of Becoming*, Jon Mills, ed., Amsterdam: Rodopi, 2002, pp. 219–228; "Valuational Species" originally appeared in *Review of Metaphysics* 51 (1997), pp. 297–311; "Improving Life," is also published in *Passing Dewey By*, Wm. Gavin, ed., Albany: SUNY Press, 2002; "Transcendence in Philosophy and Everyday Life" was originally published by the *Journal of Speculative Philosophy* XI (1997), pp. 247–255; "The Vague Hope of Immortality" originally appeared in *If I Should Die*, Leroy S. Rouner, ed., Notre Dame, IN: University of Notre Dame Press, 2001, pp. 127–139; "Both Better Off and Better: Moral Progress amid Continuing Carnage" originally appeared in the *Journal of Speculative Philosophy* 15 (2001), pp. 173–183; "Grand Dreams of Perfect People" originally appeared in *The Cambridge Quarterly of Healthcare*, v. 9, issue 03, July 2000, pp. 323–329; "Researchers and Their Subjects as Neighbors" was originally published in *Politics and the Life Sciences* 17 (1998), pp. 24–25; "Dying Old as a Social Problem" originally appeared in *Pragmatic Bioethics*, Glenn McGee, ed., Nashville: Vanderbilt University Press, 1999, pp. 194–203; "The Insignificance of Individuals" was originally published in *Transactions of the Charles S. Peirce Society*, XXXVIII (2002), pp. 79–93; "Neoplatonic Elements in the Spiritual Life" originally appeared in *Neoplatonism and Western Aesthetics*, Aphrodite Alexandrakis, ed., Albany, SUNY Press, 2002, pp. 143–152; "Peirce: Inquiry as Social Life" originally appeared in *Classical American Pragmatism: Its Contemporary Vitality*, S. Rosenthal, C. Hausman, D. Anderson, eds., Chicago: University of Illinois Press, 1999, pp. 75–84; "Metaphysics and the Social Construction of Human Nature" originally appeared in *The Philosophy of Paul Weiss* (*The Library of Living Philosophers*), Lewis Hahn, ed., Chicago: Open Court, 1995, pp. 73–83.

10 9 8 7 6 5 4 3 2

Cataloging-in-Publication Data is available from the Library of Congress
ISBN 0-415-94172-5 (hb)
ISBN 0-415-94173-3 (pb)

To my family and the community that made us feel at home

Contents

Introduction

The ideal of independent, self-determining people who care for each other intensely has haunted Western ethics and political thought. Unfortunately, a large number of obstacles stand in the way of any society coming even close to embodying this ideal.

On the side of individuals, we face problems with establishing centers of decency and mutual support in the educational system. Self-sacrificial courage to act on one's convictions remains difficult to sustain. Who counts as treasured neighbors or even as human beings is unclear. The content and scope of self-determination are also problematic, raising questions about how best to improve life and attain final values.

There are just as many problems on the side of community. Here we find ourselves driven by dreams of perfection. Wanting to right every wrong can lead to inhumanity and a painful confusion of aims. The goal of advancing science seems to justify the use of human beings. Valuing life too highly makes it difficult to allow the old to die in peace. We are ever ready to substitute our judgments for those of the young and old, the weak and the different.

Nevertheless, a look at our condition in historical perspective makes it clear that progress toward a better world is not a dream or an illusion. We enjoy healthier, richer and longer lives than any previous generation. The ties of commerce and communication bind us ever more closely to each other and educate us in benevolence. Our habits and emotions change as a result of improved material conditions, nudging us in the direction of decency, even if not of love.

The essays included in this book are unified by concern for how individuals can balance self-determination with caring for others in a humane community. They also display a unified vision that is identifiably American in its philosophical sources and in its melioristic attempt to do justice to the demands of individuality and communal life alike. I am not so optimistic that I ever forget the crushing reality of problems and the possibility of disaster. But, so long as I live, I live in the light, supposing that energy and intelligence can resolve many of our difficulties and that, in any case, the effort is worth making.

Those who have read my earlier work may notice a significant expansion of its scope. I have never before addressed issues connected with progress, transcendence and immortality. The courage of intellectuals and the calling of teachers also constitute new areas of interest for me. And the chapter entitled "Education in the Twenty-First Century" is an altogether different approach to teaching and learning from those I took in prior books.

Even where there are apparent similarities with earlier work, the careful reader will see significant differences. Although I have addressed the ideas of Peirce, Dewey and Santayana before, I did not do so on the topics included here. I have dealt with issues in bioethics before, but not from the perspective developed in these papers. And although the chapters "What Humans Did Not Make" and "Valuational Species" are continuous with my earlier work on human natures, they carry that argument significantly further.

In addition to an expansion of the scope of my work, this book also displays a change in its tone and emphasis. Although I am not in any simple sense a pragmatist, I have a growing appreciation and sympathy for many aspects of the pragmatic way of dealing with philosophical (and human) problems. The community is beginning to occupy a far more central place in my thought than I made for it in earlier work. Many of the problems I discuss here are deliberately cast as issues for communities. The distance I have traveled in this direction is shown by the argument in "The Vague Hope of Immortality" that any satisfying idea of the afterlife must involve salvation in the midst of our loved ones and not individual blessedness.

I hope that my readers will see the complexity of the issues with which I struggle even if they disagree with my approach to them. I am profoundly uninterested in technical philosophical problems. But I wish with all my heart to help solve the difficulties facing us at this stage in history and in our daily lives. If I don't succeed in solving anything, perhaps I can at least stimulate others to do better. That is the hope with which I offer these thoughts, in gratitude for the community that enables me to flourish.

I
Intellectuals and Courage

CHAPTER 1

Intellectuals and Courage

The will to group is one of the most profound characteristics of the modern world.
Julien Benda, The Treason of the Intellectuals *(1969), p. 4.*

Intellectuals do not enjoy a distinguished history of courage. There are, of course, shining exemplars of heroism among thinkers, writers and scientists. Some told the truth unmindful of the consequences; others were dauntless in their criticism of the established powers; a few even went to their deaths for principle. Zeno bit off the ear of a tyrant, Gandhi spent years in jail for his beliefs, and a number of Russian scientists lost their health, their freedom and their jobs for their resistance.

Most intellectuals, however, are compliant workers who don't want to bite the hands that feed them. Some, unfortunately, feel they are little people whose insignificance entitles them to cowardice. A few—we could all provide names—combine bad judgment with ambition and servility to emerge as particularly despicable human beings.

This is no different from the course of affairs among ordinary people. But intellectuals receive a great deal more public attention, and that is how the few courageous ones among them come to serve as icons of moral achievement. We focus on Dr. Schweitzer and on Dr. King, overlooking the acts of valor and endurance that surround us on all sides. Yet the proportion of fortitude among those who earn their living by the use of their minds is not likely to be greater than in the general population.

This is unfortunate for two important reasons. Being in the public eye, intellectuals serve as exemplars of how one is to behave. Thinkers and scientists seem to or ought to know what is acceptable or right. So people look to them for guidance in life, and such reliance imposes obligations. Furthermore, intellectuals in fact know or at least could know better than anyone else what is worth having and what we need to do to obtain it. The social investment such knowledge represents also confers serious, potentially burdensome responsibilities.

Freedom of thought and investigation, for example, is a structuring value of all the arts and sciences. Without it, we cannot hope to attain novel and sustainable results. Writers and scientists know the importance of being unhampered in their own work, so they have every reason to generalize this value and to support its application to social life. Although some parts of moral life are full of problems and doubts, there is no uncertainty about what is right in this case. Yet many intellectuals are willing to live with whatever restrictions church or state imposes, instead of acting as steadfast champions of freedom.

How can we understand such disappointing failures of nerve? A distinction might be helpful. Writers and scientists exhibit considerable intellectual courage. In the privacy of their studies and labs, they investigate boldly. They experiment with ideas and are always ready to abandon those that do not work. They follow the argument wherever it leads and are happy to embrace any conclusion the evidence warrants.

Intellectual courage, however, does not make for courageous intellectuals. One does not have to be very daring to think dangerous thoughts in quiet privacy; the test of valor is one's readiness to publish them. Opening one's mind to the public may have dangerous consequences, and it is just these consequences that one can avoid by remaining silent and letting the world go its way. Intellectuals worthy of the name do not lack the courage to think, but many of them lack the courage to speak, to act on what they believe, and to expose themselves to the effects of being unpopular.

We know why the people who run established institutions do not wish to be criticized. They think objections hurt their image and thereby diminish their power. To retain their privileged positions, they withhold information, which then entitles them to claim that things are vastly more complicated than any outsider can know. But why are intellectuals, who know that criticism is essential for the vitality of institutions, hesitant to provide it? There are at least two powerful reasons.

The first is well expressed by Benda in the claim that nowadays everyone wants to run with the crowd. The desire to be, at least in our opinions, indistinguishable from anyone else exercises great influence over us. Intellectuals no less than other people find it safe and comforting to fade into the group, to mouth favored dogmas and prejudices so they may convince their friends and employers that they are just regular folks, after all. The day of the great British eccentrics is gone. Perhaps they could afford not to care what others thought about them; for us even the bizarre is governed by universal rules.

The second reason for the failure of intellectuals to offer criticism is the sad one that they are afraid. In most of us, petty concern for self overshadows all other allegiances. Intellectuals want to be safe, they want to do well, they even rationalize and say they want to take care of their families. The fact is that they know criticism draws punishment, and they can't think of a principle for which they are willing to suffer. The great ideas of humankind are only abstractions, after all; concrete flesh and feelings, on the other hand, can really hurt. They reason that if the truth is destined to triumph in the end, it certainly doesn't need their measly contributions.

Pervasive misunderstandings of the function of scientists and writers lurk behind this avoidance of responsibility. Managers and the public at large think of intellectuals on an analogy with other producers of social goods, and those normally do not, and perhaps cannot, threaten the stability of the existing order. At a minimum, "knowledge industry" employees are expected to be team players, although they are always welcome to do what Marx claimed they were hired for and develop justifications of the status quo. Intellectuals themselves seem not to understand that their social role, like that of doctors, firefighters and the police, involves the potential for self-sacrifice: it requires that they value truth more highly than their private good. This is what renders being a writer or a scientist not just a wonderful privilege, but also a costly duty.

What makes thinkers and researchers different from other producers is that their job is to generate ideas. Nothing is potentially more destabilizing and revitalizing than a new idea. Many major advances and major collapses in the history of humankind were precipitated by ideas whose time had come. In spite of the known connection, however, we have not learned to deal with thoughts in a way sufficiently deliberate to capture their potential. This is particularly surprising and distressing today, when the availability of information and rapid reaction to it are essential for commercial, social, political and national success.

A society's thoughts constitute its most striking and most precious possessions. Learning to view the studies and laboratories of intellectuals as factories for manufacturing ideas might help the leaders of nations to keep this in mind. If they could think this way, they would insist on finding out about everything writers and scientists turn up: they would demand that each new idea be made public for assessment and potential application. It goes without saying that some notions are too clever or abstract or impractical to be applicable, while others have no conceivable use. Public laughter might eliminate a few of them, and open debate would show the weaknesses of many others. But that would still leave some whose potential value could be learned only by small-scale social experiments.

Politicians have, from time to time, paid lip service to just such trials, calling them pilot projects and hoping to learn valuable lessons from their successes and failures. Unfortunately, however, no one seems to have the courage to let them fail. As egos and careers become invested in them, they begin to be viewed as potential solutions to problems rather than as experiments. Moreover, knowledge that any experiment, once started, is difficult to stop makes us reluctant to try anything: we do not want society saddled with a string of enduring failures.

Convincing national leaders and the managers of institutions that ideas constitute our most important resource is, unfortunately, not enough. To be sure, it would make these individuals revise their view of their own roles: they would begin to welcome, even to seek, criticism and to think of themselves as initiators of improvement through change. But the public also needs to be taught to expect intellectuals to speak their minds. The central problem here is to keep people listening, in spite of the fact that a good deal of what thinkers and scientists and writers are likely to say will be of little value. Yet we can treat food with respect even if we do not carry home everything we see in the store. Similarly, we can dismiss many ideas as worthless, even as we look with interest to future fruits of thought.

Most difficult of all, we must find ways to overcome the diffidence and fear that beset intellectuals. Institutional reforms to eliminate punishment of criticism promise some results. But in the nature of the case, it is impossible to safeguard against secret retaliation. So a more positive approach might work better: we must bestow the highest honors on those who undertake to assess our practices and to pronounce judgment on them. Support of the existing state of things is necessary only when it is under external attack; for the rest, it has enough power and momentum to sustain itself. We can expect far more good from constructive, well-aimed critique. Criticism must, of course, be viewed as serious business. Fortunately, if we place a high social value on it, even those who engage in it will tend to respect its dignity and refrain from making it cheap or capricious.

If encouraging intellectuals to engage in public debate does not work, we may have to make it mandatory. As part of the job description of thinkers, writers and scientists, such participation would become a matter of habit. To get things going, we might have to impose the obligation that each intellectual undertake two or three critical sallies a year. Mechanical as this sounds, it would tend to break the cycle of fear and withdrawal in which many of the most intelligent humans are now caught. In the long run, intellectuals have to understand that they are on the payroll of the community in order, among other things, to warn us about our ways, to help us see our practices in perspective, to present arguments against what we are bent on doing and, again and again, to present interesting alternatives. Their job is to shake up state and institutional orthodoxies, instead of working to preserve them.

In unstable societies, intellectuals have an even more pressing obligation to contribute to public dialogue. Economic problems, social upheaval and political turmoil prepare fertile soil for irrationality. In hard times, it is attractive to look for scapegoats, to resort to desperate measures, to substitute naked power for consensual policy. Under such circumstances, thinkers, writers and scientists must have the courage to act as the consciences of their communities, even if they are the only people who speak on behalf of sanity and good sense.

The spectacular failures of human history hold important lessons about what simply does not work or works only for a short, painful time. The American philosopher George Santayana once said that those who do not remember their mistakes are doomed to repeat them.[1] Who but intellectuals are in a position to remind us of these errors, to warn us of impending folly and to present sensible alternatives to failed or suicidal policies? Who but thinkers and scientists have the knowledge and the trained calm to overcome panic and point the way out of our difficulties?

When intellectuals take public positions, they may find themselves drawn into the political power struggles of their society. This is dangerous because once they are perceived as partisan, they lose their claim to speak on behalf of the good of the entire community and with that they forfeit the attention of all who disagree. For this reason, they must scrupulously retain their objectivity and remain above the fray. They do enough in providing ideas and nothing of value in trying to ride to power on their backs. They set a great example by showing that not everyone is out for selfish gain and that cool reason retains its hold on better minds.

Beyond that, they need to remind us that acting on even the best idea is not a solution, only an experiment. No one, therefore, has the right to claim possession of the answers to our social ills. As in science and in all constructive thought, we must try the hypothesis that looks most promising and continue with it if the results bear it out. Such experimental work has borne fruit in intellectual life. Although it denies us the comfort of certainty, it represents the only intelligent approach to the broader problems we face.

CHAPTER 2

Reflections on Philosophy

Philosophy at the Center

The discipline of philosophy is thriving in our institutions of higher education: in most places, philosophy classes are parts of the core curriculum, philosophy course enrollments are high, and philosophy departments enjoy the respect of students and administrations alike. Even without the assurance of reliable statistics, we can feel comfortable asserting that philosophers teach at least as many students at least as well as ever.

One could argue, of course, that this success is the very danger we face. Socrates reached only a small number of select Athenians, and most of those didn't listen. Descartes corresponded with Princess Elizabeth and a handful of others; no fraternity boys paced near his oven door waiting to hear about his latest meditations. Student evaluations would almost certainly not have picked Kant as the darling of undergraduates at Königsberg. Perhaps we surrender our mission when we water down our message to address the crowd. Perhaps philosophy belongs in the margins and marginalizes itself only when it loses its soul by seeking a place at the center.

I find it difficult to marshal words adequate to express the wrongheadedness of this view. Its principle is elitist and its practice is to invoke the intrinsic value of learning to excuse irrelevance. On one level or another, important philosophical points can be understood by every college, even every high school, student. Many of these insights have direct bearing on how well people live. Failing to make them available or shrouding them in a fog of technicalities amounts to abandonment of our responsibility. We must not refuse to acknowledge the reason why our society makes an investment in us.

Philosophy becomes marginalized only when it distances itself from the problems of life. Obscurity, abstractness and pedantic complexity kill the interest of students whose spirits yearn to soar. We must beware of getting so absorbed in developing problem-solving techniques that we lose sight of the problems we want to solve. We must not allow our desire for finality to crowd out tentative answers when that is all we can have. We must not permit ourselves to be satisfied with clever quips about texts while we overlook the constraining facts of human life. And we must not join movements and schools of philosophy, abandoning our destiny to think alone.

If, in any of these or in other ways, we fail to keep faith with the grand mission of thought to guide our days, our philosophy will be left in the desert we created to starve and die. That is its proper fate. In the meanwhile, Plato's friends, returning to the cave, will continue to lead the multitudes, if not to the final light, then at least to a better life.

Philosophy deals with vitally important ideas and indispensable skills. It belongs at the center of liberal education because it liberates us to think about what matters in the end, to think in imaginative ways and to think critically. So long as philosophers honor their calling, free societies will honor them and students will flock to their classes. Robust philosophical ideas taught in an interesting way will continue to captivate young people, some of them so deeply that they will want to teach philosophy to the next generation. We must not hope for less and we need not ask for more.

A Future for Philosophy

The compartmentalization of knowledge and the departmentalization of the university have not served philosophy well. Even for its early practitioners, the discipline included what we now call sociology, literature, political science, psychology, religion, anthropology, biology, cosmology and physics. It continues to be barren without the knowledge provided by the empirical sciences and without the pollination of the literary imagination.

Confined to a department within the knowledge factory, philosophy acquires the need to justify its existence. Talk of educating people in how to think about things sounds vague, and exploring the thought of great past masters appears to make philosophy a part of the discipline of history. The mightiest justification is to adopt the ideal of the sciences and declare that philosophy is in the business of generating new knowledge. This requires proprietary methods and technical terminology, launching philosophers on a career of talking to one another with hairsplitting precision.

Philosophy's search for method was old news even in Aristotle's day. The history of the quest coincides with the history of the field. The search for intelligible forms, for synthetic *a priori* judgments, for the sensory originals of our ideas, for intuitions or self-evident truths, for the proper analysis of concepts, and for the suppressed *différance,* among countless others, has occupied thinkers for over two thousand years and made them famous. The arcane terms and peculiar turns of thought connected with each method constitute much of the graduate education offered young philosophers.

Such methods can suggest many fascinating and a few useful ways of thinking. But they have failed to establish anything firm and beyond dispute. The fact that philosophers have not succeeded in discovering new truths may explain the relatively low esteem in which they are held by practicing scientists and the recurrent proclamations of the discipline's demise. If philosophy cannot generate what we have come to call knowledge, people focused on measuring results are quick to declare it worthless.

Those who believe this lack one of the great benefits of philosophy: they cannot use the imagination to transcend accepted modes of thought. We don't blame manufacturers of forceps for failing to deliver babies or people working to purify our water for not drinking the faucet dry. In making knowledge, as in making anything new, some must fashion tools or provide essential services. The fact that the more uncertain and problematic their theories become, the more scientists tend to turn to philosophers (or turn into philosophers) suggests that the discipline can earn its keep by troubleshooting in the world of thought.

We have seen recent confirmation of this function of philosophy in all the troubled institutions of our society. The explosive growth of bioethics is due not to the desire of physicians to learn new medical facts from philosophers. They seem to recognize, instead, that people who think for a living may offer useful ways of conceptualizing the anguished decisions they must make. Business people turn to philosophers to sensitize them to all the factors and all the perspectives that must be considered in contested choices. Even government agencies employ philosophers to help them think through the public meaning and the likely consequences of their actions.

Philosophers have welcomed these developments because they provide jobs, but have not taken to heart the message they send about the discipline. Many continue to think that the heart of philosophy is pursuit of the elusive breakthrough that will convert some small part of epistemology into a science, and that work in applied ethics is justified only if it buys time for serious research. Nothing could be further from the truth. Work in hospitals and businesses calls philosophy back to its proper vocation; the value of advanced research must be measured by the skills and tools it yields to perform those services.

In this age of atomization that lavishes attention on isolated events and results, philosophy appears a relic of the past. Its aim in any context is to understand the total situation. It deals with individuals not as role-players or as fragments of the social whole, but as complex, living persons. In education, it cannot limit itself to teaching reasoning; it engages the habits and motives of people to make reasoning effective in their lives. In its theories, it must not focus on isolated, minute issues, overlooking their relations to one another and to the larger known facts about the world. In its labors, it should not concentrate on cognitive achievements unrelated to the concerns of ordinary people (including philosophers) in everyday life.

There is no greater social need than guidance in the affairs of life. In the depths of our souls, we know that not every problem has a technological solution. Human relations are always troubled, happiness is as elusive as it was in Plato's day, and aging, defeat and death demand painful personal responses. Since philosophers have abandoned their responsibility in this sphere, the public has abandoned philosophers. There is no shortage of sophists offering advice on how to live: televangelists, pop psychologists and newspaper gurus are the self-appointed sages of our age. Even among philosophers, few realize that only they can present the treasures of mature reflection. They need to rediscover that doing so is the final perfection of their art.

This does not mean that we must reject basic philosophy even as we welcome basic science. The reason for this, however, is that sometimes the best way to get the skills and tools to help in daily life is by not attending to premature applications. Philosophizing is, for its devoted followers, pure conceptual exhilaration and dialectical joy. But philosophy for its own sake is, in the end, of value only because it makes philosophy for life possible. The time has come to follow Plato back into the cave.

Teaching as a Calling

Professor, what do you profess? That teaching is a cushy job, even if it doesn't pay much. You meet classes for a few hours a week, hold an office hour, hoping no students will show up, and grade a few tests, preferably of the objective sort that take little time or thought. Soon, two semesters are over and you can enjoy the four reasons for teaching: May, June, July and August. Feigned incompetence, orneriness or criticism of the administration can keep you off committees, and as you become a senior member of your department, you can teach what you want. That means never having to change your notes again: you can read the same sentences to generation after generation of students from the same fraying three-by-five-inch cards.

Small wonder we recommend teaching to our graduate students as a wonderful career: we are held in high regard and earn a modest but comfortable wage with minimal labor. We are supposed to think bold new thoughts and add to the sum of human knowledge but, luckily, no one outside our narrow fields can judge what we accomplish. So we can create a great stir by relying on friends to extol our achievements in return for our praising theirs. The trick is cooperation, not so much in research as in promoting one another. We enjoy the benefits of a modern guild, much stronger than a union, in which we control the conditions of membership. Whoever joins and learns to play the game can delight in a life of petty power and comfortable pleasures.

This is a terrible picture of teachers in colleges and universities. Fortunately, as any account that emphasizes the negative, it is partial and therefore misleading. We must nevertheless face it squarely so we can avoid the temptation of enacting the worst stereotype of the profession. The problem of free riders that so occupies philosophers, sociologists and political scientists is especially acute in the academic world: unannounced retirement with full salary upon the attainment of tenure is a familiar phenomenon. Lucky the department that does not harbor at least one person who, contributing little, lives off the labor of others.

Professors are supposed to be both searchers after knowledge and teachers of the young. In what does teaching consist? According to a favored theory, it is simply the act of conveying information, whose quality can be measured by the quantity of transplanted truths. If this is correct, computers that send messages to other computers serve as their instructors, and the Internet may well be the greatest teacher of them all. But even if we exclude computers, the consequences that follow from this view are silly. For if I overhear my neighbors fighting, for example, I would have to say that they are giving me instruction about their feelings. And I would be acting as a teacher when I yell "Drop dead!" to the motorist who does not let me pass.

Conveying information is surely involved in teaching in some way, but it doesn't even come close to capturing its nature. If it did, we could simply dispense with human instructors and get our knowledge directly out of books. This, in fact, is an attractive option and constitutes a serious challenge to the person in front of the class. As students, all of us spent hours in the lecture hall in painful contemplation of how much more we could have learned by reading a book than by listening to a muttering bore. Teaching in our universities would be vastly improved if instructors aimed to transmit in each five-minute segment of their classes more knowledge or skills of a different sort from those one can get by reading books.

Admittedly, this by itself would not make for good teaching, but it would show respect for the time students invest in listening. The result would be similar to the work of a colleague I once had in history, whose speed in covering material was such that students who dropped their pencils missed an average of ten years.

Why would such teaching not be good? Because it misses the purpose of instruction, overlooks its context, and ignores its essential condition. The aim of teaching is the *creation of human beings,* its context is *personal caring* on the part of people who are older for those more inexperienced or young, and its essential condition is *intergenerational faith.* Without respect and at least an instinctive feel for these realities, teachers cannot succeed at their art. They remain highly trained employees of educational institutions whose lectures and seminars never quite display them as human beings who set standards of knowledge and caring by offering themselves as exemplars to imitate.

In teaching chemistry, for example, it may be attractive to think that our purpose is to convey as much as possible about the properties and interactions of elements. If this is the view we take, we may feel tempted to maximize learning by covering vast quantities of material and devising frequent, momentous tests of student memory.

Things look different if our primary objective changes from teaching the facts of chemistry to making good chemists. The emphasis then shifts from exercising inorganic memory to the development of such living skills as imagining consequences, reasoning about possibilities, and investigating with ingenuity and energy. Of course, none of this can be achieved without some knowledge of facts. But understanding the facts in their vital contexts is very different from remembering detached and therefore relatively meaningless data.

Teaching chemistry has an even more different complexion if we think its point is not to make good chemists but to contribute to the development of excellent human beings, some of whom may incidentally become chemists. Now even the skills of the chemist find their place in a broader context of activities and responsibility. Teachers must surround the growing skills of their students with awe at the power of human knowledge. They must present and endorse cautionary principles about the use of knowledge so that students will be inclined to enhance the human good or will at least find it unthinkable to rent themselves out to the highest bidder to supervise the manufacture of anthrax.

How does one create or contribute to the development of human beings? By caring enough to offer oneself as a model students can imitate. That, in fact, is the heart of good teaching, and it is not nearly as egomaniacal as it sounds. Good teachers don't have to be, and should not think they are, perfect in any aspect of life. No one is, and there is no reason to impose unreasonable demands on people. They just have to be good enough to be living embodiments of a standard worth attaining. If they aim to teach only facts, they have to show remarkable command of them. If they want to create good chemists, they have to be good chemists themselves. And if they want to contribute to the growth of humans, they must be grown human beings.

The reason for this may well go back to the evolutionary roots of human nature. Herd animals, particularly animals that hand down a culture, learn largely by imitation. The young follow the lead of trusted elders, thinking, feeling, and doing what they do. The search for role models is visible among children from the earliest stage of their self-possession. Parents who preach to their offspring without acting on their own precepts often find that their children follow what they do, not what they say. And the wearisome similarities of garb and habit among teenagers that so annoy adults cannot be understood without reference to the contagious desire to be like everyone else.

This line of thought explains why enthusiasm in the classroom is such an effective tool of teaching. Students detect the attitude of the instructor long before the transfer of information begins, and they adopt the valuations implicit in it. Teachers barely able to stay awake at their boring presentations engender nothing but tedium and disgust in those who have to survive four months of such living death for three credit hours. By contrast, I fell in love with Ancient Greek—a language required at my undergraduate institution in which I had no initial interest—because the excitement of the instructor was contagious.

If contributing to the growth of human beings is its ultimate aim, teaching is a sacred activity. The world's great religions agree that the sacred—whatever is touched or commanded by the divine—finds its focus in the creation and sustenance of human life. This is as close to an unconditional value as we need to find in order to orient ourselves in the world. The marvel of teaching, its preeminence among all the remarkable activities in which humans engage, is that by means of it we can participate in the divine process of creating the next generation. Priests and ministers labor only to bring humans to God; parents and teachers make the individuals who can be so conducted.

This is what people mean when they say that teaching is a calling; it is as if a voice spoke or, better, an arm reached out and made us do whatever needs to be done so the next generation can stand on our shoulders and know more, live better, and be more humane than any before. The connection between teaching and parenting is by no means accidental. Although teachers don't have to have children and they certainly shouldn't try to parent their students, both lines of endeavor offer opportunities to make a permanent difference in the lives of people and both demand self-sacrificial caring as the price.

At the risk of enraging those tempted to waltz through life thinking that a little attention and practice enable us to do most anything without grave cost, let me say that raising children does not work that way. Those who are unwilling to place the interest of children above their own should think twice about becoming parents. And, similarly, those who do not wish to devote themselves wholeheartedly to the service of young people have no business becoming teachers.

Nothing is as easy as becoming a parent—many face the prospect quite without intending. And similarly, there are few *jobs* as easy as being a teacher. But being parent or teacher in the full sense of the words is a very different matter, and exceedingly hard, because these are callings and not jobs. The problem we face is that both teaching and parenting have been trivialized or at least minimized—teaching, by converting it into a job, and parenting, by reducing it to a collection of jobs from baby-sitter to Bible-school teacher, none of which need be tackled by the mother or the father. In the process, we have lost the sense of the momentousness of what parents and teachers do, the touching and sacred intimacy involved in helping a soul grow.

Marriage as a preliminary to parenthood is one of the sacraments of many religions. Teaching has not officially been raised to this level. Yet the reluctance of some religious institutions to permit anyone but those ordained to serve as instructors is ample indication of the awesome significance of teaching. It is not too much to say that teachers constitute the lay clergy of the human race.

What I said about the purpose of instruction should be enough to convince anyone that I am an idealist about what good teaching demands. But lest you think that my standards are not only idealistic but also unrealistically high, let me ask you this: Would you rather have a teacher who is a nurturing mentor or one who is suspicious of your motives, oblivious to your feelings and contemptuous of your mind? And which of the two would you rather retain as the teacher of your child? In important matters, we should not be reluctant to affirm the ideal; we should hold it aloft as a banner, so that people learn what is expected of them if they decide to undertake the task.

Agreement concerning the purpose of teaching brings marvelous clarity to its context and conditions. Teaching, as all gifts, must be offered with appropriate style. If such words had not changed their meanings, the silk box in which we must present it would be marked "Caring" or "Love." Unfortunately, however, today, caring for someone tends to suggest that the person is ill or infirm; health care, for example, largely means caring for the sick. Saying to acquaintances that we love them, moreover, embarrasses them or suggests improper sexual advance. Yet love or caring in the sense of vital interest in their good is what students need from their instructors. They must be viewed as human beings with valid preferences, people who are full partners in the educational enterprise.

Too often, what we find instead is suspicion of student motives and disdain for the minds we must educate. Worst of all, instructors in institutions of higher education seem susceptible to the persistent error of supposing that their teaching responsibilities extend only to meeting their classes—that, in other words, they educate only the mind. Separating the intellect from the rest of the person is an act of pernicious abstraction that works poorly for professors even if they try it with their mates. It brings terribly distorted results in education, fostering the illusion that knowledge and decency are separable commodities. We see the result in the growth of the number of experts without conscience, of people who rent their fine minds unencumbered by moral concerns or fellow feeling.

The tendency to focus education on what can be taught in class is reinforced by the professionalization of disciplines and the competitiveness of universities. Seeing oneself as a chemist or a philosopher shifts the focus of loyalty from the local institution and its students to a discipline with international standards of achievement in research and publication. Teaching undergraduates plays no role in the life of one's profession. Even the training of graduate students must be incidental to one's research and can be justified only because it assures the continuity of one's discipline.

Universities competing for high rank in the ratings sweepstakes find it advantageous to take pride in the professional standings of their faculties. As a result, they hire and promote on the basis of peer-reviewed publications and letters of recommendation written by faculty peers. In an odd but very real way, this surrenders universities to the mercy of the disciplines: chemists determine the chemists to be hired, and philosophers, the philosophers. Teaching awards constitute a halting affirmation of the independence or the separate, local, nondisciplinary interests of the institutions. I call these efforts halting because they are inadequate to motivate the faculty: the reward for fine teaching is a few hundred dollars, while high disciplinary standing achieved by research yields annual salaries well in excess of a hundred thousand.

When I say that teaching must envelop the entire human being with its caring or love, I emphatically do not mean to direct us back to the coercive education in virtue associated with boarding schools, required chapel attendance and colleges acting *in loco parentis*. Love, even of students, is long-suffering and does not arrogate to itself the right to define the good for others. Students need guidance in self-discovery, not the imposition of uniform standards or ideals. The alternative to mindlessly enforced conventional wholesomeness is not the abandonment of character education but removal of the demand for uniformity and of the force applied to assure it.

The survival of the human race depends squarely on intergenerational faith. Adults may beget children unintentionally, but they don't raise them and educate them by accident. Many people get delight out of nurturing the young, yet there is also a deeper connection: in taking care of their children, they act as if they were repaying the love lavished on them in their early years. There is an obligation to return that love by caring for aging parents, but brightening the last years of existence is inadequate compensation for the gifts of life and personality. So we repay what we got from our parents by what we give our children: we return life for life, love for love, sleepless nights of worry for worried nights of sleep.

In spite of the stupid wars and hatreds that cloud the history of humankind, in spite even of horrid incidents of child neglect and child abuse, the faithfulness that passes the gifts of one generation to the next weaves a garland of continuity through human life. Teaching is a central part of what creates this fabric of human connectedness. By means of it, instructors return the gifts they received from their instructors and contribute to the continuity of human culture and shared life.

Surprisingly perhaps, from the moral standpoint, teaching is even more remarkable than parenting. For the concern of instructors is focused not on a few members of their families but on a multitude of strangers. The fact that these young people do not remain strangers for long takes nothing away from the self-sacrificial generosity of instructors who truly care. The idea that teaching is not a job has as its correlative the thought that it must be done with passion out of a commitment to human self-improvement and not primarily for pay.

Those who instruct without caring break the faith that safeguards the continuity of life. If the love of parents and teachers ever fails, there will be no new generation of humans, only an ordered multitude of humanoid machines.

Education in the Twenty-First Century

with Shirley M. Lachs

The fast pace of the modern world has at last defeated the risk-aversive conservatism of the human soul. We have come to accept, to expect, and even to welcome change. For a while, sound business practice was described as "management of change," and periodic alterations in product line, advertising and the appearance of things have become standard, though by no means always effective, marketing techniques.

Surprisingly, the conversion of universities to primarily business institutions has not imbued them with this veneration of change. The marketing efforts of institutions of higher education have moved in line with the state of the art in the promotion of business, but the product line has remained largely unimproved. This may reflect the imperfect control administrations exert over slow-moving, recalcitrant faculties. The faculty's jealously guarded power over educational programs has made curricular innovation difficult to achieve, especially in traditional degree offerings. Administrations can start new programs here and there, but when it comes to the all-important bachelor's degree, for example, they are selling nineteenth-century lipstick to smear on twenty-first-century lips.

The rapid development of the information industry may force major changes in the quiet hamlets of the academic world. At the very least, it is beginning to raise the question of what, if anything, the genteel and cumbersome residential university can offer beyond what is or will soon be available in information from the Internet. The question is likely to be-

---

Dedicated to Beth J. Singer, whose life as a philosopher and educator has been devoted to thoughtful caring.

come more immediate with each annual increase of tuition. It will become pressingly urgent with the next major expansion of the Internet and once ordinary Americans begin to feel truly comfortable seeking information by electronic means.

At that point, the monopoly colleges and universities enjoy over credentialing young people may no longer be enough to justify and sustain their existence. They may face the fate of industries built on outmoded technologies. Just as e-mail and the fax machine have displaced the telegraph, so learning at one's computer at home may squeeze out the lecture hall. Universities may go the way of Western Union.

Those who see college education with unclouded eyes readily admit that it is a tedious and inefficient process. Dull teachers, uninterested students, fragmented disciplines and forced study unmotivated by real-life concerns make progress slow and the long-term retention of knowledge improbable. But what good would retention accomplish, in any case? The volume of information conveyed in the undergraduate classroom is a tribute to the cognitive achievements of the human race, but very little of it is of any direct value to young people trying to make their way in the world. Hoarding it is like stockpiling old bottles, shopping bags and pieces of string with the justification that one never knows when they might come in handy.

Even the packaging of college-level courses reveals the essential unconcern of faculty for the natural beat of intelligence. Curiosity is fed by problems we encounter and respects no disciplinary bounds. It takes us wherever we must go to get the answers we need. The results are memorable even without the attempt to memorize them. The typical college course, by contrast, covers a mound of loosely connected facts and theories in disciplinary isolation. The selection of topics rests in the hands of instructors who rarely bother offering a rationale for what they require or teach. The emphasis is on covering material, as if salvation or insight into the hidden recesses of reality depended on learning no less than the approved quantity of calculus or Chaucer.

Should it surprise us, then, that students show little interest in their work and that possibly as many as three in four cheat in writing papers and in taking exams? The fact that students admit to this level of dishonesty is a sign not of remorse but of open contempt of the system whose interest is in evaluating and not in educating them. If they must pass tests, they will pass them in whatever way is easiest or most effective; they see faculty-talk of the dignity of learning and of the intrinsic value of knowledge as self-justification by funny little people who could never hold down regular jobs.

There is, of course, another side to faculty-student relations. Some young people come to admire some of their teachers and become their life-long friends. A few find their lives changed or at least their purposes redefined as a result of meeting thoughtful adults who care. And more, perhaps, than we suspect carry away with them a small part of their teachers in happy memories, endearing habits or a distant enthusiasm for the life of mind. But these are unplanned by-products of the system, not its primary goals.

Do such occasional fortuitous outcomes justify the expenditure of vast amounts of money and effort? The continued existence of colleges and universities is due as much to their power and position as to a vital need for their services. If the social inertia that allowed them to establish and maintain their power is swept aside by the electronic revolution, perhaps we should greet their decline as well deserved. No one grieves over the fate of the dinosaurs; why should we shed tears at the death of state universities?

Traditional defenses of liberal education are beside the point in the face of the electronic challenge. No one, after all, suggests that we abolish liberal arts colleges and send the next generation to engineering school. Reading good literature and having some idea of how the physical world operates may well be of great personal value to people, but they need not be connected with spending four years in a dorm. At question is not what good reflection and learning might do, but how we can best get people interested in and competent at pursuing them. Will schools of liberal education still provide something special when the sum of human knowledge is at the fingertips of anyone with modem and monitor?

The answer is clearly yes, and exploring it points us in the direction of what computers cannot give and what is, at least in one of its forms, the most neglected service of universities. Human immediacy in the form of new friends and the lasting companionship of peers constitutes one of the warmest and most worthwhile features of the residential experience.

Cynical outsiders among the students charge that many young people go to college to make contacts and to find mates, and they suppose that this is a devastating objection. But there is nothing wrong with making preparations for life at any time and in any context. And in any case, the benefits of the campus are significantly broader: the mixing of students of differing values and lifestyles from varied family backgrounds, divergent social classes and distant parts of the world broadens their horizons and enriches their sympathies. They remember work in student organizations and adventures in the dorms with a fondness reserved for the best days of one's life.

Although such immediacy could be achieved by other means as well, the residential university is a convenient instrument for getting young people together under civilizing conditions. The educational value of this togetherness has never been fully utilized. Colleges and universities make occasional, halfhearted attempts to integrate what students do and learn in the residences with the intricacies of the curriculum, but faculty visits and dorm seminars fall far short of what could be done. Better coordination of practical life on campus with the abstract materials of the classroom offers a splendid opportunity for improving education and providing a more attractive alternative to the Internet.

Important as student camaraderie is, it does not constitute the most valuable contribution of the residential college to the growth of young people. Another sort of togetherness—intergenerational immediacy—defines the work of education. Surprisingly, this vital interaction between teachers and students is poorly understood and therefore inadequately supported by institutions of higher education.

Small colleges used to pride themselves on the close connection between professors and those enrolled in their classes. There were legendary figures in many schools whose devotion to young people structured or took over their lives: they were friend, adviser, savvy mentor, older brother, loving uncle and patient confidant to generations of students. They were available to listen and to help, to comfort and to make small loans at any time of the day or year. Their students were their children or their grateful family, and the wells of their generosity seemed never to run dry.

This is an ideal that cannot be imposed on people. It was freely chosen by a few who viewed teaching as a calling and instinctively understood its profound, even sacred, significance. Though this may seem an absurdly romantic ideal to professional teacher-researchers today, there were and there continue to be some individuals who conduct their lives in its light. Nearly everything pulls against it: the busyness of the modern world, family obligations, the demands of the profession, even the physical distance at which faculty live from campus make it difficult to spend a great deal of time with students.

Colleges and universities, of course, acknowledge the significance of contact with students. They oblige faculty to hold office hours. They also operate advising systems and some of them organize painfully artificial "fireside chats" to encourage faculty to invite students into their homes. Such formal initiatives never amount to much. Many faculty members think of the mandated contact as a nuisance and an interruption; students quickly detect faculty displeasure or lack of interest and learn to stay away.

The most effective student-faculty relationships may well occur in the labs when researchers take a promising student or two under their wings. But even there, the contact is limited and professional, and tends to lack depth of human encounter and of caring.

What makes extensive student-faculty immediacy so important? To understand this, we must get a clear grasp of what faculty, at their best, represent. In addition to being accomplished professionals, they are also expected to be mature human beings. The rigorous standards that govern hiring, retention and promotion in a market where jobs are relatively scarce yield assurance of professional competence. Age, experience and service in a humane and responsible institution make the expectation of maturity reasonable. The obvious fact that this demand frequently goes unmet is of no significance when we speak of what faculty do *at their best* or what they ought to be and do. That cars may not start and that mechanics may be unable to fix them present no threat to our knowledge of what they ought to be able to do.

In one respect, faculty are no different from other mature adults, contact with whom is of genuine value to young persons in the process of defining themselves. From another perspective, they are special, and especially useful for purposes of self-formation, because they have devoted their lives to intellectual pursuits that involve criticism and reflection. Persons of that sort will, of course, make their share of mistakes. But even their relations to their failures are likely to be, or at any rate ought to be, more intelligent than average. They tend to want to understand why they failed in order to prevent the same mistake from snaring them again. Such reflection establishes habits that not only reduce costly errors in the conduct of life but also provide a sweet sense of assurance that we can deal with problems.

Perhaps it is best to make the point we wish by calling attention to two different ways of storing knowledge. We safeguard the information we develop by writing it down, publishing it in books or putting it on the Internet. We also stockpile knowledge in living human beings in the form of experience and the products of reflection. The information contained in books is inert; it does not reorganize itself as knowledge in persons does. It remains safe, unchanged and accessible, always ready to be supplemented but never growing deeper or more complex than we made it.

What is stored in persons, by contrast, is living knowledge constantly in the process of transformation. Perhaps because much of it does not exist in the form of sentences, its depth is indeterminate; people questioned about what they know can surprise even themselves. This is because a single well-formed query can add to living knowledge by causing a reorganization of existing materials, the way a spark of electricity fuses hydrogen and oxygen to create water or in the manner that tapping the side of a kaleidoscope rearranges colors into a new picture.

In more familiar language, asking people questions gives them an opportunity to think, draw on their experience, and come up with something new. The demands of communication are such, moreover, that participants in the conversation may have to reformulate their questions and their answers in terms they have not used before and thereby contribute to the creation of novel ideas and insights.

Nothing like this is available in today's machines. We can, of course, learn new things by surfing the Net, and those who are inventive about where to look can uncover a great deal. But often the information runs out before the questions do, and machines don't improvise. They are incapable, moreover, of particularizing their answers, that is, of adapting their information to the needs and situations of the people who want to know and of presenting it in terms suited to different levels of understanding and states of mind.

The simple way to say this is that we cannot have a conversation with Web sites. The more complete and more accurate way of putting it is that human beings are, among other things, vast collections of experience, organic systems of storing and using the living past. This is why talking with reflective older people can be so rewarding; their years of experience, crystallized into ideas, can give us stunningly rich perspectives on life. And this is also why it would be a great privilege to be able to question Plato or Napoleon one evening over a glass of wine. We have the words and know the exploits of the famous dead but, as a wonderful student we once knew used to say, we have a few more questions. No one can answer those questions but the people concerned and, alas, they took their share of knowledge with them to the grave.

What colleges and universities can offer that is unavailable from the computer is what they have always offered at their best: firsthand contact with remarkable people whose knowledge of their fields and experience of life have been integrated into the unity of a person. Such conversation is of benefit to both students and teachers. Students gain access to the accumulated wisdom of the human race through a dynamic medium that rewards searching and novel questions with thoughtful and often surprising answers. Teachers, in turn, find stimulation under the scrutiny of inquisitive young minds. Much human knowledge is unfocused or tacit; the opportunities and irritations of dialogue force the articulation of thought and bring indistinct ideas to the clarity of explicit consciousness.

Sustained communication between mature scholars with a measure of life experience and young people in the early stages of charting their course meets the most exacting requirement of education: it results in the transmission of knowledge to a new generation. In assessing its value, we should not overlook the role it plays in creating new insights and in keeping established truths vibrant in the minds of those long familiar with them. Nor should we underrate the importance for the future of society of the intergenerational faith engendered by such nurturing contact.

Lectures on videotape, on audiotape and—if delivered from detailed, antique notes—even in the lecture hall come closer to the way knowledge is stored in books or on the Internet than to the manner in which it can be created and obtained through open questioning and collaboration. As a method of conveying information, lectures lack the speed and the free-ranging exploration typical of computer access to data. The information they present is rarely the reason for our interest in them; the source of their fascination is the eloquence and angle of vision of the lecturer. What makes such presentations worthwhile is the opportunity they afford of seeing and asking questions about how another human being perceives the world or some intriguing portion of it.

Laboratories have for centuries provided a setting for cooperative enterprises in which intellectual sparks can fly. But in scientific work, as in every activity in which persons meet, the central variable is the quality of the interaction. In spite of the claims of people who disguise nasty imperiousness as the defense of high standards, benevolent mentoring is not incompatible with the demand for top performance. To the contrary, high expectations in a friendly, supportive environment are more likely to bring results than the terror imposed by moody tyrants.

Hands-on education in scientific inquiry and laboratory investigation in which faculty adopt students as their junior partners are, therefore, permanently valuable services that electronic media cannot supplant. Their benefit derives from the same source as that of face-to-face work in the humanities and the social sciences. Searching, unimpeded intergenerational communication informs the young and stimulates their elders. The unpredictably rich results of questioning can make students the teachers of their teachers and their interchange a source of exhilaration and delight.

We are in greater need of what the residential college experience offers than perhaps any prior generation. Our world is disablingly busy. The demands of their jobs and of their complex lives make it difficult for parents to devote extensive attention to their children. Child-care workers and teachers, whose professional services are supposed to assure the moral growth and intellectual development of the young, are overwhelmed with people they must benefit. They cannot spend much time in direct personal contact with any of them. As a result, a significant number of individuals grow up without getting to know older, more experienced persons and without the benefit of feeling their sustained love.

This loss can be devastating. Intergenerational friendship is the sole method of handing down the habits of caring without which human life remains empty and bitter. As with any skill of the heart, this cannot be taught through words or through exercises devised by counselors. It is the grateful response of people to a happy childhood in a nurturing community, the desire to pay the next generation for what was received from the last.

Even at their best, residential institutions of higher education are poor substitutes for loving families. But they are among the few alternatives available today. College students are old enough to appreciate the deeper reaches of intergenerational friendship yet not so jaded as to have ceased looking for warmth and guidance. Under the right circumstances, they can develop rich and caring relationships with their teachers. Though most of these remain temporary partnerships, some grow into lifelong commitments to intense mutual support.

The windstorm of the electronic revolution feels like a zephyr in the sheltered valleys of the academic world. Colleges and universities have not even started to assess the changes they will have to undergo to survive in the new world of the twenty-first century. They appear to trust in their credentialing power to stave off disaster. But before long, some reputable institutions are bound to recognize the windfall of offering legitimate degrees through electronic distance learning. This will set off a competitive stampede, resulting in a squeeze on prices. Will students short on money and time not prefer the cheaper and faster electronic degree to spending years at marginal institutions?

A painful consolidation of residential colleges and universities is as near a certainty as anything in the future can be. Rich schools are likely to survive, but even they will find their missions and their curricula transformed. To move in the direction of providing closer and more extensive contact with faculty, they will have to revamp their educational strategy. The imaginative use of new technologies that alone makes this possible will, in the process, altogether transform the undergraduate program.

Full recognition that books and the classroom do not constitute effective ways of teaching facts is likely to revolutionize what teachers and students do. Electronic access to all the cut-and-dried material of education will liberate faculty from lengthy exposition and boring drill. Students will have all the facts they need at their fingertips, with easy machine checks that they got them right. Since they will uncover the facts as needed for the solution of problems, they will master them in their context and remember them better.

This should enable faculty members to attend to the tasks of education proper: to teaching skills of investigation, hypothesis formation and theory testing, and to enhancing critical judgment and the scope and depth of appreciation. The resulting growth involves expansion of both the rigor of thought and the sweep of imagination, conferring on students some of the same pleasures that critics, scientific investigators and creative artists enjoy. We hardly dare say it: education might, in this way, become as joyous for students as it has always been for the best of their teachers.

We do not mean to suggest that utopia is just around the corner. It never is. But the ingenuity of human beings has now put tools at our disposal that enable us to do what prior generations could not even dream. Transmission to the young of important portions of the accumulated knowledge of the human race need no longer exact the pain of dozens of years of rote memory. Much more material than any one person could ever remember is now available in response to simple commands typed into or spoken to machines.

Before long, we will find ourselves tied to our computers as we are tied to our cars; they will become integral elements of the self. The critical question is how we will learn to use this external memory for the purpose of improving human minds and, through them, human lives.

The effects of externalizing memory are likely to replicate the effects of finding a machine solution to providing the conditions of any important practice. The ease with which the activity can be performed makes for a vast increase in its frequency and a decline in the value we place on performing it the old way. So, for example, when writing was invented and accounts of past events could be stored in libraries or on walls, oral histories passed from bard to bard were nearly eliminated. And the advent of the typewriter brought with it a flood of writing along with decreased appreciation of fine calligraphy.

Our veneration of the power of memory is also likely to evaporate as we learn to replace factual information stored in individual brains with communal data banks. Contests such as the College Bowl may come to look like freak shows without a point, much like the performances of people who try to play eight instruments at once to imitate an orchestra. Forcing students to remember large bodies of information and rewarding them for feats of recalling disconnected facts may appear sad or even bizarre to subsequent generations.

This is the context in which we must understand the impact computerized storage will likely exert on educational practices. Even a cursory assessment of how much time is spent on memory work suffices to indicate the extent of the changes we face. The optimistic interpretation of these impending events is that the development of technology is at last lifting from humans the burden of brute or unfitting activities. Dishwashers have liberated us from the daily imperatives of the sink, and backhoes have taken over the hard work of digging. Why should the task of carrying with us the irrelevant details of the world not pass from us, as well? Thought and appreciation constitute more worthy uses of our time and capacity than the storage of dead facts.

Such an optimistic account of developments is clearly better than the alternatives. But to make it acceptable, we must dispel a possible misunderstanding and call attention to a peril. When we speak of handing over the work of memory to machine substitutes of the human brain, we do not mean to imply that we will walk around with empty heads, unable to recall anything that happened to us. On the contrary, investigation and appreciation are themselves impossible without mastery, and that means storage and integration, of skills. Thought requires a subject matter held fast in memory, and we cannot decide on the direction of inquiry without sustained knowledge of the shape of facts and of what about them needs to be explained.

Evidently, such contextualized ordinary memories are not what computers are in the process of replacing. Human minds, particularly the interested intellects of the young, are like flypaper: everything they come in contact with sticks to them. Such effortless remembering is a condition of operating in the world, and it enriches life in incalculable ways. Without it, we cannot know whether tires go on the car or as decorations around the neck. And we fail as friends if we are unable to distinguish strangers from those we love.

We have in mind, instead, the forced ingestion and periodic regurgitation in educational institutions of vast quantities of unrelated facts. At times when information is difficult to come by, such privately stored knowledge is invaluable, in just the way a flashlight comes in handy when the lights go out. But it is a mistake to organize education as if we perpetually faced the dark.

The danger confronting us is that our success has become our problem: the wonderful aids we have devised for mastering facts and understanding the world may diminish the felt seriousness of education. Traditionally, the discipline of compulsory memory work has carried the burden of conveying the momentousness of learning. The cry for a return to basics in education may, in fact, be simply the desire for effort and earnest respect to infuse the enterprise. Prosperity has supposedly made young people soft or unambitious. Since human nature, at least in its current incarnation, has no respect for the easy, eliminating the pressure of rote memory may make education painless or even fun, and thereby sap the energy with which we tackle it.

The long-term challenge facing educators at all levels is to find ways to sustain the motivation of students and to convey to them the life-creating power of appropriating the culture of the past. Fortunately, early indications point to success. Access to vast reaches of the Internet keeps young people riveted to their seats in front of monitors for hours. Such natural curiosity, combined with desire for the companionship of caring adults, should give teachers everything they need.

In any case, simple as access to information has become, there is nothing easy about interpreting and explaining the facts. Learning more about the world, therefore, will always be a challenge that the contagious excitement of good teachers can convert into the work of personal and intellectual growth.

II

Issues for Individuals

What Humans Did Not Make

The question of how much humans contribute to the sum of reality has haunted modern philosophy since at least the days of Kant. Interest in the issue did not arise by accident. A central element of modernity is the effort of humans to take charge of their lives and to achieve control over the physical and social circumstances that affect them. This historic quest, involving the development of technology and the tendency to make political changes, if necessary even by revolution, displays human beings as active in a world-transforming way. It was natural for the thought of such large-scale constructive or reconstructive activity to penetrate philosophical reflection and to raise the question of what, if anything, in the world is not a product of our exertions.

Answers to this question have suffered, unfortunately, from misunderstandings of the nature and exaggeration about the extent of our contributions to reality. Kant believed, for example, that we structure the totality of the empirical world solely by means of our cognitive apparatus. Space, time and all the relations that constitute physical objects, he thought, were added by human subjectivity to the otherwise-indeterminate raw material of our senses. Pragmatists, by contrast, overstated the amount we contribute to reality by actions that redistribute physical energies. Others laid undue stress on the world-creative power of language, of symbol systems, of the imagination or of the will. Some even claim that we created not only the world, but God as well. No one appears to have taken the trouble to develop an adequate and sensible classification of what we contribute to reality and how.

The best way to begin this task is by being careful to avoid hyperbole. We cannot reasonably maintain that the world consists solely of facts independent of human agency. If we were creatures of pure light viewing a still landscape of eternal truths, we could suppose that our vision adds nothing to what has always been real. But we are active, needy, interested beings, and we know that many of the facts surrounding us would never have come to be without our work. The fact that these words fill this page and the fact that they are being read could not exist without human contribution.

I need not spend long on the current point; an objectivism that sees everything as independent of us is both implausible and unattractive. Total constructivism, on the other hand, though it is just as unlikely to be true, continues to fascinate many thinkers. The pattern of this family of views is invariant: consciousness, thought, language, discourse or social meaning is declared to be a universal human structure nothing can escape. These realities are supposed to be the solvent in which everything independent of us disappears. If we object by kicking the curb or pointing to the stars, we are asked to explain what we have in mind. Philosophers find such invitations irresistible, and the moment they begin, the constructivists triumphantly convict them of bringing the putatively alien reality within the orbit of discourse or consciousness or thought.

Although this argument is difficult to defeat, I cannot shake off the suspicion that it is phony. So much is beyond our will, beyond our control, beyond understanding that the tightest argument designed to show our mark on everything still fails to convince. William James, a far more sensible soul than current advocates of the inescapability of discourse, struggled with this problem and concluded that though the *what* of realities is largely a human contribution, their *that,* their sheer existence, does not come from us. Perhaps surprisingly, the arch-constructivist Kant shared this belief. In his attack on the ontological argument, he made it amply clear that existence is a brute contingency we cannot lead back to the mind's conceptual apparatus. Even though both reality and actuality are categories or modes of thought, only perception can put us in touch with what truly exists. And perception itself yields evidence of existence not by means or on account of its formal features (what Kant called "the pure forms of intuition"), but because its content, derived from the sensuous manifold, connects it to what is not generated or controlled by the human mind.

James and Kant appear to be on to something important. Nothing brings home the limit of human power more directly than a recalcitrant or uninvited existent. The tragic loss of loved ones, the absence of needed food and drink, the oppressive presence of bullies or disease, painful inability, insurmountable obstacles, the crushing experience of the *no more* all point to powers we did not make or cannot master. Existence as a brute reality is the central nonhuman element in facts. I conclude, temporarily for now, that wholesale constructivism is indefensible; we are not gods who make the world unaided.

Nevertheless, let me make the best case I can for the constructivist. From one perspective at least, a great deal appears to be the work of humans. But in surveying our proud creative activity, we may also discern its outer boundaries. Those limits reveal what is permanently beyond human power to make and to undo.

Humans create facts by what they do, by what they choose, by what and how they perceive and think, and by how they feel. That we act and choose and think and feel are, of course, themselves facts, but they are less interesting than the further facts we create by means of these activities. By actions that redistribute physical energies, we make airplanes and make them fly. By choice or social agreement, we create rules about when to fly them and how. By perception and thought, we note weaknesses in the performance of planes and design improvements. On the basis of how we feel, we take the planes to join those we love. Evidently, these four ways of contributing realities to the world need not be independent of one another. On the contrary, in many cases they are inextricably connected. Choice often precedes thought and makes it possible, and on some felicitous occasions we think before we act. Feelings are always there to color our choices and to help us evaluate the results of our actions. The point is not to isolate these creative activities but to distinguish them so that we may acquire a better grasp of what we do and how.

1. Facts Created by Action

The novel objects we make constitute our most obvious additions to the furniture of the universe. Houses and pens, bathtubs and hybrid corn, canned soup and cans of mace would not exist if humans did not. This suggests that existence is, after all, not the ultimate element free of human contribution: our activities richly enhance the variety of existents in the world. The suggestion, however, is misleading. All the new existents we devise are constructed out of other existing materials, and even though some of those may be humanly contrived, it does not take very long to get back to ingredients we found and did not make. Toys are made of plastic, and both toys and plastic are made by us. But plastic is made of oil, which we did not create. Human creativity is limited: we can make new things out of old, but not something out of nothing.

We live in a world of objects, very many of which were constructed by human beings. In cities, the ground is covered by asphalt, and nearly everything above and below it bears the mark of human hands. Buildings and the elevators that serve them, the music in the elevators, and the instruments on which the music is played are all human products. To be sure, trees grow of their own accord in the middle of wide boulevards, but only because we put them there and guide the traffic around them.

The achievement of the city—the city of man, not of God—has impressed empirically minded constructivists to such an extent that they think they can see our mark on everything. They are so busy looking for the human all around us that they rarely lift their eyes to the sky and hardly notice beetles in the cracker box. Evidently, the vast majority of things in the universe are not our handiwork, yet it is difficult to deny that, to ordinary people, the objects we make seem the most interesting and the most important.

The progress of industrial civilization will render the humanly created ever more central in our lives. In the process, it will foster the appearance that the entire world is made by us. The more sanguine among city-dwelling, verbal philosophers already maintain that the real cannot live beyond the confines of human language, discourse or symbolic activity. In the face of such tempting foolishness, it is important to keep in mind the regionality of our achievements and to savor the thought of the vast stretches of nonhuman nature that surround us.

2. Facts Created by Choice

We tend to think that facts generated by human choice are primarily of the sort we know as "conventional." The names of countries, the moves permissible in chess, the acceptability of "ain't" in the English language constitute conventional facts, because they are the outcome of agreements alone. The agreements may be tacit, but they are binding as long as we do not change our minds. We are, however, free to change them at any time we wish, and the altered compact creates novel facts.

This provides a glimpse of the power of human choice but does not come near to grasping the variety of facts it can create. The introduction of the three-point shot in basketball may appear to be no more than a change in conventional facts (even though realists fought it as somehow changing the essence of the game), but it alters behavior on the court, the work of coaches, and even recruiting in a profound way. A simple change of rule, one could sensibly argue, is thus adequate to make vast changes in the world. This will come as no surprise to those who watch the economic and social effects of the frequent changes in our tax laws.

The moment we begin to think of rules as created by social choice, we realize that the entire world of human institutions is the outcome of tacit agreements. Government itself rests, if not on the consent, then at least on the voluntary compliance or the indifference of the governed. Institutions are not physical realities brought into being by collecting, dividing, arranging, moving, grinding or gluing material objects. They are, from the physical standpoint, fictive entities held in existence by the continued readiness of human beings to act in complex, characteristic ways.

To be sure, as a social structure General Motors is eminently real. But its existence consists simply of what human beings can and are prepared to accomplish for it or in its name, along with what others freely permit to be done. If a banker attempted to empty its accounts, its employees would resist and call on the legal system to back them up. But if GM's financial officers shrugged their shoulders and if district attorneys, judges and the police showed an equal lack of concern, the corporation would burst like a soap bubble and disappear. Such institutions are built on the stable sands of human commitment; in acting within them, nothing constrains our choice beyond the choice of others to enforce the rules.

All of this reminds us that the most pervasive and most immediate realities constructed by human choice are the actions in which we engage. In addition to creating and sustaining social institutions, the choices and the actions that flow from them also endow physical events with novel meanings. Travel to New York becomes, in this way, something more than relocation in space: it is also fulfillment of my promise to meet a friend. Through institutions, moreover, we generate a variety of novel sorts of events that, although they have physical components, cannot be understood by reference to material facts alone. Part ownership of a company through stocks is one such reality: the paper certificate or equivalent computer entry is part of an elaborate system of symbols that invites or commands assent. Some situations are perhaps even more remarkable. The same physical event can constitute radically different acts in different contexts. Clubbing another, for example, is banned as a criminal action. But it may be legal and even right when performed under certain circumstances by individuals entitled to wear the symbolically powerful clothes of the police.

Choices also play a central role in creating the facts we call beliefs. In these matters, philosophers wish to give up choice and surrender to the compulsion of the evidence. William James was right, however, in seeing a significant element of will and improvisation in the opinions we hold. Some humans, of course, resist believing everything they wish and take pride in reserving their commitment to ideas they have reason to embrace or at least love too much to be willing to give up. The general growth of so-phistication has, however, helped most of us recognize that the facts are in-adequate to determine what we think and that, as a result, the imagination can weave its wonders everywhere. James was also right in noting that some of our beliefs can, astoundingly, create their own objects: in acting on the innocent conviction that the people I just met are worthy of my trust, I may well gain them as trustworthy friends for life.

Last but not least, we create new facts by deciding how far to apply im-portant concepts and by choosing schemes of classification. When we question whether or not abortion is murder, we ask about the limits of the application of the concept of person. Though the existence of all manner of beings can be terminated, only persons can be murdered. To permit the ap-plication of the concept to relatively undifferentiated collections of cells is a decision, not a discovery. We need, of course, to find and to cite reasons for such extensions of normal use, just as we need to present considera-tions in favor of using a particular scheme of classification over others. That we have reasons for these choices does not convert them into discov-eries of essence, and we must be careful not to allow them to masquerade as intuitions of preexisting fact. The life of choice pulses under nearly all of our cognitive efforts.

3. Facts Created by Cognition

We have no reason to embrace Kant's notion that everything in the human world results from the monolithic power of our cognitive apparatus. Such massive determination presupposes timeless and uniform transcendental structures, whose existence is, to say the least, improbable. The details of what and how we think, however, clearly create facts that can influence our choices and guide our actions. We learn more by looking at these particu-lars than by inventing views of cosmic generality.

Though some of the concepts we use are optional, others constitute a part of the gift of history that cannot be refused. These empowering yet paralyzing presents are borne by our language and by the categories of common sense. Activity, passivity, thing, process and causation are notions that structure our world; using them to understand what surrounds us feels natural and right. They are, of course, neither necessary nor in-escapable, but ridding ourselves of them is difficult and perhaps unwise. The concept of causation, for example, enables us to create facts of respon-sibility in the world and to raise institutions of punishment and reward.

The ideas of activity and passivity can lead to facts of self-assessment and through those to constructive efforts to improve our lot.

Our perceptual apparatus also contributes to the generation of facts. Although we do not know the colored inside of the worlds of other creatures, there can be little doubt that the mosaic-like eyes of certain insects breed experiences different from ours. Just as the constitution of my color-defective eyes produces perceptions rich in browns but devoid of purple and red, so our structures of sensation and thought create a world alive with qualities and relations particularly appropriate to them. We have no difficulty in gaining contact with existents beyond our organs of cognition, but the picture we paint of them owes an amount that is difficult for us to determine to the pigment and brush of our minds.

Additional facts show the creative power of what we think or believe. In flying over land, for example, I see geometrical fields carefully tilled and planted in green crops. The cultivated land constitutes a reality shaped by human action, but the sights I see are, in no small measure, the work of thought. Without the beliefs that I am high in the air, that what stretches below me is arable land, that good land tends to be owned and worked in small segments, and that the green I sense is more likely to be due to growing plants than paint, among others, I would never manage to *see* tilled fields. Many of the realities of which the human world consists owe, in this way, a deep debt to knowledge and belief.

4. Facts Created by Feeling

Few have not experienced the transformative power of moods and emotions. A philosophy anxious to draw sharp lines might suppose that feelings make a difference only subjectively. This, however, pays scant attention to the overwhelming reality of the colors of mood. People who live surrounded by feelings of inferiority, depression or fear do not doubt the reality of their world. When the exhilaration of invincibility or the glorious sunlight of young hope fills every corner of life, it is more real by far than any of the mundane objects it lights up. How we feel creates facts no less than what we think and what we do, if for no other reason then at least because it can change our thoughts and actions.

In fact, of course, it can do much more. Choice envisages a future and action attempts to bring it about. In both cases, what is to come appears removed. In our feelings and moods, by contrast, the future and the past are present directly: their influence sets the ground note of the symphony of life. When their operation is social, it creates great periods of national exertion or lethargy. In addition to shaping such momentous realities, feelings also have a magical power that can convert one's homely love into an airy and magnificent creature.

With so much of surrounding reality indebted to human activity for its existence or nature, is there anything truly independent of us? There is, and we can see it best by focusing on the ultimate limit of human power— death.

My car is a fully individuated object in the world and it is in that sense unique: only mine contains the materials of which it was made, only it rolled off the assembly line at Hamtramck on the first Monday of September, 1986, at 3:31 in the afternoon, only it was bought by me and stood for years in my driveway, with a scratch on the left brake light, under the old oak tree. Nevertheless, should I wreck it, it will be easily replaced by another vehicle. Should the love of my life die, on the other hand, she simply cannot be replaced. To be sure, other women may be available, even others perhaps who look like her, carry her first name and wear their hair in the same soft curls. But they cannot take her place. With her passing, something special, something of very great value would be gone.

Her uniqueness is different from the uniqueness of a car; it cannot be explained by reference to individuation alone. Beyond what it takes to be a singular, identifiable item in the physical universe, she has developed a collection of significant features and abilities that make her unique in the world of social relations. This assemblage includes the generous ways she acts, the subtle turns of her thought, her understanding of herself, her feeling for the plight of others, her uncompromising independence, and the way in which she tries to secure that independence for everyone she loves. All of these characteristics can be plausibly subsumed under the three general categories of self-knowledge, self-determination and self-communication that a recent writer identifies as the marks of personhood.[1] My love appears irreplaceable, then, because she is unique beyond physical uniqueness—because she is a singular and valued person.

Just as infants are products of human biology, persons are products of human society. Mature adults, therefore, are human creations through and through; they constitute, according to Mill and others, our finest handiwork. We may be tempted to embrace ancillary beliefs to cushion the shock of this remarkable fact: we may maintain, for example, that only God can provide the person-seed, the spiritual molecule with the potential for personhood that is necessary for our labors. Such opinions express agreeable sentiments, and one is sure to be viewed as mean-spirited for resisting them. Yet we can summon precious little evidence to support them: though our modesty murmurs that we can't have done it all, in this sphere at least, the only processes we see are ones we initiate and control.

Whether they are divine endowments or the genetic fruits of evolution, the hidden gifts that enable us to start building persons are conditions of our activity that fall within our power. The human genome, with all its potential, is alive in all of us. We have taken the first, halting steps to modifying it in accordance with our wishes. We have devised medical aid for those who cannot reproduce with ease. And once the infant is born, we can trace and quicken the social processes that develop the great marks of personhood.

Self-knowledge grows through painful years of experiments in the art of social interaction. The fact that the human body operates under central control serves as the ground of self-determination: we first learn to control the movement of our parts and then take over regulation of much that we as integrated organisms and as social agents do. Self-communication is also an acquired social skill. Fostering the projection of self through speech, action and the products of creative imagination[2] is one of the primary functions of education. Admittedly, some people surprise us by their striking talent at such self-expression. But there is no reason to seek an explanation of such achievements beyond what genes and natural bent, good teaching and superior drive and, ultimately, repeated experiment and reinforcing success provide.

The self we know and communicate, the self that guides its own fortunes, is itself largely a social product. I say "largely" because the demarcation between the part of the world we feel directly—our bodies—and surrounding realities may well occasion the first thought of our separate, perhaps even insular, nature. From that reflection on, however, parents and teachers can follow how circumstance and social interplay create the layers of drives, habits and structuring values of which selves are made. Nothing in this natural development suggests forces beyond what humans bring to bear or permit to operate.

Having created bodies and the persons that live in them, humans take endless trouble to sustain them in existence. We breathe to stave off death, we eat, tend to our wounds, and avoid the dangerous. We take physical exams, undergo operations, seek organ transplants, even have ourselves attached to invasive machines to gain a few more days in the sun. These strategies have proved immensely successful: in the last few hundred years, we have managed to triple the life expectancy of the average person. But however long we live, we don't live forever. At some point, human power breaks down: neither he nor the ministrations of his monstrous empire could give

Stalin another minute of life. The processes of the world spin—here, there, everywhere—out of our control and that which we neither made nor desire presents itself as the ultimately real.

Death, nonexistence in the teeth of our efforts to live on, is therefore the paradigm of what is beyond the human world. We can generalize this and say that uncontrolled processes of existence and uncontrolled processes that lead to nonexistence constitute the elements of the world we did not make. We dip into these streams of events as we dip for water into the sea; what we pull up and manage to put to use is the raw material of the things, experiences and persons we create. The sea surrounds us and in a mysterious way, as does water, it suffuses our bodies and operates in and through them. Although we create a world, we know little of how we manage to do it. Viewed from one perspective, we can readily see this world brought into existence not by us but by the nonhuman, natural processes that live in us and carry us along.

If death is the outer limit of the collective power of humankind, it is not surprising that we devote exceptional efforts to delaying it. In the last hundred years, we have targeted it as the enemy and used medicine, engineering, education, public health initiatives, legislation and government power to reduce its hold on us. Nevertheless, the survivors in our war with death fill the coma wards of our hospitals. Knowing that total emancipation is a futile quest, the wiser among us have devised a subtler strategy. Instead of eliminating death, they want to gain control of it by determining when it can come and how. This is the deeper meaning of Dr. Kevorkian's work. With generations of Stoics, this assistant in suicide reminds us that though we must die, we can do so at will. Even if humans cannot do everything, they want the ultimate power to draw the limits of their power.

CHAPTER 6

Valuational Species

Physicians and nurses training in city hospitals are in daily contact with the richness of the actual. The surprising, the unusual and the abnormal assault them on every side. Their work requires that they recognize every shade of the strange, the marginal and the deviant as parts of a spectrum of cases, no two of which are altogether alike and each of which demands differential treatment.

Attorneys practicing divorce and criminal law often encounter the irregular and the bizarre; specialists in tax and bankruptcy law see endless variations of the shady. Psychiatrists meet with so much eccentricity that they find it hard to agree on how best to categorize its exotic varieties: each new edition of their *Diagnostic and Statistical Manual* presents significant classificatory changes. Even social workers and state employees dealing with the public confront vast ranges of human emotion and behavior and learn to make few generalizations about what people are likely to do. Although we often remark that only the full moon brings the depraved and the deranged out of hiding, they are in fact around us all the time.

Such variety must be given its due. This suggests that philosophers, the people most interested in formulating general theories about human nature and behavior, should be particularly mindful of the vast range of our differences. Unfortunately, however, here as elsewhere, those who need the most possess the least. Sheltered within the academic world, philosophers lack access to human diversity. Their experience is limited to the stable and the normal, to smart young people searching for knowledge or social success.

The institutional location of philosophers exerts a profound influence on their theories. The population of universities is among the most uniform in the world; though students love appearing odd, few of them really are. The truly different don't qualify for college or tend not to apply. The folders of the few who do end in the back closets of admissions offices. When philosophers pursue their passion of searching for essence, therefore, the range of samples available to them for generalization is sharply restricted. Where could they come in contact with the monstrous and the grotesque? Service stations and grocery stores on the well-ordered side of town offer only the ordinary.

Small wonder, then, that oddly unreal theories emerge. Who but intellectuals reflecting on their friends and students could have come up with the idea that humans are rational animals? And would even the thought of identifying the essence of things have occurred to people, had they not been surrounded by crushing similarity on every side?

Seeking the essence of things makes sense in a world that lives by the manufacture and sale of vast quantities of familiar objects; tubes of lipstick must resemble each other closely enough to meet customer expectations. But searching for the discrete, immutable forms of species of living organisms, including humans, seems neither necessary nor appropriate over a hundred years after the general acceptance of the theory of evolution.[1] For Darwin and his followers established the continuity of life forms on the planet, developing an account of how changes in the germ plasm and subsequent reproductive success lead to the emergence of novel groups of beings.

A static cross section of the living things that surround us suggests stable, discrete species. Cats and dogs, the goldfinch and the hawk seem to be utterly distinct from one another, and where we see little divergence, as with alligators and crocodiles, we readily believe the experts that more than habitat separates them. A dynamic account, on the other hand, sketching development over time, presents a very different picture. It shows an uninterrupted flow of life in which creatures display complex sets of overlapping characteristics. When a sufficiently large number of individuals exhibit sufficiently similar features, we say that they all belong to the same species.

Sufficiently? That is a matter of judgment, and judgments depend at least in part on the ends they serve. There are different degrees of similarity among individuals in a population, but the level required for belonging to the same species is not a fact on a par with these resemblances. Likenesses of genetic makeup, of anatomy, of physiology, of ecological niche and of behavior are open to public inspection or exploration. By contrast, claims that one or a group of these similarities of a certain degree defines a species are proposals open to public debate. The former are matters to be ascertained, the latter, decisions to be made.

The notion that the same form is imprinted on every member of the species is making its halting last stand as the claim that all humans share the same genetic makeup. Yet recent estimates put the average difference in genetic material between human beings at 3,000 nucleotides, or roughly a tenth of 1 percent of our genetic endowment.[2] This means that differences at the extreme between individuals even of the same generation can be several magnitudes higher. Hopes for simple species essences disintegrate upon careful examination of the empirical facts.

In the Darwinian flow of life, the sharp lines between species are our own creations. At the margins, species can overlap either in the historical development of one out of another or in the extreme divergence of individuals from the norm. Typically, we proceed by choosing the cluster of characteristics on the basis of which we wish to classify, and then identify some individuals who clearly display those features to serve as paradigms. The procedure is nominalistic to the core, for we determine species membership by the resemblance of candidates to the designated samples.

That species are made, not found, is shown by the presence in this procedure of decisions at three points. We select the traits we wish to stress in our categories from among the very large number each group of organisms displays. We choose the core members of the class from among those that manifest the traits to varying degrees and in combination with diverse other characteristics. And when we find individuals not very similar to the samples, or similar to them in some respects but not in others, we decide whether the similarity is sufficient for them to belong to the species.

Such decisions create facts, though not of the sort that serves as their material. Our choices presuppose realities not open to choice; in the case of constructing species, these are the living creatures that resemble one another to varying degrees. Many of the features of these organisms are *independent* of what we think or want. The structure of their bodies, their method of respiration and their diet are facts that require, and allow, very little contribution by us. These are things we have to face up to or live with, or at least discover and acknowledge. I would use the term "objective" for facts of this sort, were it not for its history of abuse from Descartes through Kant to our own day. What I would mean if I employed the word is that some things exist and exist with certain characteristics, especially causal ones, quite without the knowledge and consent of anyone. That my cat has sharp claws that shred the furniture is one such fact, and that my father is no longer living is another.

Since these matters touch on existence and nonexistence, they tend to be objects of grief or celebration. Our contribution to them resembles what makeup artists do for actresses. Emotion, perception and thought paint them the colors of the rainbow, but the features of the face always show through. The destruction of old furniture may be seen through the pleasure of being at last forced to buy new. Belief in another world might present death in a light different from our normal conception, stripping it of its sense of finality. But whatever interpretation we place on the event, the element of existence, of what we might call brute reality, lurks under our modes of thinking about it, the way the formed body hides under or fills out fancy clothes.

We might say that, with respect to such particulars, the world is determinate. We can of course add relations to these existents (and nonexistences), such as when we catch the cat sharpening its claws on the sofa. And under favorable conditions, we can even change some of their features, such as when we take the cat to have its nails trimmed. But these are accretions and substitutions that embellish or alter otherwise fully formed beings. With Peirce and against Nelson Goodman,[3] I find it difficult to believe that there would be no world without our symbolic or volitional determining activities. That we can make worlds solely by the manipulation of symbol systems is even less plausible.

Though things are determinate with respect to some of their features, they are relatively indeterminate with regard to others. We classify animals, for example, on the basis of the determinate characteristics of individuals, but such features underdetermine the taxonomy. The complex interrelations between the traits of living creatures permit significant leeway in how we group them. We can categorize them by the number of their feet, in which case we will end with a spectrum ranging from the snake to the millipede. But we can arrange them also by the hardness of their bodies, in which case seashells and turtles will belong to one species and slugs and my very fat friend Ed to another, or by their height, placing basketball centers with llamas, and corgies with cats.

Some ways of carving up the world carry vast significance. The difference between mushrooms and toadstools is largely that the former nourishes while the latter kills. And much of the history of agriculture revolves around the distinction between those animals that can be trained to do heavy physical work and those that can't. This suggests, once again, that in sorting creatures into groups, we always keep an eye on our needs. Objects open to multiple classifications, as plants and animals always are, invite our interests and purposes to determine where they belong.

Though animals are determinable with respect to their classification, they are not indefinitely so. In spite of the fact that both move with remarkable speed, it is inappropriate to think of a herd of gazelles as a sort of summer storm. And, even though we can classify kangaroos with animals that jump and with animals that use their tails for balance and even with animals that suckle their young, we cannot sensibly say that the pouch in which they carry their newborns makes them kin to pita bread.

The extent to which living creatures are determinable for purposes of classification is as individual as the creatures we wish to classify. Since such determination involves a relation to us, it is also a matter of how attentive we are to similarities and how inventive we prove ourselves in coming up with interesting new groupings. Generally, richness of the structure, behavior and relations of an organism enhances its taxonomic determinability: the more and the more complex characteristics it displays, the greater the number of groups to which it can be seen to belong.

Objects are completely determinate with respect to their sensory features. So if we wish to sort animals into those that are brown and blue and red, little is left to choice beyond disposing of borderline cases. We have immediate acquaintance with the defining characteristic of the class; those that display it belong, and others don't.

The situation is very different when we invent such notions as mouse and rat. Organisms are relatively indeterminate with regard to such categories, and there is no single, visible mark that settles whether or not any of them properly belong. A part of the reason for this is that we pick many features to define the kind, weighting them differentially, though not expecting all of them to be present. Another part of the reason is that some of the features we pick are vague, and their empirical manifestations require interpretation. The inevitable result is reliance on complex human judgments and a consequent looseness of sort.

The idea of species essences must have occurred to people to counterbalance this undesirable consequence. Why should it be more difficult or more problematic to recognize rats than it is to recognize brown things? If we suppose that being a rat is a characteristic of some living things, we can take key empirical signs of rattiness as conclusive evidence of the presence of that essence. Just as seeing the blue of a thing settles its color, so seeing two beady eyes and a scraggly tail on a scurrying smallish form settles its species. Seeing colors is then matched by intuiting the essence of things, and we gain the comfort of direct acquaintance with the natural kinds to one and only one of which each living thing belongs.

The latter assurance is, of course, entirely fictive. It remains spurious even when we restate our workaday distinctions between species in the more technical language of biology or genetics. The essences of species are not enshrined in the physiological structure, the reproductive capacity or even the genetic endowment of individuals, for the simple reason that there are no such essences. The notion of a species is pieced together out of a collection of features displayed by large collections of individuals. Its core characteristics are determined by choice, its domain is limited by human decision, and its edges are always fuzzy.

Customary modes of thought paralyze the imagination. We are surrounded by uniformities, some obvious and some enforced: cats seem to be pretty much alike, and it has become taboo to say that there are different sorts of human beings. We wonder how we could even think of classifying organisms in a way that diverges from what is sanctioned by biologists and looks, for all the world, to be confirmed by daily experience. Yet, as philosophers, we must not let current practices captivate us to the point where we no longer see the contingency of what we do. We must not allow our schemes of classification to blind us to alternatives that could be just as blinding if we committed ourselves to them. We must, in brief, see our attempts to classify living beings as variable, optional ways of ordering the wilderness of facts. In pursuing the task, we must be respectful of what is determinate in the world and we must be intelligent about our interests.

What is true of classifying living organisms in general is true also of classifying humans. The conception of a human species is pieced together out of characteristics observed in large populations of individuals. No single feature or invariable set of traits is necessary and sufficient for someone to be declared a human being. Such pronouncements result from complex judgments made on the basis of considering candidates with regard to dozens of features.

Physical appearance is the first test we impose on those we might admit into our midst. The requirement is not that they meet some conventional standard of good looks (though the question of what level of hideous deformity deprives individuals of human status has occupied writers of horror fiction for ages), but that they resemble in some general way the appearance of sample humans. A creature that looks like a large sponge lacking bilateral symmetry could not pass for one of us. Generally, beings without heads and faces would be unlikely candidates for humanity.

With looks goes size, though as an independent variable. Tom Thumb and eight-foot wrestlers clearly qualify, but a being no larger than a flea may not, even if its voice could be amplified enough to be heard. And a creature that needed all of the state of Maryland to sit down would almost certainly not be accepted as human even if it had a soothing voice and interesting things to say.

Behavior has to be appropriate, as well. The wax figures in Madame Tussaud's museum have the right look and size but they do nothing, while the humans we know can hardly stand still. The actions must, moreover, not look mechanical, unless of course the context (as, for example, singing Olympia in the first act of *Hoffman's Tales*) makes it clear that such angular motions are mimicked and not natural.

Actions must show sustained purposiveness, unless of course one can imagine reasons why the being we try to classify keeps abandoning its tasks. There must, moreover, be need for things we recognize as important—for food and water, and for novelty, caring, communication and sleep. But even these needs are under the thumb of the almighty *unless;* there are exceptions and counterexamples to everything.

Next, candidates must be able to make mistakes and to show affection. Unflappable infallibility is not a promising sign of the human, and we are ready to call stoic reserve downright inhuman. If possible, we also want to ascertain that the being to be included was born of woman rather than manufactured in a local factory or grown on a banana tree. And today, if all else fails, we may even have the individual's genetic structure examined, to see if it resembles that of sample humans closely enough.

None of these indicators is decisive as evidence for inclusion or exclusion. In ordinary life, we are rarely in doubt; a glance or two is sufficient to foreshorten a complex judgment. But when serious questions arise about the humanity of some creature, we find ourselves canvassing all the considerations I have adduced and many more, including the social and economic costs of a decision either way, in search of a balanced judgment.

Such judgments can be difficult and politically charged. Freaks and monsters seem to dwell "in an intermediate zone between the species";[4] they appear to "call into question, to problematize, the boundary between humans and other animals."[5] John Merrick the elephant man, Jo Jo the Russian dog-faced boy, Fred Wilson the lobster boy, Avery Childs the frog boy,[6] humanlike creatures raised by wolves, speaking no language and running on all fours, and the beastly, bizarre and deranged individuals we find in every city present problems of classification that have important moral consequences. We are currently engaged in a bitter public debate about viewing the fetus as a human being and may eventually face the same decision about advanced computer-driven robots. In all such cases, the central thing to remember is that we seek not a discovery but a responsible decision. Taxonomic classification is a matter of choice that always remains in our hands.

There have been unfortunate attempts in the course of history to simplify such complex decisions by introducing irrelevant criteria and making them decisive. The tribal origin, the skin color and the religion of individuals were at one time or another considered easy ways of telling whether one was human or an unworthy beast. Refusing to admit any one mark as conclusive is one of the safeguards that exclusion never again becomes automatic or easy.

I have indicated that such judgment calls bring our purposes and values into play.[7] This makes it sensible to ask what good it does to sort creatures into the single, uniform category of humans. One may argue, with John Dupre, that "*Homo sapiens* is much too broad and coarse a category for understanding human beings."[8] If, as he claims, our behavior cannot be explained by reference to properties characteristic of our taxonomic place,[9] what is the point of viewing all of us as belonging to the same species?

Such objections make the mistake of supposing that the primary function of classification is epistemic. But saying that some beings are human conveys less about what they are like than about how we are to treat them. The humanity of a creature is not a fact discovered but a status conferred. It means, among other things, that if found hurt or ill, it is to be taken to a doctor, not a vet. As a signal to us, moreover, that it *is* to be taken for help instead of being discarded or being allowed to bleed to death by the highway, it exposes us to blame and perhaps even legal action if we fail.

Establishing effective signals of this sort in relation to a broad range of individuals constitutes a grand but late achievement in history. The idea of expanding the compass of humanity, and with it caring, beyond the tribe or beyond the confines of beings narrowly like us is the foundation of decency and the guaranty of at least the possibility of a happy life. Being classed with humans endows individuals with rights and dignity. It protects them from the sort of abuse endured by poor blacks in the Tuskegee syphilis study and the mass murders faced by Armenians, Bosnians, Tutsis, Hutus, Gypsies, Christians, Jews, Moslems and Native Americans, among countless others.

The notion of a simple human nature that spreads its protective umbrella over a broad spectrum of individuals is, therefore, of vast moral significance. As with all benefits, however, there is a hidden cost. Sameness of nature invites us to expect similarity in behavior. When this expectation rises to the level of demand, we feel justified in prescribing to others what they should and what they must not do.

The idea that, as Aristotle would say, nature determines perfection occurs to us virtually without prompting. Since our primary acquaintance with human nature is in our own persons and values, it is understandable that we should want everyone to treasure the things we do. The uniform human nature that protects us from atrocities is transformed in this way into a fountainhead of conformity. In the hands of the powerful in society, this call to act alike can come to justify coercion.

We see this tendency in the attitude of some Western countries toward the Third World, in declaring certain sexual practices to be against nature, and in the demand (which we are now trying to unlearn) that women should be like men. A vast number of disagreements that masquerade as ethical are in reality differences in taste and preference due to genetic or cultural or historical contingencies, leaving neither side entitled to claim the high ground of moral rightness.

Moreover, even where the controversies bear moral significance, there may be no universally correct answers. Of course some acts are morally right and others wrong; error in valuation is a painful and prevalent reality. But casual outsiders cannot determine the values appropriate to any living soul and have, therefore, no defensible basis for coercing behavior or even for condemning those who continue to act by their own lights. Our values differ not only by one set being right and others wrong, but also in that within the compass of what ought to be permissible, only unlike things can satisfy us.

The idea that our nature determines our good opens a line of thought that helps us see and appreciate our diversity. For, to use Kant's language, if nature is the *ratio essendi* of our values, our values constitute the *ratio cognoscendi* of our natures. The insight that who we are determines what life is good for us thus suggests the equally sensible notion that people have no better way of learning about their natures than by seeing what fulfills them. This way of putting the matter leads inevitably to the conclusion that one human nature cannot accommodate all of us. If values emerge from nature, the wide and irreducible heterogeneity of human goods clearly points to a multiplicity of human natures.

Our current needs offer added support for acknowledging not only a single human nature, but also many of them. The reasons for both acknowledgments are the same: to secure the dignity of human beings and to make it possible for them to seek their good lives in their own ways. Inclusion in a single species guarantees rights to all; differentiating us into a variety of natures safeguards against a natural consequence of such inclusion, namely the oppressive demand that all of us pursue the same ideals. Our shared nature forms the foundation of decency, our divergent natures provide the ground of toleration.

The moment we begin to talk about different human natures, however, we face grave dangers. For fear of reinstituting exclusion, we must not speak of such differences outside the context of our unity as members of a single species. Moreover, we must be especially careful not to define human natures in such a way as to breathe new life into pernicious distinctions and old prejudices. As we have seen earlier in this century, unchecked national-ism can, for example, mutate into a system of supremacy based on hierar-chically arrayed human natures defined by racial characteristics. And in practice no less than in theory, throughout much of the nineteenth cen-tury, people associated human natures with stages of cultural development.

By contrast with such gross and for the most part irrelevant indicators, we need to structure the taxonomy of human natures in a fashion that pays particular attention to the satisfaction of individuals. Racial and sexual identity are not much more relevant to this than is the height of people or the porosity of their clavicles. Stage of cultural development can be ger-mane because it influences taste and satisfaction, but it is not determining. The human natures we seek are not biological and not even cultural in the sense suggested by a recent writer.[10] Genetic and cultural features may sub-tend them, but they are centered around the affective and valuational affinities of individuals.

It may be instructive to relate the human natures I have in mind to the culturally defined multiple human species John Dupre urges us to recog-nize. Dupre thinks our single human nature constitutes a biological species whose characteristics are not very useful for the explanation of behavior. He introduces cultural speciation as a way to boost the explanatory power of the properties typical of the group to which we belong. His view is that "cultural distinctions within the (biological) species should play a role in our understanding analogous to that played by distinctions between species in biology generally."[11]

As a critique of sociobiology and a call to understanding behavior at the social level,[12] this is right on target. But Dupre himself admits that the interconnectedness of the modern world has hybridized whatever cultur-ally distinct species might have existed before. This strips the notion of cul-tural species of most of its value, and Dupre ends with the idea that "the appropriate typology for modern humankind is going to vary according to the context of inquiry."[13]

He is certainly right about this last point, which constitutes an excellent platform for assessing the value of my position. The suggestion that we dis-tinguish human natures by the valuational affinities of individuals leads to a human typology useful for enhancing both our understanding of what people do and our toleration for how they differ from us. Values are prime determinants of behavior and central targets of alien attack. To group individuals by what they treasure is, therefore, of great epistemic and moral utility. Instead of being inapplicable to globalized society, as is the notion of cultural species, it captures the very heart of the modern world, adding to our grasp of why people act as they do while providing a spur to act in a way that is morally better.

What might a system of such valuationally differentiated human natures look like? A great merit of the history of philosophy is that nearly every interesting intellectual problem has been worked up in its course, even if in a strange or unreal context. So, for example, Plato recognizes the valuational affinities of individuals in his search for a community that would be characterized by order, stability and the satisfaction that attends virtue. He thinks, of course, that such persons should be seen as constituting classes rather than species, and he is, unfortunately, quick to impose hierarchical order on them so they may be ruled by intelligence in their service to the state. But the peace of the *polis* and its permanence are built around the differential though complementary satisfactions of its elements.

We need to overlook Plato's eugenic and educational efforts to generate these human types, along with his manipulative communitarianism, focusing only on the central insight that humans quite naturally group around certain values that, if permitted dominance in their lives, make them happy. He is right that some people love war and adventure with all their souls, and nothing but fights and danger and risky exploration can make their existence worthwhile. Even such a peaceful person as William James acknowledged this when he wrote of the need for a moral equivalent to war[14] for, the usefulness of martial virtues aside, some people just cannot be happy without being pugilists.

If we expand Plato's three classes to an indefinite number, we come near to the conception of human natures I have in mind. Whatever the source of our preferences, when they crystallize in the form of habits that define our constitutions, satisfying them ceases to be a matter of fortuitous happenstance and acquires centrality. Someone who thrives on public attention, for example, can suffer no greater punishment than to be deprived of it. To people who seek power and wield it with unceasing delight, continuing exercise of it is an imperative above all others. And individuals used to quiet reflection on the world may find that nothing else satisfies in quite the same way, or that nothing else satisfies at all.

Persons who share any such life-organizing value display pervasive similarities to each other. We can best understand what they do and how they feel by reference to their structuring, though possibly unarticulated, commitments. In order to construct a life, the purpose or devotion must be relatively general and pervasive, and in order for us to permit it to construct lives, it must not be aggressively antisocial. How encompassing it must be is a matter of circumstance waiting for leisurely, judicious assessment. How far it can go on the scale of abrogating shared values before we stop those who live by it is a matter of far more urgent judgment.

Acceptance that our natures differ commits us to mutual respect and toleration. But high-mindedness can go only so far, and, like it or not, we find ourselves constantly engaged in wiping out or at least preventing the spread of certain human natures. I speak not of opportunity criminals or of people who, embittered by an impersonal world, feel tempted to make a violent statement, but of individuals whose nature resembles those of mass murderers and serial rapists or simply Jeffrey Dahmer's. We do everything we can by education, by incarceration and if necessary even by execution to make sure that this species of humanity does not replicate itself.

With respect to other sorts of human beings, all of us would be well advised to learn more about them and to learn to appreciate them. As William James eloquently pointed out, we all suffer from a certain blindness, a grave inability to see the world as others see it.[15] A central component of this sightlessness is the difficulty we have in understanding how others can live by the values they do. Yet it is not so hard to get a feel for what such lives are like; sympathetic observation quickly takes us there. Caring acquaintance makes what at first seemed monstrous a harmless matter of course. The greatest benefit of recognizing different human natures is that it makes our differences natural.

Purists among us may find it odd that the real distinctions metaphysics attempts to capture should respond to the call of our purposes and values. But Plato and much of the rest of the great tradition held that there is no deeper principle than the good. Metaphysics must, accordingly, always remain in the service of ethics.

CHAPTER 7

Improving Life

In an otherwise astonishingly abstract and tedious essay, Harry Frankfurt argues for the interesting thesis that the unidirectional relation between means and ends is insupportable.[1] He points out that Aristotle, the father of the Western tradition of thought concerning means and ends, maintained that means are valuable only for their tendency to bring about desirable ends, while ends are valuable in and of themselves. The relation is asymmetrical because means derive their value from the ends to which they lead, but ends gain no benefit from the relationship.

Frankfurt argues, by contrast, that even if ends do not profit from having certain means necessary for their attainment, people do. For the actions in which one must engage to bring about certain ends endow one's existence with meaning by providing purposive activity that is complex and "radiates extensively within the person's life."[2]

So just as means have instrumental value because they lead to certain ends, ends have instrumental value because they require certain activities as means. Further, ends have "final" value because we care about them and they are worth having on their own account, and means have final value because they are worth having as necessary constituents of a meaningful life.

This point appears remarkably similar to Dewey's idea of what is sometimes called "means-end integrated actions."[3] According to that view, human actions are at their best when each one of them is both means and end, that is, useful for what it produces and enjoyable for what it is. Is this "coalescence"[4] of instrumental and consummatory value what Frankfurt has in mind? If it is, Dewey has at last made his much-awaited appearance in the precincts of analytic philosophy. Unfortunately, however, his arrival continues to be delayed. Frankfurt's ideas are different from Dewey's for at least two reasons. First, he speaks of ends acquiring instrumental value because they require certain means that have final value. The means obtain such intrinsic value, however, only because of their relationship to a meaningful life. Frankfurt says that the means are necessary for such a life, but not that they constitute it. This indicates that the means lack intrinsic value after all. They simply serve as means to two desirable ends instead of one: they are useful for obtaining the specific final goods at which they aim and also a meaningful life of purposive activity.

Frankfurt could amend his view, I suppose, and say that the connection between means and meaningful life is more intimate than he initially implied, for such a life is constituted by purposive activity rather than being merely brought about by it. But this still keeps him a distance away from Dewey. The hallmark of what Dewey calls an "external means" is substitutability.[5] Working as a waiter is an external means to earning the money necessary for life, for nothing about earning a living specifically requires it. This is but another way of saying that working as, say, a taxi driver can easily and adequately replace it. Similarly, what we need for meaningful life is not this or that specific purposive activity, but only some purposive exertion or other. So means acquire final value not for what they are but for the sort of thing they represent. This is at odds with Dewey's commitment to the value of individual activities and events and also with what we treasure and how we treasure it in everyday life.

The second difference between Frankfurt's and Dewey's views is closely connected to the first. Frankfurt is satisfied to talk about generalities of the order of meaningful lives, suggesting that some activities acquire intrinsic value for contributing to them. With characteristic common sense and commitment to the denotative method, Dewey avoids speaking of such totalizing abstractions, restricting his account of the coincidence of means and ends to specific activity sequences. Instead of arguing that nibbling one's lover's ears contributes to something as nebulous as a meaningful life, he points out that such small bites are both intrinsically delightful and truly helpful in getting where one wants to go. This strikes me as a far more interesting and promising approach to the improvement of life than anything Frankfurt has to offer.

How far can Dewey's ideal of means-end integrated actions take us in the quest to improve human life? I examined this question once before, but there is more to say than I had a chance to develop there.[6] Here, I first explain why this topic and Dewey's response to it are of great significance. Then I outline historically important alternative approaches. Finally, I examine Dewey's proposal in detail and evaluate it against the background of these alternatives.

Since the beginning of the historical record, humans have enjoyed the pursuit and possession of valued experiences. Unfortunately, the pursuit was often painful and the possession disappointing. But even when the enjoyment was deemed worth its cost, it could be attained only at considerable labor or sacrifice or pain. The Bible testifies to this element of the human condition and identifies it as a consequence of original sin. God's punishment of Adam's and Eve's transgression condemns women to bearing children in pain and all of us to earning our daily bread by the sweat of our brows. The situation has not changed much since those early days. Although life today is immeasurably easier than it must have been thousands of years ago, we still face having to delay gratification, having to do much that we don't care for and having to submit to the discipline of enduring painful means to obtain satisfying ends.

Perhaps the first systematic response to this lamentable condition was the establishment of class structure, shifting all onerous activity to large groups of unfortunate slaves or laborers. This allowed the tribal chief or king or lord to devote his time to the enjoyment of the goods of the world. Hegel describes this strategy well in the master-slave dialectic, noting the struggle by which the lord attains control over the lives of his slaves.[7] The result is that the slaves work the ground to produce the necessities of life, while the lord retains for himself "desire and the enjoyment of things."[8] Whether the lord ends up bored, dependent on his slaves or desperately in search of a challenge, it remains true that he does not have to do much he does not want to and lives with far fewer demands on him for unpleasant exertions. Since his happy self-indulgence is gained at the cost of great misery to others, this procedure solves the problem only for a few, while it exacerbates it for everyone else.

Another strategy to deal with unavoidable misery, as Hegel aptly points out, is the slave's. He has no opportunity to shift the burden of the painful cost of delight onto others and thus no choice but to face endless labor with equanimity. The Stoic solution is to accept whatever comes one's way without complaint and to do what one must as though one wanted to. "Do not wish that things go the way you desire," Epictetus, himself a slave, says, "but wish them to happen as they will, and things will go well for you."[9] Such control over desires or refusal to acknowledge the unpleasantness of the unpleasant can presumably be attained by anyone. But its cost is too high, requiring the extinction of natural human preferences and feelings. Indifference to the painful quickly turns into indifference to all things, exacting loss of the joys of life as the price of subduing its pains. If the lord lives at the expense of others, Stoics hardly live at all: they despair of our ability to improve the human lot, abandon all hope, and satisfy themselves with changes to their attitudes even when the drive for objective changes would succeed.

Aristotle's famous distinction between processes and activities is a highbrow variant of the class-structure strategy. Processes involve the usual separation between potentially painful means and desirable ends. Their hallmark is that their ends are external to the means used to attain them, and the ends can be attained only with effort and over a period of time. In activities, by contrast, means and ends coalesce or else means simply drop out. Each activity is pursued for its own sake, and we can engage in it directly, without having to perform any antecedent acts. This means that activities involve no instrumentalities at all. They are ends-in-themselves that require neither preparation nor time for their performance: they are instant accomplishments and hence transcendent moments of delight.

The way to eliminate the painful labor of life, then, is to concentrate on those experiences that are possible without it. Such experiences tend to point away from the material underpinnings of life, consisting mainly of the higher achievements of what Aristotle calls "intellectual virtue." Thinking and seeing and contemplative enjoyment are activities in the required sense: to do them, he says, is to have done them,[10] meaning that in them, doing and deed, process and product are indissolubly one. Small wonder, then, that the life of the philosopher is second only to God's. Thinkers know how to engage in activities and thereby to liberate themselves from the dissatisfactions and drudgeries of life. Free of the incomplete acts to which we are condemned in the temporal world, philosophers can live, at least for a few moments, in the eternal.

Aristotle's plan for bettering life is not as harsh as Hegel's lord's, but it is just as elitist. The difference is that class divisions rest on discrepancies of power, whereas Aristotle's strategy relies on divergences of taste and training. But in reality, a division of labor underlies Aristotle's proposal as well. The material needs of life don't disappear while we contemplate; only when they are met, in fact, can we enjoy the leisure necessary for thought. So the shift from processes to activities does not solve the problem of unavoidably painful instrumentalities. It redistributes the pain to those who must produce the goods of the world and to those times in the lives of the educated when they are not busy contemplating.

A variant of the Stoic slave's strategy has for long enjoyed popularity among morally serious people. The approach is reminiscent of Kant and is, in at least one version, powerfully supported by the promises of religion. Instead of recommending indifference to joy and suffering alike, this strategy isolates necessary but undesirable labor and designates its performance a matter of moral obligation. Calling it duty removes such misery from the realm of what we could expect to like; that what we ought to do should be no fun is unsurprising and irrelevant. Kant sums it up neatly by asserting that morality has nothing to do with happiness. Its austere edicts derive from reason and bind us to obedience through respect for a law we impose on ourselves. Whether we like it or not is never to the point; it would be not only hopeless but also wrong to try to change the course of things in such a way that duty becomes less onerous or, God forbid, something we can happily embrace.

Self-development, for example, is a duty we must not avoid.[11] Boring teachers, endless practice and painful self-control must be endured without complaint. That we experience them as torture testifies to the fact that they do us good; they could surely not be as beneficial if they were fun. Pain, therefore, is a natural, inevitable and wholesome signal that we take our obligations seriously. In the *Critique of Practical Reason,* Kant goes a step further and converts the traditional promises of Christianity into philosophical support for the view that we must overlook the painful instrumentalities of life. For those who put up with them and do what duty demands are entitled to heavenly rewards.[12] Over the infinity of our immortal lives, God will adjust happiness to match virtue and thereby compensate the upright for their pains. Evidently, this does not erase the suffering in this world, but it holds out the hope that things might go better in the next.

A central characteristic of modernity is the unwillingness to leave it to God to set things right. For the last five hundred years, Western civilization has been in the business of showing God how He might take a more active role in bringing improvements to the world. What I will call "the technological strategy" consists in identifying undesirable features of reality and launching intelligent efforts to change or to eliminate them. This has been a hugely successful enterprise, enabling us to extend human life, defeat disease after disease, and make daily existence vastly more comfortable than earlier generations could have imagined. Many of the pains previously thought unavoidable no longer plague us. Machines have taken over much undesirable labor, and resort hotels testify that social life is organized so that at least some people can enjoy stretches of time as uninterrupted series of ends.

Intelligent industrial and commercial activity have been so effective in dealing with human problems that we hear more and more sanguine appraisals of its ultimate promise. Various forecasts predict an end to wars, the expansion of life expectancy to a hundred and fifty years, the elimination of hunger and all disease, and mastery over both depression and aggression. Manipulation of the genetic material of our species is supposed to enable us to create problem-free individuals whom we can clone into societies of happy and responsible people. Distinctions of class, race and gender will melt as we educate or breed prejudice out of people. Everything unpleasant will be recognized as unnecessary or at least as unworthy of humans, to be accomplished by metallic or silicon machines. Utopia, in brief, is just around the corner, offering ever greater benefits at diminishing cost.

The promise of such unclouded days is curiously at odds with the reality of industrial and commercial life. No matter how much better off they are than prior generations, people today seem no more happy. The incidence of mental illness is increasing, and suicide, especially among healthy young persons, is a baffling and distressingly common phenomenon. Even the best adjusted find themselves engulfed in a whirl of immediately pressing but otherwise meaningless activities. Our workdays are filled with busy preparations for consummations that are fleeting or that never come. Most important, the tedious labor we used to have to expend to secure the necessities of life directly has been replaced by equally tedious but different service to huge institutions.

This last point is crucial. We do not have to go hunting each day; we do not even have to fertilize the garden and kill and clean a chicken for lunch. But we do have to go to work and serve in whatever ways our employers direct. Many of these activities are of little interest and carry no intrinsic reward. They involve pushing paper and attending meetings on issues of momentous indifference, or moving physical objects from one place to another, or attending to things that are difficult to see as anything but insignificant. No matter how many external means we succeed in eliminating, others no better rush in to take their place. The servant of modern corporations may enjoy fewer satisfying ends-in-themselves than the hunters and farmers of old.

This brief look at historical alternatives highlights the importance of Dewey's idea of means-end integrated actions. His view promises permanent improvements to the human condition. Instead of solving the problem of how to dispense with undesirable labor for a few people only, as do class-structure arrangements, Dewey offers a strategy that is universally or at least generally applicable. Instead of proposing a subjective, attitudinal adjustment, as do the Stoics, or a trick of reclassification, as does Kant, he presents a way of objectively reconstructing our relations to our activities. Although he strongly favors intelligent improvements in the material conditions of life, he has no difficulty in seeing through the excessive optimism of the devotees of technology to the travail that underlies the achievements of civilization.[13]

Dewey's view of means-end integrated actions consists of the following three general ideas:

1. Each event and action has an intrinsic quality that can be enjoyed;
2. Each event and action is connected to others by means of causal or sequential relations;
3. Events and actions can be arranged in sequences so intimate that their earlier and later phases are united.

Although Dewey was deeply indebted to Hegel, he learned from Peirce not to be satisfied with mediation or thirdness alone. Peirce's category of firsts reminded Dewey that there is an inexpressible immediacy in all of experience. Enjoyment or suffering of the qualities of what happens is the outcome of paying attention to them for what they are, independently of the relations connecting them to other events. I am satisfied that experiences have such qualities and that, in a stance of immediacy, it is possible to enjoy many of them. I am by no means sure, however, that all of them can be enjoyed rather than suffered, but I will wait to discuss that issue until Dewey's position is clear.

Dewey's second claim also strikes me as unproblematically correct. What he calls "the sequential order"[14] consists of naturally connected events, that is, of processes or natural histories. These orderly connections make it possible for us to achieve some measure of control over the environment. I may note, for example, that sunflower seeds falling on the ground tend to germinate and grow into new plants. I can exploit this connection and place sunflower seeds where I want the plants for decoration or maximum yield. The procedure works equally well in situations in which we wish to prevent a natural process from prevailing. I may notice, for instance, that rain soaks my head when I am outside, but not when I have a roof over my head. I can then design a small roof, called an umbrella, to carry with me to prevent nature from having its way. Such useful interventions presuppose no special theory of the nature of causation: we simply need to observe sequences and find the time or the place to direct, abort, or redirect them.[15]

The first idea affirms the possibility that each experience can be enjoyed as end; the second points to the fact that every event is instrumental in bringing others into existence. Important as these claims are for Dewey's view, the characteristic feature of his theory is the third idea, addressing the way earlier and later events must be connected in order for a sequence of actions to be means-end integrated. In general terms, the relation needs to be one of unity. Dewey seems to have identified two different sorts of unity that may obtain between means that are not external and the ends to which they lead. The weaker condition for escaping the status of being an external means requires that means be enjoyable as ends-in-themselves and that ends be useful for further attainments. This suggests that such processes must exhibit unity at least in the sense that their elements are similar in being both useful and intrinsically valuable. This condition, if met, would be adequate to eliminate the drudgery of life by rendering means inherently and not only instrumentally valuable.

The stronger condition for a means being "intrinsic" demands an internal relation between means and ends. According to it, sharing final and instrumental value is inadequate for means-end integrated actions. There must also be a more intimate connection which takes one of two forms: either the means must be a part of the end or the end must be a completion of the means. Dewey explains the first version of the relation with great rhetorical power, returning to it again and again. He attacks the view that means are antecedents that must disappear before our desires are fulfilled. On the contrary, he says, they are vital ingredients of what will come about, in just the way flour is both a means to and an element in the bread we bake. He uses a variety of other illustrations to make sure his point is clear: he notes that sound institutions are both means to an orderly society and elements of it,[16] bricks and mortar are both necessary instruments and valued components of houses,[17] and paints are means to the pictures they constitute.[18]

The second version of the relation is a little more difficult to explain than the first. Dewey suggests that means and ends must be related in such a way that the means foreshadow the ends and the ends complete the means. An example may make this relation clearer. Baking an apple pie is an activity united by the identity of purpose and outcome. When all goes well, my objective and the eventual object produced are the same, and the entire process is directed by what I want to attain. I may begin by looking for apples to peel, rejecting squash and carrot; I buy pie shells instead of cheese pizza; I place the unbaked pie in the oven rather than in the disposal unit. Dewey insists that such intimately interconnected processes occur in nature even without human intervention. He has in mind sequences the ends of which are fulfillments and not merely cessations.[19] The mating of animals and the creation of islands as a result of volcanic activity may be instances of such fulfillments, though the question of whether they are or not is irrelevant to what Dewey wants to say about means and ends and, accordingly, does not need to be decided here.

In perfect accord with his method, Dewey developed the weaker and the two versions of the stronger account of how means and ends may be unified by observation of experiential sequences. He may not have realized that he was dealing with three independent requirements for means-end integrated actions or he may have thought that any one of the three involves or entails the others. I see no obvious or simple connections among them. One could subscribe to the demand that all elements of an experiential sequence be both means and ends while rejecting the idea that means must be parts of ends or ends fulfillments of means. Similarly, even if a means is eventually incorporated in its end, it need not be an end on its own account when experienced as an early element of a process. However this may be, meeting three criteria, even if interconnected, is a heavier burden than Dewey needs to bear. For this reason, I will examine them one at a time and credit Dewey with a significant advance if even a single one of them can be generalized enough to help us improve human experience.

What sort of generalization do we seek? We want to see whether, by using Dewey's criteria of nonexternal means, we can convert displeasing experiences into ones that satisfy. Such conversions cannot be matters of adjusting attitudes alone. They require reconstructions of experience and possibly even significant institutional changes, albeit none that is utopian. Such a test of Dewey's ideas is clearly in line with his meliorism and expresses in concrete terms his commitment to philosophy as the critic of social practices.

The idea that ends are fulfillments of purposive processes is, among the three requirements, the one most expressive of Dewey's commitments. His notion of purposive process connects to his ideas about meaning and intelligent control. Viewing ends as completions of human efforts, therefore, amounts to placing them in the context of our desires to bring about outcomes favorable to life. Careful attention to the conditions of what we do enables us to achieve the consequences we want, and outcome controlled by our own actions is what Dewey calls "meaning."[20] He adds that "The characteristic human need is for possession and appreciation of the meaning of things."[21]

For ends to be fulfillments of means, they must be meaningful and therefore humanly constructed outcomes. Dewey's idea is that anything so constructed involves effort and victory, and he finds it impossible to believe that such successful activities could fail to be joyous. His prescription, then, is to make the employment of means intelligent so that we can take delight in the effective exercise of human powers. This is thoughtful observation of what pleases us, and generally good advice. As early a student of human nature as Aristotle remarked that unimpeded activity directed upon worthy objects is naturally accompanied by pleasure.[22] The joy of possessing the end spreads to the means used to attain it and is reinforced by the exhilaration of experiencing our power. What we have to do to carry the day is, then, not an alien necessity but an affirmation of what we want and who we are.

The obvious problem is how we can experience means-end sequences as self-controlled exercises of our power. Clearly, most of the ends we enjoy are fulfillments resulting from our intelligent efforts—if "we" and "our" are taken to mean "human" or "social" or "institutional." "We" manufacture airplanes and fly them all over the globe. "We" build skyscrapers and fill them with corporations that bring goods from the far corners of the world to satisfy our cravings. "We" create systems of communication that enable us to know what happens in Australia or in outer space. Modern life is full of stunning institutional achievements of which we, if we manage to identify ourselves with the human race, can be genuinely proud.

The difficulty resides in the relation of the we to the I. Normally, the grander the fulfillment, the more people are required to secure it. Participants in such social acts must be organized in chains of mediation,[23] with a clear division of labor between those who plan, those who execute the plans, and those who enjoy or suffer the consequences. An astonishing level of ignorance pervades these chains: though everyone is busy contributing to the ultimate result, very few understand how what they do is integrated into the larger whole. This means that even the people whose direct agency attains the end find it difficult to see the achievement as their own. They are familiar with but their own small fragment of the means; control of consequences is not in their hands.

We find, therefore, that agents in our highly mediated society experience themselves as instruments of causes they do not adopt and may not even approve. Contributing but an insignificant ounce of power to the megawatts needed for large-scale social acts, they cannot adopt the end as the fulfillment of anything they know about or labor to achieve. Their alienation is an outcome of the magnitude of institutional acts and the multitude of people required to carry them out. For this reason, it is very difficult to overcome. Eliminating large-scale mediated chains sacrifices the attainments of industrial civilization. Quite apart from Dewey's abhorrence of psychological manipulation, the last hundred years provide ample evidence that increasing social-mindedness or identifying the I with the we in peacetime cannot be achieved for long by propaganda.

How could individuals come to see the ends they help attain as mean-ingful fulfillments of their own efforts? Three conditions would have to be met. They would have to understand the social acts in which they partici-pate much better than they do now. They would have to be partners in the decisions to undertake such acts. They would also have to share equitably in the benefits such acts generate. This is but another way of saying that our society would have to be organized to provide effective and universal education, openness in institutional, social and governmental decision-making, participatory democracy in all human interactions, and social jus-tice for all. Human life would, indeed, be immeasurably better if we lived under such circumstances. But no one can seriously contemplate such de-velopments outside the realm of dreamy utopia.

Is the other, simpler form of Dewey's strong criterion for nonexternal means applicable to much of human experience? The wide range of Dewey's examples suggests that means that both generate their ends and become parts of them constitute the rule and not the exception. Flour cer-tainly is both instrumental to and an ingredient in bread, bricks are neces-sary for houses and also parts of them, and colors are required for paint-ings and also constitute them. If this relation obtained generally in experience, means and ends would be at least partly identical, recognition of which would tend to transfer to means some of our enjoyment of ends. Instead of viewing means as oppressive necessities, we could welcome them as early, incomplete appearances of what we hope to achieve.

Unfortunately, convincing as Dewey's examples may seem, they all share a common, limiting feature. The means he selects for attention con-sist of enduring physical and social objects. Bricks are not used up when we build a house and flour does not pass out of existence when we convert it into bread. The cultural objects he identifies tend also to persist: a "good political constitution, honest police-system, and competent judiciary"[24] are continuous patterns of activity. These examples overlook all the elements of means subject to the destructive power of time. Bricks must be carried to the masons, and they must fit them in the wall hour after tedious hour. Flour must be mixed and kneaded at night by a baker who would much sooner be home sleeping with his wife. The integrity of institutions is achieved by the agonized self-control of those who could abuse it, and must be safeguarded by painful vigilance.

All of these activities disappear with the doing, and most of them in-volve undesirable labor. None of these elements of means can be retained and raised to glory as parts of what in the end satisfies. They torture us with their boredom, their repetitiousness and their unavoidable pain, filling our days with what no one wants and no one can escape. The long, uncomfortable journey does not end up as part of the fun of visiting distant places. A sonata beautifully played does not incorporate years of youth lost in involuntary practice. The starving person's anguished search for food is best forgotten when the meal begins. Even if some elements of means survive and reach fulfillment in their ends, most of them do not; they remain as the bitter costs of getting what we want.

That leaves us, alas, only with Dewey's weak criterion of means-end integrated actions. This conception presents means and end as a continuous process, each part of which is useful on account of its relations to other events and enjoyable because of its intrinsic qualities. Dewey thinks so highly of this coalescence of means and ends that he employs it to explicate the nature of the esthetic. His point is that artistic creativity aims to produce works each element of which is delightful and yet leads seamlessly to the rest. Symphonies are like this, and our lives can be lived this way as well, if we do not permit enjoyment and utility to be separated.

The Enlightenment dream was to make life rational. Dewey adds to it the nineteenth-century hope of making it a work of art as well. This creates a grand ideal that we can, here and there, approximate for a time. There are activities every element of which is rich in consequences and rewarding to experience. The play of children comes to mind, as does the sexual play of adults; sports qualify, as do good conversations. I discussed this at greater length elsewhere[25] and I continue to think that having such experiences suffuse one's life would make for an exceptionally satisfying existence.

The problem for those of us wishing to improve life is that some of our experiences are already means-end integrated actions, and it is not clear how the bulk of those that are not can be reconstructed on that pattern. Giving a cat a pill, having a rattle found and fixed in the car, and preparing one's tax forms are just not joyous activities, and there is nothing we can do to make them that. One can bribe oneself with rewards for undertaking such tasks, and if one is gullible one can make oneself believe that they are fun. Such psychological manipulation, however, is not what Dewey has in mind. His idea is that every experience has a quality intrinsic to it that, if we focus on it properly, can be a source of joy.

There is no denying that careful attention to the details of things elevates the human spirit. Intricacy of pattern and richness of involution still the human mind with grateful amazement at the actual. But such resolute focus requires leisure and peace of mind; interest in the utility of the perception tends to negate concentration on the immediate. Many qualities, moreover, are not agreeable to experience. Attention to the distinctive features of agony, of foul smells and of human failure is not rewarding, and it is best to move through such deserts without looking long and hard.

We can, of course, imagine the world without deserts, but that is utopian. For Dewey, rightly, the issue is how to make incremental changes, improvements that add up in the end. And that is just where the notion of means-end integrated actions is supposed to help but does not help enough.

But how much is enough? In spite of occasional statements that demand and promise more, Dewey himself seems satisfied with modest progress in the affairs of life. Perhaps no one should hope for more. Difficult problems have no grand solutions; it may be wise to settle for ideals that leave us a little better off here and there. Combined with the power of technology to relieve us of the worst suffering and of the most inhuman labor, Dewey's idea of means-end integrated actions may help us achieve some, though by no means all, of the little improvements of which the human frame is capable. Not wishing for Utopia, or even for universal improvement, is a sign of maturity. Yet it is a sad sign: relinquishing the hope for more decisive and more permanent betterment of our condition leaves a living wound in the human soul.

CHAPTER **8**

Transcendence in Philosophy and in Everyday Life

Philosophy lost something important with Kant. Prior to the advent of his critical thought, we could with good conscience pursue the transcendent. Philosophy appeared capable of giving us insight into what lies below, behind or above ordinary experience. It seemed possible that the ultimately real is a transcendent God, that time is an illusion and, that when all is said and done, the world really consists of one or a very few or an infinite number of imperishable substances, ourselves among them.

Systematic thought offered hope of learning about these hidden realities. Philosophers were convinced that if only they used the right method of reflection, the ultimately real would open to them like a flower to the sun. It seemed at least possible that all the travail of this universe was but an overture to the grand opera about to unfold. Many serious people thought it likely that humans are in temporary exile in this life and that we will soon find ourselves recognized as children of a king, in disguise briefly for purposes of instruction.

Those were the childhood days of thought, the centuries of its uncritical innocence. To be sure, there always were sceptics and empiricists who resisted the speculative drive. But it is worth recalling that even empiricists were people of faith: Locke believed there was a God, and Berkeley thought there was hardly anything else. Only Hume challenged everything, but he was a night raider of the sort who creates havoc in the dark, though in the morning the world looks the same once again.

With Kant, however, everything changed. Even the possibility of philosophy giving us knowledge of transcendent existents was eliminated. From the standpoint of cognition or theory, the concept of such an extraexperiential item as the noumenon could have no content; it had to be a negative, a nearly empty notion.[1] This means that our everyday experience is the final standard of truth—that nothing can overturn this workaday world's claim to be, at least for cognitive purposes, ultimate reality.

Kant himself could not quite bear his own message, so he dropped tantalizing hints about a kingdom of ends and about what we might infer about a divine governance of the world from beauty and the purposiveness of organic life. But he remained unequivocal that such transcendent matters were not proper objects of knowledge, so that even if one part of our nature demands that we think them without cease, another part makes sure that those thoughts never acquire ultimate cognitive warrant.

The outcome of this line of thought is denial that we can ever make the big discovery. For humans, no such discovery is possible: we cannot transcend the condition revealed in our daily experience. With robust knowledge of another ontic sphere denied us, the only transcendence open is internal to experience. Kant and his successors thus turned transcendence from an ontological and epistemic to an axiological affair. They taught that instead of searching for a world beyond space-time finitude, we must content ourselves with trying to find something of intrinsic value in daily life. The stamp of the divine can no longer be some small but revealing signal to thought but a value in which we can find true satisfaction, in which the striving self finds rest.

Any general description of a trend, such as I have offered so far, has evident exceptions. Nevertheless, it is striking how few thinkers since Kant have even dared to engage in the ontological quest. Hegel and Kierkegaard, Whitehead and Sartre, Heidegger and Dewey, however they may disagree with each other, have all long given up on the simple hope that there may just be a reality deeper, finer, less evanescent, more secure, more humane or simply better than the world we inhabit today.

Since, intellectually at least, we are all children of Kant, I do not propose to speak of transcendence of the ontological/epistemic sort. But I want to be sure we note, and I personally wish to mourn, its passing. We lose something precious when we give up a noble quest, however apparently hopeless. Sensible as it may be to rein in our expectations, limits imposed on the human mind exact a price. And I cannot help thinking it at least *possible*—not only logically but in a real, living sense—that, to our great surprise, Plato or St. Thomas or Leibniz gave the right account of ultimate reality, after all. It is just *possible*, though I do not believe it, that Spinoza was right in thinking of time as due to a defect in our grasp of things rather than as a final reality.

So while I do not wish to add to such metaphysical speculations, I certainly want to leave the door open to the idea that one or another of them represents a genuine discovery. My attitude is complicated by modern skepticism that such discoveries can be made. We all know that there are fewer things in heaven and earth than have been dreamt of in philosophy. Yet, my soul whispers, perhaps one grand philosopher may just have dreamt aright.

Transcendence today is the search not for a reality beyond the everyday but for a value of unquestioned finality in daily life. This shift to axiology seems to fit the realities of modern industrial society focused on the control of nature. The desire to escape to another world is proportional to the misery we have to endure in this one. As physical suffering and need have lifted in the last few hundred years, interest in consolatory realms has waned. The price we pay for our improved condition, however, is ceaseless, and some think senseless, labor. The industrial world invites and rewards hard work that leads to delayed gratification; as a result, people find their lives consumed in activities of little direct value.

The deferral of satisfaction to the lunch hour, to the weekend, to vacation and ultimately to retirement leaves us in a recurring cycle of necessary labor—in what some call "the rat race." The desire for transcendence is the longing for something that breaks this cycle of means and ends and enables us to escape the everydayness of the everyday. The unconditional value we seek is supposed to liberate us, even if only for a short time, from meaningless routine.

Where can we find such a supreme value? Portions of the philosophical tradition since Kant can be used to provide a helpful hint. Kant himself is characteristically ambivalent on the issue: he thinks the experience of beauty provides a unique sort of value, but he cannot let the matter go without the winking suggestion that the disinterested pleasure involved offers a deep ontological insight. Since beauty engages the reflective and not the determinant judgment, we cannot *know* the purposive harmony of our faculties and of our faculties with their objects. Yet we are propelled to suppose that there is such a harmony,[2] and on the basis of that, to *think* of the world *as if* it displayed an intelligent and benevolent design. The bittersweetness of the *as if* is an apt symbol of Kant's own hesitations concerning the reach of cognitive life.

What is all caution and subtlety in Kant turns to simplicity with a touch of exaggeration in Schopenhauer. Although the credit goes to Kant for identifying beauty as a unique value, it was Schopenhauer who established the centrality of it for transcending the everyday. To be sure, Schopenhauer himself has a metaphysics that houses his account of the beautiful, but his advance on Kant is the idea that the disinterested contemplation of forms is an escape from this world rather than insight or entry into another.

Schopenhauer's description of existence is a remarkable amalgam of the psychology of romantic aggressiveness, the biology of the food chain and the unfettered competition of social and economic life. Driven by insatiable will, everything wages war on everything else, everything tries to eat or defeat whatever surrounds it.[3] The struggle for a moment in the sun defines who we are and what we do, exhausting our energy and consuming our lives in endless need and fleeting pleasure. Even memorable victories evaporate and leave us facing disaster anew and, in the end, certain death. The futility of it all makes Schopenhauer's world look like a cosmic version of the rat race, a great commotion in which insignificant activities lead to unsatisfying results.[4]

Humans can make only two meaningful responses to the universal disaster that is life. Approaching the demeanor of the saint, they can eliminate the pull of need and desire by slowly withering into death. Since this involves the disappearance of will and existence, it is not transcendence but an odd form of escape. Through it, we evade suffering by having nothing or nothingness take its place.[5]

Transcendence can be achieved only by the disinterested contemplation of beauty. What we transcend specifically is servitude to the will, that is, worry concerning our interests and the resulting cycle of gain-oriented means. In the encounter with beauty, we overlook the particularity of the existent, and with that, all the use we might make of it. Individuation drops away, and we attain immediacy with a shining, though lifeless, world of universals.[6]

To see the universal in the particular is to liberate ourselves from practical interest, from what is, for people living in industrial societies, the power and temptation of the *world*. Beauty lifts the oppression of need and circumstance. Though it cannot eliminate the moral incubus that surrounds us, it can at least yield temporary relief by providing something beyond the values of struggle, survival and success.

It took philosophers only one step beyond Schopenhauer to reach a truly interesting account of transcendence. That move was the universalization of beauty by means of the radicalization of universals. Schopenhauer acknowledged only generic universals, that is, forms defining the kinds of things that exist. Reminding his readers of the first appearance of such a notion in Western thought, he called these forms "Platonic Ideas."[7] To restrict universals to such types or archetypes is to limit them to a relatively small number. This makes the contemplation of beauty a rare and refined activity that requires the ability to abstract and is hence open to only a select few.

In one of the many ironies that dot the history of philosophy, it was an aristocratic thinker who democratized beauty to the point where anyone can be thought to have access to it at any time. George Santayana was in love with universals and could see no reason why they should be restricted to the forms of *sorts* of things. All particulars have identifiable structures, and each quality and every relation is just what it is. Such repeatable specificities are as much universals as the generic essences of natural kinds.[8] Why, then, should we deny the status of timelessness to all the definite features and relations that, without themselves changing, make change possible?

The simple insight that there is no necessary connection between the general and the universal invites the thought that we are surrounded by eternal forms. Any sense quality, such as the white of this paper, and any relation, such as its lying on the desk, is a universal in which the mind can rest. The complex shape of the paper with all these marks on it can be seen as a universal as well, and so can the even more complicated pattern of the-paper-with-its-marks-on-the-desk. Each focusable simplicity or complexity becomes, in this way, an eternal form, as long as we arrest it in consciousness and view it apart from its practical connections or vital significance.

The smell of morning sausage sends a powerful message to hungry people. They pay little attention to the intrinsic character of the scent, overlooking it in the haste to understand its meaning and, having done so, to make it to the table. The function of the smell overshadows its features: it mobilizes us into action instead of capturing our attention for an appreciation of what it is.

This is how we react to nearly everything that enters consciousness. We note what we see because we are interested in what it means, in how it relates to our welfare, in what use we can make of it. We do not linger over the grand meadow dotted with black cows because, being in a hurry to get home, it signals that we are still miles away. In our excitement to do something with them, we rarely take time to savor the beauty of ideas. Even in old age, when we have time to tarry with memories, we do so with longing and regret, instead of delight at the distant picture show.

After retirement, my father, who had been a lumberman, confessed to me that he had never looked at a tree without seeing a log. Only when the haste of life subsided was he able to notice and to take peaceful pleasure in the movement of the leaves. A moment's pause to gain a degree of removal might have enabled him, as it enables us, to achieve the same appreciation at any time in life. The radicalization of universals calls systematic attention to this ability to see the enjoyable universal in the useful particular everywhere. It makes it possible for us to give a philosophical account of the remarkable fact that if only we opened our souls to the world, we would find ourselves surrounded by beauty.

The experience of beauty has become, in this way, the point of transcendence in the modern sky. As a point and not a door, it promises only momentary rest from the travail and suffering of this world, not admission to the next. The calm, however, is real enough: beauty frees us from the oppression of time and lifts the burden of care. Our encounter with it is, as it has been tacitly and technically speaking for Kant, the peace, the joyous peace that passes all understanding.

When beauty is seen as universal, however, it loses its unique features. If the Mona Lisa is no more magnificent than the hideous scratchings of a lunatic, the usual distinction between the beautiful and the ugly disappears. There is a difference, of course, between seeing the world as splendid in all its details and seeing it as raw material for meeting our needs. But that difference is not internal to the landscape of transcendence and is, moreover, the distinction between the beautiful and the useful and not between the beautiful and the ugly. And without the latter contrast, it makes as little sense to call everything beautiful as it does to call everyone a winner in the race.

So, as it has always been supposed, transcendence—even of the modest axiological sort—takes us beyond common predicative oppositions and thus even beyond its own origins in axiology. It opens the possibility of joyous absorption in the present and in anything present to consciousness.[9] The selectivity that is the heartbeat of life loses its point, and whatever comes our way is embraced with glee. The irrelevance of choice calls attention to another traditional feature of transcendence: although humans achieve it, transcendence takes them beyond the merely human and humane. Our cozy values become, in this eternal landscape of frozen immediacies, distant alternatives with no power to attract.

If human life in our brave industrial world is all haste and striving, it should not surprise us that the peace of transcendence feels inhuman and cold. The cozy heat of existence derives from our exertions, from our beloved goals and the comfortable tools used to achieve them. To many, a single moment without a pressing plan feels like death itself; hence aimless, and therefore useless, immediacy with whatever happens our way must seem icy, meaningless and unengaging.

As Schopenhauer and nearly every sad thinker in the nineteenth century pointed out, the alternative to busy strife is boredom.[10] Removing their overly dramatic claim that all of life is a struggle leaves us with the contemporary notion that all is planning and busy labor. Boredom as the only alternative to this has been replaced by the television set and, more recently, by surfing the Internet. But those who feel dissatisfied with struggle and tedium or busyness and entertainment as the poles of life continue to search for something of greater significance or more satisfying.

Since transcendence is meant to take up the space between action and boredom, we must be sure to distinguish it from the cold of entertainment that is the death of mind. That death is surrounded by a warm glow, testifying to less than affectionate relations between humans and persistent thought. Transcendence, by contrast, is the death of will, a generally lamented event that chills us to the bone. We are far more intimately connected with our drives than with our intellect, so when transcendence puts them on ice or declares them irrelevant, we feel as though life itself has fled.

To many, the most worrisome feature of transcendence is its presumed conflict with moral values. Novelists, in particular, tend to be fascinated by the ways in which acting on aesthetic values destroys decency and goodness. The pursuit of transcendent beauty is supposed to result in moral disaster. At the very least, aesthetes do not take considerations of goodness into account. Worse, as explored in the literature of the turn of the century in such fictional characters as Dorian Gray,[11] they may take delight in the dark beauty of depraved, forbidden or horrendous acts.

If we understand transcendence as immediate enjoyment of what is present, however, concerns about the clash of moral and aesthetic values are unwarranted. The reason is that, as I noted earlier, immediacy dissolves everyday valuational oppositions, removing the conditions of the search for beauty. By eliminating the differential attractiveness of alternatives, it undercuts the possibility of valuation altogether. In moments of transcendent joy, we do not prefer the aesthetic to the moral because preference itself ceases to be an exercise of will and becomes, instead, an object of attention. So we choose nothing and simply enjoy whatever is present without an interest in its hidden features or in what it may enable us to do.

We must not infer from this that transcendence is incompatible with action. Absorption in what is present to consciousness suggests a spectatorial stance, a viewing of the distant scene. But the suggestion is misleading: one's actions can fill the mind as readily as what the world sends our way. A wonderfully expressive smile and the way my clenched fist hits the handball are as immediate and enjoyable as seeing the moon behind magnolia leaves. Of central importance is focus on what is already there. The magic bursts the moment we care about how the smile will be understood or whether the ball will hit in bounds. We can take delight in our actions, therefore, but not an interest in their results.

This, however, resuscitates worries about the detachment and unconcern of transcendence. Such apprehension would be appropriate if we thought of immediacy as structuring entire lives. But the notion of our bodies operating on automatic pilot while we self-indulgently enjoy the scenery is absurd. Transcendence occurs in happy moments when we manage to shed the cares of the world to embrace it for the marvels it presents. Like balloons in the sky, these high points of existence must move in an ordered space: they work best when they relax, decorate, complete and fulfill lives rich in other activities and values. Just as balloons are no substitute for the ground, transcendence cannot replace the life that needs, generates and enjoys it. If morality aims to enhance human flourishing, it will make room for transcendence rather than fight it as a rival.[12]

Does this account of immediacy as the locus of transcendence have anything of value to offer to everyday life? As any worthwhile philosophical view, it touches experience at two points. It originates in some interesting observations about what tends to give human beings carefree joy and then returns to present the activities that do as possibilities for all of us. Its value lies in offering a counterweight to guilt and regret, with their emphasis on the past, and to hope and planning, with their commitment to the future. Important as it is to learn from the past and to work for a better future, we must not forget that wedged between the two is the neglected present, which, on any sensible account, provides our only, moving life.

The special virtue of such an account of the value of the present is that it demonstrates the instant accessibility of joy in everyday life. If we attend to what is before us, it promises, we shall experience unceasing delight. But more: the satisfaction will not be of the sort normally associated with the belching immediate hedonism that sings *carpe diem,* if in drunken stupor it can remember the words. Instead, the pleasure is airy and wholesome and innocent, a song to celebrate that we can feel and think, that we are alive and awake and alert.

Nevertheless, in one respect at least, this view of transcendence promises too much. In principle, it may well be true that any object considered in its immediacy before the mind yields a special delight. But in real life, only relatively few things function in this way for most of us. Atlanta when the dogwood is in bloom forces transcendence, perhaps even spirituality, on us. To the majority, however, the smell of the dungheap does not, and it may take extraordinary efforts to overcome our revulsion for long enough to attend to its intrinsic qualities. Is it worth trying to do that? Should we not simply enjoy what we can find lovely with ease, and avoid the sights and objects we naturally abhor?

A sound philosophy of transcendence must serve both as an inspiration and as a consolation. It must applaud and support our natural tendency to surround ourselves with objects we can delight in and embrace. In this way, it aids and completes the enterprise of making human life better. But at times we travel through dark nights and long valleys, and we have little choice of what besets us. In these parts of our journeys, it is important to know that even if we have no power to improve our material condition, we can make the terror disappear by reducing the most frightful force to an appearance of itself and savoring it as a glorious or a comically self-important picture. This is the ultimate revenge. Transcendence to the immediate enables us to disarm the world by enjoying its deadly power and, while it crushes us, at least to laugh.

Laughter at such moments of pain may seem distant from disinterested joy. It may, in fact, appear to be the triumph of will over circumstance and, as such, thoroughly different from transcendence. But the appearance is deceptive. As a strategy, seeing things under the form of eternity is indeed an expression of our desire to prevail—by understanding if we cannot by physical or social means. The moment of pure laughter, however, is beyond all strategy: in it, our desires recede to the same distance as the oppressive power. Our struggles and our fate become incidents in the history of a remote universe, a world viewed through reversed binoculars.

The difference between the joy of easy transcendence and the laughter of release or resignation is only the price they exact. With the former, we achieve delightful absorption in the present spontaneously, at no cost. In the case of the latter, we suffer wrenching preparation for transcendent joy. We have to learn to give up, to feel that nothing really matters in the end. In the laughter that follows, we die to the world and are at last alive.

CHAPTER 9

The Vague Hope of Immortality

The easiest way to understand the desire for immortality is from the standpoint of the isolated individual. Marco Polo went to China and lived on; why could the soul not seek its fulfillment and retain its integrity in alien worlds? If the quintessential I is a substance, as Descartes surmised, it could travel from one universe to the next, from here through purgatory to the place above, without losing its bearings. The worlds it would visit might seem strange at first, but such a universal spirit would soon feel comfortable anywhere.

The demand for immortality might also express our love of existence or our desire not to relinquish the satisfactions of communal life. Such desires betoken the social commitments of people, but they lead to insuperable problems for developing a conception of immortality. I will deal with these issues later.

The idea of self-sufficient individuals, on the other hand, is compatible with virtually any notion of the afterlife precisely because such persons are strangers in every world, floating as detached globules of intelligence on the surface of events. The problem here is that even if we manage to come up with some consistent notion of immortality, we have no sensible idea of the self on which to graft it; the idea of the isolated individual is incoherent.

So my argument is this. A sound conception of the self leaves us without any helpfully concrete notion of an afterlife, and any notion of immortality worth a second look presupposes an indefensible idea of who we are. I begin with this popular but wrongheaded account of the self.

I

A very large number of things and facts have no bearing on our lives. The age of the universe, the precise distance from my wife's skirt to the outskirts of the Andromeda Galaxy, and the intensity with which Tristan loved Isolde hold little significance for any of us. The existence of two or three people who play basketball better than I fails to disturb my equanimity.

Some matters should not be of concern to people, but they are. I wear glasses in an odd fashion, perched an inch above my ears. A few weeks ago, an acquaintance walked up to me and said wearing glasses in that way was stupid. The angle of their tilt annoyed him. I invited him to look the other way, where there might be sights to please. Leaving others alone is a virtue in desperate search of people to embody it.

Yet some elements in the alignment of the world are of vital significance to us in the prime of life and even when we prepare to die. Interestingly, these are not the usual concerns about future prospects and health, but solicitude for the people, even the objects, dear to us. The birdbath and cherry tree that shaped and shaded many a day in my young life matter to me even today. In gratitude, I wish them well; I want them to continue to exist, partly for their own sake because they were splendid, and partly so they may fill other young souls with peace and pleasure.

We feel the same way about people who share our lives. I want my wife, children, students and friends to thrive after I die. In fact, it cheers me to think that they will, carrying a small part of me in their souls. I know very well that *I* will not in any significant sense *live* in them, yet that people vitally important to me will continue and do well matters profoundly.

In this and in many other respects, we differ from brutish tyrants. When Attila died, his wife and servants were slain so that they could serve him in the other world or at least not enjoy the benefits of this one. Attila's heirs are those who, having tested positive for HIV, seek unprotected sex with a multitude of partners. Angry over their fate, they want to take as many people with them as they can.

There has been a striking change in the sentiment of humans since Attila's day. Forcing healthy individuals to share a dead ruler's fate was then considered unobjectionable and perhaps even right. Today, by contrast, people who attempt to spread their misfortune by force or guile create revulsion in their neighbors and invite prosecution under the criminal code. For now, it is still alright to take as many down with us as we can when we are at war. But feelings run deep that members of our own community must never be treated that way.

The matter is not one of enlightened self-interest. Wishing others well and aiding them may be the best strategy for a long and happy life. But when death is half a block away, plans for a long journey are beside the mark. For egoists, imminent death dissolves the restraints required for successful life and opens the door to whatever promotes immediate delight. If humans were expressions of a selfish gene, nearness of the end would make them sociopaths.

That this happens only on rare occasions shows how deeply we are entwined with our world. The view of humans as isolated, self-centered pools of aggression derives its plausibility from a narrow selection of examples. When Hobbes says, for example, that "the condition of man . . . is a condition of war of everyone against everyone,"[1] he is universalizing the occasional experiences of ordinary people and the state of mind of many a king and ruler. Careful observation of human life discredits such remarks: mothers tend not to wage war on their children, and lovers sometimes protect each other at the cost of their own lives.

Human relations are not always cooperative, but nurturing activities are no more aberrations from our warlike stance than going to war is love by other means. If war is the paradigm of human activity, selfishness does not look foolish; but if we start from the tender support we offer those we love, narrow self-seeking seems to have no hold on our nature. At the very least, therefore, we must acknowledge a selfish and a social side to who we are.

But this still gives too much to the loner and the egoist. The war of "everyone against everyone" is not the struggle of one against the world or of individual against individual. War is a social act in which the combatants are ever in search of comrades and allies. Friends or fellow citizens feed and clothe the soldiers; those who risk their lives have children and lovers waiting for their return. Without cooperation, war would be impossible.

Collaboration, as any human activity, does not leave the soul untouched. The self expands to embrace the persons and objects close to it. The line between self and other melts when the other is a companion of many years, a well-loved dog, or one's familiar and comfortable home. The economy of the self expands in this way to include a portion of the world much larger than one's body and one's soul; it spreads from the center of the narrow self into the surrounding community, mixing its substance with whatever shares its interests or aids it.

This expansion of the self is not unique to humans. Dogs defend their territory and protect their owners loyally. With them, as with humans, gallant actions follow naturally, almost automatically, and not as the result of inferences or calculations. Assaulting the owner's child is no different from aggression against the dog; which of them was threatened cannot be gleaned from the fury of the counterattack.

Some people are so committed to others that they fear their own end less than the thought that those they love with all their hearts may die. This may explain why humans can reach a level of heroism in their defense of beloved others. If actions are reliable signs of commitments, we have reason to believe that some of them, when they face a forced choice, opt unhesitatingly for the welfare of others over their own. Mothers interpose themselves between their children and danger. Soldiers throw themselves on hand grenades to save the lives of their comrades. And though I fight fiercely when anyone attacks me, that energy is insignificant compared to my rage at seeing someone hurt my children or my wife.

When the ego expands to encompass a multitude of things and persons, these initially external realities do not remain foreign objects: they are incorporated into the self and become constitutive of it. People who love what they do define themselves by their professions, treasuring the tools they use and the places where they work. Many humans live primarily in their relationships and view themselves as mothers, fathers or friends rather than as individuals whose wants deserve first consideration. And we tend to think that referring to the country of our birth or the region where we grew up is adequate to explain what we value and who we are.

Seeing individuals as separate from one another and confined within their bodies provides, therefore, a distorted picture of the facts. On the contrary, persons overlap with one another in all sorts of ways, some of which create the tenderest relations while others serve as sources of deadly conflict. Under favorable circumstances, father and mother merge into each other and unite once again in the joint embrace of their child. But when rivals seek the same mate, incorporating it through the relations of constant attention and fierce desire, the overlap is unbearable and leads to strife.

With selves that overlap and crisscross in a multitude of ways, it is not surprising that we take an intense interest in how we leave the world. In departing it, we leave large portions of ourselves behind. The persons and things that satisfy us do so not as alien forces; they are elements of who we are. Death is horrible, therefore, not because it threatens nonexistence but because it cleaves the person and imposes an inevitable parting. When we close our eyes for the last time, we are separated from a world we love, that is, from our very selves; the severed person bleeds, as what gave us such delight remains behind and the impulse to caress it is no more. We are not self-centered, independent globules of consciousness.

II

The desire not to die may also be a natural outcome of our love of life. So many of the things we do delight us that we never want to stop; if we can run and laugh and eat and love well, why should the fun not go on for century after glorious century? We are reluctant to close down the activities of a prosperous life because they are going so well, and of a life of suffering and loss because we might soon turn it around. In either case, whenever the end seems imminent, we think that just a little more time might get us ready to go.

Yet what would it be like to live on without a natural conclusion? The Sibyl was granted endless life without eternal youth; such an existence of wheezing decline and chronic pain over thousands of years cannot be attractive to anyone. Since the body wears out, causing misery, any life worth continuing has to be in a realm free from decay. There we may enjoy the peace of blessedness, singing the praises of the Lord and perhaps seeing God face-to-face. In that shining world, time and the losses it exacts are forgotten, and we can rejoice in the glory of what we do and who we are.

But what can we do and who exactly are we in that world? The only positive ideas we can entertain about this realm are those we steal from life here: we speak of peace and singing and seeing someone face-to-face. The humble origin of such words as "shine" and "rejoicing" reminds us that their spiritual function derives from what the animal in us appreciates. The rest of the ideas that give content to the notion of heaven relate to our existence by negation. That the afterlife is free from the ravages of time and that neither loss nor disappointment can touch us there amount only to reassuring denials that that world is not as flawed as this.

The origin of the constituent ideas of heaven and the negativity of much of our conception of it are nevertheless inadequate to strip it of legitimacy. There may well be realities we can approach only negatively or by analogy. Yet a careful look at the concept calls attention to what in our fervent desire for blessedness we may forget: that what we hope for is baffling or hopelessly vague.

If I were an individual of the sort Hobbes, let alone Descartes, imagined, heaven would be easy to define. It would be life that is the opposite of "nasty, brutish and short"—let us say pleasant, perhaps even elegant, humane and very long. As a single agent pursuing a private good, I could feel at home in any cozy corner. As long as I remained free and secure and in possession of such instruments of pleasure as the goodwill of God, I would need nothing; the fortunes of others would sound like tales from a distant planet.

But we are not insular individuals whose direct relation to God suffices for satisfaction. Heaven would be like a concentration camp if entering it separated us from those we love. We are complex social beings who cannot flourish apart from companions and family. We incorporate them into our larger selves just as they find room for us in their souls. Such inclusion is not an occasional or accidental nicety; it constitutes the fabric of our being. We are parts of each other, and the parts others constitute account for the bulk of each of us.

I have already spoken of the indissoluble bonds between the self and its community. William James speaks of this remarkable unity in terms of the expansion of the boundaries of the self. G. H. Mead and others think there could be no self and hence no broadening of its horizons without the environment, the impetus and the materials the world of others provides. In either case, satisfaction of the individual is impossible without the concurrent well-being of significant portions of the community. Heaven must, therefore, be a friendly and social place where the good fortune of all is the condition of the delight of anyone.

III

So far so good for our idea of heaven. For our moral convictions confirm that this conception of an afterlife is on the right track. People generally agree that it is wrong to be indifferent to the fate of others and repugnant to take pleasure in their distress. So it should be unacceptable for those who enjoy eternal bliss to delight in invidious comparisons between their good fortune and the sad fate of those whose pleas for blessedness are denied. The morally right conception of the afterlife depicts heaven as the fulfillment of our social impulses, achieving at last the perfect coincidence of the good of the individual with the interests of the community.

The desire for such a harmony of people with their neighbors reveals the struggles of which we wish to be relieved. Yet it is in these and other struggles that we have our lives, and that is the source of the trouble for our idea of heaven. In the natural course of events, fulfillments flow from efforts and bring them to a smiling end. We can distinguish the two, but we cannot separate them. Effort without result is frustrating and vain; pleasure with no need for exertion is curiously hollow. Only the two together satisfy, the one as price and preparation, the other as conclusion and reward. We might think of them as two parts of a natural human act in which, in the absence of endeavor, even pleasure does not please.

Admittedly, nothing seems easier than to detach our moments of delight from the events that generate them and to think of benefits without their costs. Adolescent males notoriously dream of being objects of the attention of exquisite women showering pleasures on their grateful parts. They think of themselves as quivering sensoria absorbing gratification without having to do anything to earn or to sustain it. A ready receptivity, they believe, is all we need to lead the good life.

This, however, is the stuff of daydreams. Two considerations show that it is fantasy. The adolescent mind, anxious for quick release, sees all labor and deferral as pain. It needs much attentive experience to carry it from chugging beer to the discriminating pleasures of wine-tasting. The revelation that the pleasures of eating come to more than gulping food and that hasty orgasms never do justice to love dawns on it slowly. Perhaps only later in life does the role of process in pleasure become clear. Then we realize that the bulk of our delight in eating resides in what might be seen as grinding labor but what in the performance is experienced with a measure of satisfaction—in biting, tearing, chewing and swallowing. We also learn that much of the pleasure of love is in foreplay, in the fevered movement of bodies and in the play of building to, yet resisting, consummation.

The element of the human condition to which these comments point is not that our satisfactions are bought with suffering. If we were speaking merely of a causal connection, we could always try to substitute alternative conditions to generate what we want; we could hope to eliminate the pains and burdens of life by the comforts of technology. But the relationship is much more intimate. We can enjoy only or primarily what is laborious and requires effort. Since pure sensation and unadulterated pleasure are past our ken, we feel little delight without the process of working for it. God's malediction that "in the sweat of thy face shalt thou eat bread" is even more horrendous than it must have sounded to Adam and to Eve; it decrees not only that we must pay for everything we get but also that we cannot take joy in anything unsaturated by the agony of our labor.

We are, in brief, condemned to pain and cursed in our pleasures. The theology of this twilight condition has been only partially explored. We know that Adam's sin erased the possibility of a life of easy harmony. But the punishment for disobedience is typically supposed to take the form only of pain. Little attention has been paid to the wrenching adjustment God's curse wrought in our nature, making our pleasures dependent on our pains and turning our lives into a sad and glorious victory in defeat. The Fall rendered us masochists not in our intentions but in our activities and enjoyments, in the innermost recesses of our nature.

The way pleasure occurs constitutes the second reason for the inseparability of satisfaction from exertion. When things go well, fulfillment appears to be effortless or automatic. The ease with which it comes may lull us into believing that when we enjoy pleasure, we *do* nothing. This impression is reinforced by the sense of passivity that accompanies some sensory indulgences. A back-scratching or a hot shower generates delights that seem to involve no activities on our parts. We simply need to let another's fingers walk or the hot water run, and be present for the sensory consequences.

This, however, is an incomplete picture of what actually takes place. The feeling of passivity supervenes upon the humming activity of the sensory and the nervous systems. But more, the enjoyment has to be varied and sustained. Visions of beauty lapse unless they are renewed again and again by keeping the head stable and refocusing the eyes. No satisfaction is lasting without exercising sufficient control over circumstances to maintain the feeling. Even in the shower, the passivity we experience is framed in activities of the sort required for standing up instead of collapsing on the floor, remaining erect under the stream of water rather than leaning until one falls out of the tub, and moving from time to time to let the water hit different parts of the body.

In truth, we do not know how to be passive, no matter how much we try. And the point is that we have to *try*, meaning that we have to expend energy to reach the stage where exertion is not needed. Yet, or just because of this, we never actually get there: attaining the level of passive enjoyments or costless benefits is impossible. This, again, is the human condition of being unable to enjoy anything to whose existence or nature we make no contribution. Whether we read this in theological terms as due to the Fall of Adam or in naturalistic ones as the fate of animals struggling in an adverse environment, the fact that, for us at least, enjoyment without labor is inconceivable remains a structuring feature of our lives.

IV

What, then, of our notion of an afterlife? I exclude from consideration ideas according to which death is followed by absorption in the life force or in the peace of nothingness. However reassuringly such views are expressed, they invariably imply personal extinction. I am interested in what content we can give the hope that our individuality will not be erased without a trace. Sitting in a delightfully seedy McAnn's bar in New York one day, I heard a distinguished philosopher say: "If heaven has no McAnn's, I'm not interested." Though the sentiment is easy to appreciate, an afterlife no different from or no better than existence today cannot serve as a motivating ideal. A life worse than this, moreover, is not an object of hope. We can, of course, always conceive of a world better in some particular: one, for example, in which I have hair, you more money or all of us fewer terrible diseases. But such worlds constitute objectives of reasonable striving; to achieve them, we need knowledge and luck rather than life everlasting.

That leaves a life that is problem-free and consists of an unbroken string of satisfactions. Such a heavenly existence would have to be social, but without the usual costs of communal life, that is, without friction, anxiety, destructive competition, conflicting interests and debilitating hatreds. We simply have no idea what such an existence would be like. On the personal level, we cannot even think of enjoying what we did not labor to attain or to sustain. On the social side, we cannot imagine human interaction free of conflict and struggle.

Marx thought that such harmonious social life would become possible after the socialist revolution. But when it came time for him to say what it might consist of, he had nothing more positive to offer than that it would allow us to fish in the morning, hunt in the afternoon, and do philosophy in the evening. If these were its hallmarks, heaven on earth would make for a painfully boring, deeply dissatisfying world. Would we want to go angling if the fish jumped in the boat when we embarked? Would we enjoy hunting if the quarry rushed up to us, died on the spot, and promptly turned itself into a savory dish? Could we get anything out of philosophy without criticism and disagreement? A world of diversified but easy activities is particularly tedious precisely because it lacks the problems that give a keen edge to life. The bulk of human togetherness is focused on solving or at least on coping with problems, not on flaccid enjoyments. Without shared difficulties, the meaning and the small victories of existence quickly dissipate.

Just as we cannot embrace the joys of private life without becoming heirs to labor, so we cannot feed on the pleasures of community apart from the troubles social life resolves, and causes. The very structure of human caring is determined by the problems we face: our love for children and aging parents is saturated with concern for their well-being. We worry about them, fight to protect them and work with them to overcome the obstacles in their way. Love unburdened by the predicaments of life is a single note tediously sustained, not a symphony. Good music, as good living, requires variety and enough discord to struggle with and to subdue in a broader harmony.

Our finite, ambiguous state affects not only individual activities and social life but also the architecture of our selves. We are what our desires, struggles and satisfactions make us. Much as we hope for the costless delights of heaven, we also seek the interesting—that means the problematic—in life and look for challenges to test our powers. We are made for this twilight world, and nothing shows the ambivalence of our condition more clearly than that we both love this life and wish to escape to something better.

I conclude that, given a proper understanding of the nature of selves, we have no specific, clear and viable idea of a heavenly afterlife. This does not mean that we fail to survive the dissolution of our bodies or that there is no better world to which death opens the door. Since we lack adequate information, it is wise to withhold judgment on such issues, though the want of positive evidence should concern those who hope for eternal life. But even if there is an afterlife, we are not in a position to determine or even to imagine its nature.

To be sure, we can refer to it from a distance by external designators, just as we can speak of the millionth prime number by reference to the sequence of our systematic search, even though we do not know which number it is. But, alas, our idea of heaven is even vaguer than our current notion of the millionth prime number. For we know at least that the millionth prime number is a number, and we know precisely how we can find out which number it is. When we speak of costless pleasures and unproblematic social lives, by contrast, we literally do not know what we are saying. Joy and labor are indissolubly connected in this world, and if there are "pleasures" not surrounded by problems and supported by exertions, they are nothing like the delights we experience and know. We cannot grasp the nature of such satisfactions, and it is not even clear what right we have to refer to them by that honored name.

Aside from forming a concrete idea of heaven, supporters of the afterlife face an unanswered question concerning our identity there. Human self-identity is a function of experiences undergone and problems overcome. We are styles of operating in the world, built up over years of dealing with the contingencies of life. How could I be anyone in particular if I consisted of the same unproblematic joys as my neighbors? And how could I be the same person in heaven as I am here if my labored life becomes, past death, an ethereal song?

I cannot say that my two selves are united as are hope and its realization, because without a clear idea of heaven I cannot form meaningful hopes relating to it. And even if the later self knew the struggles of the earlier, it would have no basis for viewing them as its own. More likely, it would regard them as the butterfly does the travail of the distant worm that must die before the birth of wings and flight. So the beings that may succeed us would not remember us at all, and if they did, they would look upon our strivings and our joys as the experiences of aliens rather than as the bumbling indiscretions of their childhoods.

Might it then be that the hope for immortality is a vague, ill-thought out wish? When Shelley speaks of "the desire of the moth for the star," he has in mind a yearning both for what is difficult to reach and for what cannot be clearly grasped. Such longings are not uncommon among human beings; they often take the form of wanting something whose nature or consequences are inadequately explored. King Midas came to grief because he wished for everything he touched to turn to gold, and Icarus plunged from the sky because he overlooked that the sun melts wax. Wanting to have all the money in the world or to have sex with everyone in the 82nd Airborne might sound like legitimate desires, but they engage the attention only of people who do not fully understand what is involved.

I suspect something like that is the case with the desire for immortality. A heavenly afterlife sounds like a good idea, so long as we do not examine it enough to realize that there is not much of a concrete idea there at all. The quest for endless life and limitless delight blinds us to the cognitive shortfall at the heart of our notion of immortality. Descartes was right when he pointed out that the human will and, hence, human wants are infinite but the intellect is finite. And he knew that the resulting pursuit of infinity gets us in trouble.[2]

Our tendency to break down barriers and to surmount all obstacles makes the magnitude of the trouble difficult to assess. The desire for immortality of the sort I have discussed is a transcendent or a religious version of our current social and scientific drive to overcome all the difficulties standing in the way of human fulfillment. The failed Marxist experiment in resocializing us is now supplanted by the hope for a wholesale genetic reengineering of our natures. We think we can defeat aging, eliminate disease and turn each of us into an exemplary specimen of our kind. Scientists tell us that nothing can stop us from converting this small planet into heaven but failure of resolve.

The cost of such grand but foolish drives is the loss of our souls. We are finite creatures with limited potential for satisfaction. Like cats, we love enclosed spaces and terminal movements; nothing pleases as much as a good beginning, a little progress along the way, and a cozy conclusion. The open-ended is a wound in the ordered world. Everything we deal with—sneezes and suppers and sentences—comes in small units, and we view the unfinished as gapingly incomplete. The infinite leaves us hungering for closure and sadly forgetful that everything is more precious when in short supply.

Why, then, would someone seek the infinite and want everlasting life? Only because intelligence has not extended its dominion over the heart. That we never perish and upon dying face a better life is an understandable hope of hard-pressed animals. That "we" in some sense are "immortal" in some sense may even be a proper object of faith. But it is a mistake to count on personal survival of death, and a pernicious error to think we need it to redeem this life. So long as we do the Lord's work and do not ask the Lord to do ours, we can make this world good enough for us. And when we die, it should be adequate consolation that we lived well and that our loved ones stay behind.

III

Problems for Communities

CHAPTER 10

Both Better Off and Better: Moral Progress amid Continuing Carnage

To victims of twentieth-century atrocities, my argument may seem sinister and hollow. To intellectuals who equate sophistication with cynicism, it will appear naïve and perhaps shallow. To seekers after perfection who find each number wanting because it falls shy of the infinite, it will be a lesson in futility. But to the rest of us, what I have to say may serve as a useful reminder of how fortunate we are to live today and not even just a few hundred years ago. It may also evoke reasonable hopes for the future and establish a standard by which to measure the magnitude of the tasks on the road ahead.

I wish to show that in spite of the misery and wickedness that still remain in the world, the human race has enjoyed significant moral progress over the course of history. Only fools would deny that, on the whole, there has been striking material progress. But many believe, quite wrongly, that there is no connection between material and moral advancement or even that growth of comfort entails loss of character. At the very least, the ways in which being better off contributes to being better are poorly understood and inadequately appreciated. I hope to be able to clarify the connection.

The facts fall considerably short of proving John Stuart Mill's nineteenth-century hope that humankind is by nature a "progressive being."[1] There is no assurance that the positive changes achieved through centuries of effort will continue or that we have once and for all escaped the threats of nuclear annihilation, ideological repression and murderous intolerance. I have, moreover, no desire to deny or explain away the evidence against moral improvement. Progress is not universal and unrelenting, and its presence is perfectly compatible with individual wickedness, with some contin-

uing institutional discrimination and with pockets of unmitigated nastiness. Yet one can deny its reality only by selective inattention, by the application of unreasonable standards or by astonishing ignorance of history.

Let me begin by acknowledging that the twentieth century is full of
events ranging from the lamentable to the awful. Precise numbers are hard
to come by, but it is clear that two world wars, the Holocaust, Stalinist
purges, Japanese concentration camps and the Chinese "Cultural Revolution" terminated the lives of more than a hundred million individuals.
Massacres in Cambodia, genocide in sundry African countries, ethnic
cleansing in the Balkans and other horrors added more than ten million
dead in the last twenty years. Injustices against women and minorities continue everywhere. Religious intolerance, ethnic hatreds and national rival-
ries contribute to the misery of hundreds of millions of people. Random
violence erupts even in the most civilized countries, and fraud, lying,
cheating and coercion constitute ways of life all over the globe.

These facts cannot be denied. But they must be understood. The stag-
gering number of those who died in wars in the last hundred years, for example, must be related to the vast increase in the human population since
1800. This does not explain or justify the killing, but it places it in historical
context. There were not a hundred million people alive at the time of the
Great Plague. That many killed in Descartes's day would have left few if
anyone to reproduce the race. In the twentieth century, by contrast, the
number constituted but a relatively small percentage of the global population. Moreover, a single evil intention without the aid of advanced technology can spell the doom of only a few victims; with access to weapons of
mass destruction, it can destroy tens of thousands of people.

We must also consider that morality does not progress at the same rate
everywhere. Offsetting massacres by Hutus and Tutsis cannot be blamed on
civilized or morally advanced nations. Many of the horrors of Cambodia
and Iraq must be laid at the door of dictators, who are among the morally
least developed persons in the world. And participation in atrocities by
many well-meaning people, though inexcusable, is at least in part testimony to the contagion of collective action and the relative powerlessness of
individuals. Placing people in circumstances where decency demands
heroic self-sacrifice is a telling but by no means complete measure of their
moral quality.

Determining the moral level of a society is a complex affair, involving
study of the practices and the sentiments of its people. As collections of living habits, practices are often at odds with one another, requiring examination of their relative strengths or of the frequency with which they are en-

acted. In looking for signs of the growth of decency, we must pay relatively little attention to rare heights of moral achievement and to exceptional degradation; as in assessing quality of life, what matter in the end are the repetitive patterns of everyday existence.

Even more revealing, perhaps, is what a given society accepts as commonplace and what, by contrast, is viewed as demanding excuse or explanation. In a disorderly, xenophobic world, for example, the occasional arrest, torture and murder of foreigners is a matter of course. When it happens, no special account of the event is needed; everyone knows and accepts that this may be the fate of intruders. In a law-abiding country that welcomes visitors, on the other hand, shooting at tourists from overpasses is considered an anomaly in need of explanation. Such accounts, moreover, are supposed to identify the causes of the event rather than serve as its justification. The point of understanding in a civilized world is the elimination of such incidents, not their exoneration.

In assessing the practices of various societies and historical epochs, we need to acknowledge an initial distinction between the material conditions of life and the moral qualities of individuals. Simpleminded utilitarians might suppose that only the level of happiness in a society matters much, and that is largely a function of the consequences of human actions rather than of the moral excellence of agents. But this distinction is, in the end, not very helpful. For happiness is by no means the only important value, and even if it were, it could not be detached from the internal disposition of people to favor creating it in themselves and in others. Mill himself acknowledges as much when he writes about the significance of choice in life and the intricate connections that obtain between character and well-being.[2]

So let me deal with these issues separately and examine the ways in which prosperity enhances virtue only after I have considered each of them in detail. At first sight, the idea that we are better off than any previous generation may appear as what people nowadays call a "no-brainer." Consider an example. The philosopher Josiah Royce took a trip to Australia in 1888 and 1889. He spent nearly three months at sea on the way there, out of touch with the rest of the world. He fretted ceaselessly at not being able to participate in the life of his family. His friends and his wife, in turn, were plagued by persistent worries about his health and well-being. An occasional telephone call would have allayed these concerns and made everyone involved feel happier or at least less uncertain, less angered and less guilty.

Here is another example. The invention of the solanoid made it possible for cars to start at the turn of a key. Earlier versions of the automobile had to be hand-cranked at considerable effort at the front of the car below the radiator. From time to time, the crankbar would jerk, dislocating hand or arm. Less than a year before solanoids were first installed, when a young Detroiter cranked his car, the engine started and then backfired, transmitting violent motion to the crankbar, which hit him in the face, broke his jaw, and knocked out some of his teeth. The man developed general sepsis and died. He was the last fatality connected with the hand-cranked automobile engine.

There is no doubt that automobile drivers in the 1920s were better off than people who had had to ride in horse-drawn wagons a hundred years before, and that we live better than they did because we can get in our cars and start them without having to crank them in the weather. How could one deny this? Only by insisting that increase of comfort and decrease of suffering and risk constitute no improvements in life. This, in turn, can be justified only in one of two ways: we can assert that well-being carries no moral weight at all or that increments of it come at unacceptable cost. The first line of argument is absurd on the face of it. No sensible person can seriously entertain the notion that human suffering and delight should be thought insignificant. Even Kant, who came closest to this view, believing that happiness had no moral value, found an important role for it in satisfying our entire constitution.[3]

The second justification has at least some plausibility: we know that everything desirable comes at a price. But the claim that each technological advance, for example, leads to more misery than good is simply false. The use of penicillin, to take just one case, has admittedly caused a number of deaths and its availability may have contributed to less than optimal caution in sexual relations. But the millions of lives it has saved is out of proportion to the relatively few whose loss or diminution may be attributed to it. On a simple cost-benefit basis, established and non-outmoded technologies are nearly always worth their price. Acknowledging this, opponents typically shift the ground from the discernible costs of progress to its more intangible effects in supposedly destroying human character. I will deal with this claim a little later.

Let me generalize the points my examples are designed to highlight. For most people in most of the industrially advanced countries, life today is strikingly easier, safer, richer in choices, more diversified, healthier, more just, longer, and more satisfying than ever before. We eat better, suffer less pain, are ravaged by fewer diseases, exercise greater control over our environment, face brighter prospects, have a better chance of enjoying worthwhile experiences, and live more peaceful lives than any previous generation.

To learn what life was like in prior centuries, we need to read about the travail of ordinary persons, not the exploits of the high and mighty. The little people who built the pyramids of Egypt and the cathedrals of medieval Europe were infested with parasites and found themselves at the mercy of tyrannical rulers and a poorly understood, terrorizing world. The peasants of the Black Forest whom Heidegger so admires[4] lived in cramped discomfort and suffered from painful degenerative ailments. People everywhere were decimated by war, malnutrition, persecution, tuberculosis and venereal disease. The relatively few who survived past the age of twenty-five suffered from digestive malfunctions and rotting teeth. Persons of the wrong religion were executed, people were deprived of property on the basis of accusations alone, and those in debt went to jail, never to return.

A better understanding of the human body, the development of technology and the spread of democratic values made life better in large and small ways that are nearly impossible to detail. The best summary of these blessings is to note that they improve the human lot by increasing the range of our choices. We can now do things prior generations could hardly imagine the gods performing: sending messages to each other in the dark of night, making hot rooms cold by turning a knob, and growing food in desert sand. Such choices mean that we can determine our own good: we can still permit our teeth to rot or the heat to suffocate us, but we don't have to.

The oppressive force of necessity has been lifted from our shoulders, and we can live as humans should, or at least as we desire. It is better if one out of four women don't die in childbirth and if lack of protein and calcium does not cripple one person out of every eight. It is better if people don't have to drink putrid water and eat rotting food, and if drunkenness is not the only relief from pain. It is better to live in a world in which hunger is a pleasant prelude to a meal instead of a gnawing menace that cannot be escaped. And it is better by far if families don't have to bury two children out of ten and see another three out of ten grow into physically or morally deformed adults.

A growing number of Americans believe that saying other ages and other cultures do not compare well with our own is unseemly or wrong. There is good reason for this: racist, nationalist and ethnocentric affirmations of superiority constitute important elements of much recurrent human villainy. Furthermore, the idea of progress has on occasion been used as an instrument to justify such claims of comparative or transcendent excellence. We may rightly think, therefore, that it is best to avoid grand cross-cultural comparisons and to foster, instead, a generous appreciation of the virtues of other forms of life.

Such sentiments feel instinctively so right to us that it is tempting to adopt them. But their very popularity cuts against their truth. Prior ages were, and many cultures continue to be, not at all reluctant to declare their preeminence over all others. The fact that we relate to alien value systems with self-abnegating generosity is itself evidence of moral progress. But more: people in industrialized nations tend to be ahead of others when their practices are measured by generally, though perhaps not universally, accepted standards. They take better care of the sick and the disadvantaged, they have a keener and broader sense of justice, and they hold human life in higher regard than do individuals in less-developed countries. There is no better way to show that these are shared standards than by observing the choices of people all over the globe. Most of them do not think values are incommensurable; they have no trouble comparing their condition with ours, and when they do, they find theirs wanting. As a result, vast numbers of them prefer our opportunities and our caring—that is, our style of life—to their own. They vote with their feet in moving to industrialized countries or introduce modernizing reforms in their own.

As all good things, progress comes at a price. Heroic self-sacrifice may be more uncommon today because it is less necessary. In many contexts, institutionalized care has replaced tender personal relations. We have lost the heartfelt closeness of fellow sufferers and the excitement of living in endangered communities. By no means the least, all or nearly all our hallowed values have been commercialized. But we are amply compensated for such losses. Individual generosity has placed 12 percent of our vast national wealth at the permanent service of education, the arts and the helping professions. Government considers it a sacred obligation to take care of the sick and the elderly. And though it is lamentable that there remain causes whose support requires hunger strikes and nonviolent resistance, we must remember that such tactics work only in civilized countries where the perpetrators are not summarily murdered.

The growth of the middle class coincides with the development of better ways of taming the power of nature and of making it serve human purposes. The comfort and security we associate with middle-class living is in no small measure the result of applying intelligence to the solution of the problems that face us. Even those who want to argue that humans lack goodwill or an ultimate vision of what would satisfy them cannot deny that ingenuity, inventiveness and sustained labor have made human life immeasurably better.

Some high-minded critics of progress readily grant that, in material terms, life has undergone significant improvement in the past few hundred years. But they accord no moral significance to our growing comfort. A few go so far as to claim that there is an inverse relation between well-being and virtue. They say that good living softens the will even as it hardens the heart. And, indeed, there is some evidence for this: in certain cases, the children of the well-to-do lose the work habits of their parents, and some of those pampered with luxuries find little sympathy for people in need.

I have already indicated that in assessing what good there might be in the world, human welfare cannot be disregarded. Might it nevertheless be true that growing comfort entails moral loss? If only austerity can build character, our good fortune in living well and long must surely hurtle us into spiritual decline. Active virtues are likely to atrophy, the imagination may shrivel, and we will be tempted to turn inward to wallow in our happiness. We could end in the position of Nietzsche's last man, as small persons enjoying small pleasures in an abominably comfortable corner of the universe.[5]

Older people have from time immemorial charged the new generation with having lost the ancient virtues. In truth, announcing that the young lack character may be a way of saying that they have characters of which their elders don't approve. Every desire not immediately met and automatically sustained builds habits and drives; no generation lacks perseverance in the pursuit of its ends. But the ends change and the young, growing up in the midst of plenty, may no longer hoard bottles and shopping bags—or money—in the way those who lived through the agony of the Great Depression could never overcome.

So austerity builds the sort of character needed to flourish under its strictures. Prosperity generates a different kind of person, one given to enjoying what life provides. This appears as profligate to children of the Depression as they seem irrationally pinch-fisted to those who never had to face their concerns. The question is not of which group is right; they both are to the extent their attitudes are appropriate to their situations. Indefinitely delayed gratification is just what may get us over the hump in a time of shortage and uncertainty, but we would be fools not to fiddle and dance under the moon at the end of harvest.

People of plenty have as many virtues as the hardy indigent, even though what they do may look indulgent to those given to self-abnegation. And their virtues are superior because of their superior means: when there is hardly enough for oneself, it is difficult to be generous. Flashes of heroic caring are always possible, and we heap special honor on those who take food out of their mouths to feed the hungry. But kindness is a more powerful disposition among people who don't suffer constant pain, and courage flourishes more easily when one's body is strong and one's feelings are educated. Magnanimity is not even possible for individuals without significant means, and the sentiment of justice cannot readily take hold while people struggle to survive.

Contrary to the fears and warnings of Luddites, the means our prosperous industrial world provides directly promote the growth of virtue. Consider the power of telecommunications. Medieval villages received virtually no news from the outside; their small worlds remained inescapably isolated from one another. By the time of the Vietnam War, the distant killing was replayed each night in our living rooms. Today, email, the telephone, CNN and fax machines have forged indissoluble links between us and people around the globe. Once we know what happens to them, we cannot be indifferent to their fates: Sri Lankans and Kosovars evoke our sympathy as they solicit our aid. The resulting painful involvements—in Somalia and Bosnia and Kosovo—can be explained only by reference to caring. A primary motive for such costly interventions is the interest we take in human welfare everywhere.

Those who say that it is not in our national interest to dispatch troops to save innocent people or to stop humanitarian catastrophes far away take too narrow a view of what is a proper subject of concern for citizens and for human beings. The notion of the national interest must itself be put in the context of moral evolution. Hobbes's egoist, whose life was "solitary, poor, nasty, brutish, and short,"[6] may never have existed, but the human race did survive thousands of years of tribal warfare and clannish exclusiveness. The idea that our allegiance must extend beyond service to the local warlord and encompass others in a unified nation-state hundreds of miles away was a significant innovation in morality.

The notion of citizenship, pointing to democratic equality in mattering or, minimally, in not being overlooked, represents a momentous advance in the scope of caring. The idea of national interest extends protection and fellow feeling beyond the family, the tribe, the inhabitants of a region and the subjects of a local authority. As such, the notion is a way station to universal human concern, which is now slowly beginning to take its place.

The same development in ideas occurred much earlier in religion with the emergence of universal faiths. Such religions as Christianity and Islam offer open enrollment to anyone prepared to confess certain beliefs. The proffered benefit of salvation is not restricted by birth or social status; it is available to human beings everywhere. This puts an end to aristocracy in religion and lowers—or raises—all persons to one level in the eyes of God.

Something similar happened also with the criminal code, which is the single most civilizing instrument ever devised. Those who think there has been no moral progress through the ages should recall that for thousands of years humans struggled without an impartially administered law protecting their lives and property. When laws proscribing and punishing criminal acts first emerged, as in the code of Hammurabi, they were a magnificent step in the direction of human security. Yet they were supposed to govern the behavior of only those people whom local authorities had within their reach.

Even at the height of the Roman Empire, its criminal laws were thought to have bearing solely on its citizens and on the citizens of subjected nations. Until recently, laws of universal applicability were typically restricted to areas beyond national sovereignty, such as the sea. But from the middle of this century on, we have had a growing body of law that is supposed to set limits to the activity of humans everywhere and that takes preeminence over the legislative arrangements of nation-states.

The subject matter of these laws is as important as their scope: they are designed to protect human beings from inhumane treatment. The category of crimes against humanity includes many of the atrocities that tyrants and repressive regimes used to inflict routinely on suffering multitudes. Since the indictment of Milosevic, they can no longer do so believing that they will escape prosecution. The possibility that a sitting head of state would be indicted for war crimes committed against the citizens of his own nation would have been greeted with incredulous laughter even fifty years ago. Leaders of defeated powers had often lost their lives, but for an international court to hold a king or prime minister responsible while still in office was unprecedented in the history of the human race. To demand decency even, or especially, from the high and mighty is a stunning breakthrough in morality.

These remarkable developments came about as a result of growth of concern for human beings simply because they are human and not on account of their being of the same race or religion or nationality as we are. The increase of caring, in turn, had its source in large part in the material conditions that shape our lives. Rapid transportation, instant communication and universal commerce make us participants in the lives of others. The leisure and wealth generated by highly efficient economies provide the wherewithal to aid our fellows. Without the infrastructure of the industrial world, large-scale concern for others would be impossible. One can readily suppose that there have been pockets of caring throughout human history, but nothing ever existed that comes even close to the magnitude, the reach and the institutional support of benevolence today.

At least two mechanisms support this growth of generosity; one is the way telecommunications have come to bolster the human imagination and the other is the power and pervasiveness of commerce. The only sure source of decency is the imagination that enables us to place ourselves in the position of others. This splendid faculty makes it possible for us to do much more than empathize with those in pain; it propels us into the worlds of others to appreciate their self-justifications. But it is weak and quickly exhausts itself in the extraordinary efforts required to enter alien frames of mind. So while the imagination makes decency possible, it also imposes its own limits on the moral life.

Sensory contact with the distant functions as a mechanized imagination. Television brings us the distant scene, and we are no longer required to construct for ourselves how others might live and what they believe. Crying children, a blood-splattered street and people dazed from seeing the bomb go off present a reality hardly in need of interpretation; we respond to an immediacy more vivid, or at least more extensive, than what the mind creates. Sympathies expand as more of the world enters our consciousness, until people we have never met but whose images we see daily become companions with a claim.

Even as early a writer as Benjamin Constant noted (1819) that "[w]ar and commerce are only two different means of achieving the same end, that of getting what one wants." Since commerce is "a milder and surer means of engaging the interest of others to agree to what suits [one's] own,"[7] little by little it takes the place of war. If we wage war to get people to surrender what we want, they are likely to resist; if we offer them something they want in return, they relinquish it freely. Moreover, trading keeps others productive so they may create more of the things we want, which means that we can trade again, whereas in war we may feel impelled to kill them.

Plutarch relates that Marcus Cato, in addressing the Roman senate, let a few fine figs drop out of his toga. When the senators indicated their admiration of the size and beauty of the figs, he remarked that "the place that bore them was but three days' sail from Rome."[8] If they wanted such figs, he said, they needed simply to kill the Carthaginians who grew them. The idea of setting up a trading post in Carthage seems not to have occurred to him.

Momentous changes take place in human relations when large numbers of people realize that trade is a better way to relieve others of their goods than force. It is no overstatement that replacing war with commerce is a turning point in the moral evolution of humankind. Instead of wanting other people dead, we want them to live and prosper. Our relation to them becomes internal: in trade, their good is essentially linked to ours, so what harms them harms us as well. A momentous expansion of the self follows inevitably. We begin to view our trading partners in the same favorable light in which we bathe ourselves. Their habits become interesting, their choices respectable, their fates important. We are ready to protect them, as we did in Kuwait, and admit them as valued persons into our community.

As all higher stages of development include a trace of what went before, trade retains a residue of playful or warlike competition. But this is a matter of clever gamesmanship rather than deadly combat. Its point is to gain an advantage over others, not to ruin them, for in killing them we would kill a part of ourselves. In this way, the growth of technology and the spread of commerce make powerful contributions to the moral betterment of the human race. They tie us to one another in fact and feeling, increasing both interdependence and caring. At a time when intellectuals were less cynical, we would have called them instruments of perfection. I am satisfied to call them tools of socializing humans or of unifying the human race.

Those who wish to argue that trade and wealth and communication change only our actions and not who we are need to develop a better understanding of the intricate relations between "external" actions and the inner person. Everyone does things "out of character" from time to time, but normally the habits that constitute us are built out of repeated actions. What we do again and again penetrates the soul and shapes it in its image; it is impossible to act in a generous way over many years and yet remain a miser. Here and there we can act as though we were brave or just or kind, but when we act consistently that way, no one can deny that we truly are. I conclude that, on the whole, humans today are not only better off but also better than previous generations. And by "better," I mean not only that we do good things more often but also that we are, on the whole, morally more admirable people.

I remain unrepentant if this conclusion offends our sense of unworthiness. But my view will appear more convincing or at least less objectionable if I guard against two possible misunderstandings. I do not think that moral progress is destined to continue. Some unforeseen catastrophe or the wicked work of charismatic leaders may well reverse it. In any case, it is a slow process unlikely to move ahead without the committed work of many millions of people over long periods of time.

Further, I said that we are "on the whole" better than those who went before. Being on the whole better is consistent with there having been a few people in prior ages who were more virtuous than anyone living today, and it does not even suggest that we are in some absolute and final sense "good." All injustice has not been overcome, all pain has not been stilled, all needs have not been met. Probably they never will be. As we well know, indifference, deceit, ill-will, even wickedness continue to flourish here as everywhere around the globe. We find throwbacks and face reversals again and again. The black holes of nastiness we continue to encounter set our tasks as educated human beings and especially as philosophers. But taking all of this into account, we still feel the tides of decency rising and see shafts of light to guide our actions and to feed our hope.

The Significance of Purposes
for Bioethics

Until recently, bioethics has been dominated by a sort of conceptual analysis dealing with principles and their application and by apologies for a variety of religious positions. Both of these approaches offer benefits and drawbacks. Analysis of concepts and principles improves the clarity of our vision, and powerful statements of traditional religious values remind us of important commitments that have served us well. But focus on principles makes it easy to overlook context and process, and the affirmation of old truths helps very little in seeing their relevance or their application today.

The weakness of dominant lines of thought makes the entry of American pragmatism into the field of bioethics particularly timely. Its stress on process, on context and on the concrete future promises a welcome corrective to static analysis and rededication to the past. Its commitment to community life and to democratic values is likely to bolster the best features of the other approaches without succumbing to the lure of empty abstractions or soothing piety.

The central problem of much bioethics today is that it attempts to comprehend difficult moral issues apart from the social context in which they occur. Grand principles and religious values cannot be honed at a distance from the living problems they are supposed to resolve and then applied to issues wrenched out of context and described in an impoverished abstract or general way. Bioethics is not like surgery in which the timely removal of isolated lumps can let patients get on with the rest of their lives. It is closer to what we do in managing chronic disease, in which each course of action is fraught with risk and every treatment is a compromise.

Just as physicians must remind themselves to treat not the disease but the person, so bioethicists need to remember that they deal not with issues but with the problems of living people. What constitutes a problem is, therefore, not an abstract matter one can determine from a distance, but an outcome of the condition, the values and the purposes of the individual who endures it. I will speak only of purposes here, and I will not come even close to saying everything we should concerning them. Let me begin with a broad and not uncontroversial statement: purposes constitute a central and the currently most neglected element in understanding the problems of bioethics.

An earlier generation of philosophers thought that consciousness is diaphanous; we find that, at least to us, purposes are. This should not be altogether surprising. Individual and social intentions are, for the most part, unarticulated. Supposedly we know what we want, and our actions reveal our desires and preferences. The larger purposes of the community are presumably fixed by the processes of social decision-making. So we should be able to determine who wants what by asking or watching, or by consulting the dialogue of public life. The trouble is, of course, that we don't ask and watch, and that even when we do, the evidence is ambiguous.

The ambiguity derives at least in part from the relative indeterminacy of the object we use the evidence to reveal. The irrationality philosophers have dreaded from Socrates on begins with our inability or unwillingness to shed the full light of consciousness on what we want. Many have said that the unexamined life is not worth living; to my knowledge, no one has yet remarked that unexamined purposes are not worth acting on. And the examination of purposes begins with the effort to give them definite shape, that is, to state them precisely and to measure their cost and compatibility.

The truth is that purposes arise in the process of living and capture us to do their bidding. They are powerful natural tendencies or movements that carry us along, as do the waves of the sea, allowing us to think we are in charge. If things go well, no examination of what we want is needed; if things go awry, we try to hitch a ride on the next wave. Only near-disaster makes us stop to take stock, and the pressure of such seasons makes them unsuitable for calm study. There are ritualistic times of crisis in human life brought on by maturation and aging, but without resolve and the skills of self-examination, even these are inadequate to clarify or revise our purposes.

Things stand no better with social objectives. Part of the success of business organizations may well be due to their unambiguous aims: oil refineries want to realize a profit by turning crude oil into usable derivatives. But even they face the possibility of conflicting goals or of confusion. Refineries may find it difficult to decide whether they wish to make gasoline or heating oil or some other products, and conglomerates are notorious for losing sight of their mission or frittering their efforts on a grab bag of incompatible aims.

Oddly, the purposes of communities are most easily determined under the worst circumstances—namely, when their survival is at stake. Faced with extinction, citizens unite to defend their homes, their language and their ways. The singleness of purpose that accompanies war tends to pull the community together and lend each of its members some satisfying task. Victory is often followed by the disintegration of this unity; no subsequent social purpose can command the agreement of people or match the unifying intensity of the desire to survive. In democratic societies, legislatures and judges rarely manage to formulate sound social purposes that capture the imagination of the majority. Conversely, the times at which contagious ideas infect large numbers of people are usually occasions when public discussions of policy are particularly one-sided and shallow.

The role of philosophers is, therefore, not very different from what it was always supposed to be. They need to occasion the examination of public and private purposes and assist in carrying it forward intelligently and with vigor. This is particularly true of bioethicists as they deal with decision-making in the clinical context and with public policies relating to human health. They must uncover disguised objectives, they must be alert to the emergence of new goals, and they must constantly challenge established aims and purposes.

I will illustrate this point with an example from the world of clinical encounters and another from the context of social life. Physicians, like the rest of us, carry their values with them wherever they go. Diagnosis and prognosis are not machine acts, leaving health care workers neutral with regard to what patients ought to do. On the contrary, doctors normally have clear ideas concerning what treatment options are available and which among them their patients should embrace. These notions derive at least in part from the purposes that shape the practice of physicians and in part from the purposes physicians impute to their patients.

So, for example, in the case of decisions concerning aggressive chemotherapy, a doctor's commitment to extend life may come in conflict with the patient's sense that enough is enough. Both the desire to treat and the decision to call it quits are likely to have their source in unspoken purposes. The doctor may conceive the task of the profession as combating death at all costs and the role of the practitioner as defined by the demand to live up to this aim. The patient, on the other hand, may wish not to be a burden on family or to take care of children by leaving an inheritance instead of using up resources in what seems a futile quest.

Attempts at communication are not likely to succeed without a measure of self-knowledge on the part of the participants. Each needs to have, moreover, at least some awareness of the aims of the other and respect for these aims even if at first they seem ill-advised or alien. The central facilitative task of bioethicists requires that they possess the ability to lay bare the unarticulated purposes that frame conflict and propel action. They must find ways of asking doctors and nurses and patients and families *why* they think what they do and what they wish to achieve by their actions. Knowing how our purposes diverge will obviously not eliminate all conflicts, but it will give those involved a keener sense of what they find important and what opposing commitments they must face. This is how we become more intelligent in dealing with our problems.

The emergence of social purposes is even more difficult to detect than the presence and nature of individual aims. With living persons, there is at least somebody to ask; in the case of the community, no one is in a position to supply a definitive answer. So the bioethicist must be alert to changes in social taste and behavior as these show themselves in relation to health and health care. How insensibly such shifts occur is well illustrated by the difference between current attitudes to death and those that prevailed as recently as ten years ago.

Throughout a succession of international conflicts, the U.S. Armed Forces prided themselves on safeguarding the lives of soldiers irrespective of cost. Downed pilots were retrieved from behind enemy lines at vast expense, and costly bombardments were initiated to cover the retreat of a few straggling GIs. Hospitals and health care teams mirrored this attitude to life: the prolongation of existence occupied center stage as one of the sacred purposes of the medical profession. Questions about who would pay seemed irrelevant, disconnecting life support was unthinkable, and everyone whose heart stopped was brought back.

Anyone who keeps this in mind is bound to find hospitals strikingly different places today. Discussion of do-not-resuscitate orders is widely encouraged, physicians take care not to initiate life-sustaining procedures that may be difficult to stop, and the elderly receive notably less aggressive treatment than their children. We seem no longer committed to sustaining life of every sort at all costs. A full recognition of the magnitude of the change has yet to penetrate the consciousness of the public. Shockingly, even bioethicists have failed to note it, call attention to it, and challenge it. Its implications for our practices elsewhere and its potential for undermining the intergenerational faith that sustains society have never been charted.

The point is not that our previous practices were either better or worse than what we do today. The problem is that both our prior commitments and our current ones were adopted without attentive deliberation. At a stage in our social history, we acted on one unarticulated purpose; at the present time, we act on another. Both purposes, along with the change from one to the other, escaped examination. As a result, we lived and continue to live without full benefits of the intelligence required to improve our practices. Pragmatic bioethics demands a look at what we mean to do and offers the tools for identifying and criticizing it.

CHAPTER 12

Grand Dreams of Perfect People

Male cats mate happily with any female in heat in the neighborhood. Something similar occurs in colleges as nearness and availability overwhelm all other considerations. So we see young men and women marry people who happen to be at hand when the time is ripe.

Yet there is an important difference between cats and humans. Even young people in a hurry to mate select those they view as the best among available partners. This suggests that they take an interest in their future and often even in that of their offspring. The standard by which they measure what is best may be quixotic or questionable, but there is no denying that they are engaged in a rudimentary eugenic quest. The ineffectiveness of the process renders it harmless, and the earnestness of the young lovers swept along in it makes it all charming.

But the charm evaporates with the ineffectiveness. When individuals make a science of finding mates and succeed in raising smart, hardworking and beautiful children, their neighbors are quick to cry foul. The undeserved good fortune of others can be borne with a wistful sigh, but their ability to master circumstance and control the course of their lives evokes suspicion and resentment. There is something terrible about seeing others go about life with rational deliberateness while we continue to bumble around.

The promise of genetics to introduce universally available improvements in future generations does not suffice to allay our concerns. The idea of having healthier, lovelier and happier children with no effort on the part of parents is attractive, but people are gnawingly skeptical that it can be accomplished. In any case, at least a part of the charm of children is that they are like us; if they were radically better, we could not have the cozy sense of their being *ours*.

Parents dote on children who look and act like them. Being prettier or a better athlete is welcome if the increment does not interfere with recognizing ourselves in the next generation. But purging our offspring of our imperfections makes them at most admirable strangers, not our beloved own. It makes it hard for us to believe that we had anything to do with begetting or raising such exquisite little people.

And what, after all, are our imperfections? The little mole above the curl of lip that makes a woman's smile mysterious? The tendency to dream that leads to surprising inventions and enterprises? The habits of excess that lurk behind great achievements? Most husbands and wives do not agree on the traits of which their children should have more or less. And for every family in which they do, there are five others that dismiss its ideals as grotesque or lamentable.

The diversity and peculiarity of what we want our children to be reveal profound disagreements about values. Of course, we all want them to be wonderful. But our conceptions of what it would mean for them to prosper or to excel show striking dissimilarities. Soldiers and preachers do not hope for the same traits in their offspring, and hard-drinking couples are unlikely to wish dull respectability on their young. The desires of those who live in other societies or in other historical times differ from ours in ways difficult to assess and perhaps impossible to approve.

Such differences are anything but trivial. They call our attention to the vast range of human nature and demonstrate the hopelessness of attempts to attain universal truths about what people prefer and what is good for them. Yet philosophers have always been in love with such sweeping ideas. For more than two thousand years, they hoped that their methods of investigation would lead them to incontrovertible insights into the essence of things. When the wiser among them realized that this was never to be, they switched their allegiance to physics, elevating it in their thoughts to the science of sciences.

The failure of physics to develop into a unified science of the world has not discouraged these thinkers of grand thoughts. Recently, they have shifted their hopes to genetics. The Human Genome Project, they believe, will at last provide us with a definitive and objective account at least of the portion of reality that constitutes human nature.

In one respect at least, this represents an advance. The focus on human nature carries us past the naïve view that we can examine objects without any reference to observers. In another respect, however, we are back where we began. For genetics attempts to study the observer in just the simple-mindedly objective way in which physics approaches particles and forces. Investigators promise us insight into the real essence of human beings and think they have to attend neither to the structuring conditions of their own values and purposes nor to the pervasive selectivity that underlies their choice of facts.

Love of the universal and the objective is easy to understand: they offer certainty and unlimited scope. Those captured by this love search for finality in knowledge, forgetting the humbling lessons of anthropology and history. Genetics is supposed to tell us not only about the facts of our constitution but also about the values proper to us. The hope is that in discovering who we are, we will at once learn what we need. And laying bare the mechanisms of preference will presumably enable us to distinguish proper choices from those prompted by error or disease.

Some think such lofty achievements are beyond the scope of genetics and yet look to the biological sciences in general to tell us about the proper function of human beings. Their hope is that diseases at least are objectively determinable facts. A study of organ structures may clarify their optimal operation and that, in turn, may reveal the parameters of natural activity. Even if such knowledge is inadequate to guide us in personal choice, it can be parlayed into public policies that promote favored values.

Make no mistake about it, the connection between the growth of knowledge and changes in public policy is anything but casual. New knowledge often yields new technology that promises a variety of benefits. We want magical cures for our problems, and such desires create a universal demand for what science can provide. This raises the question of how expensive benefits can be provided on a large scale, mobilizing the champions of justice to search for justifications to shift the burden of funding new programs of distribution and of treatment to taxpayers.

What justifications work when the cost of benefits is momentous? That the lives of beneficiaries would be improved clearly does not, because the lives of donors may well suffer corresponding damage. Every demand to fund a public program reduces the opportunity of individuals to improve their condition in their own way with the money they earn. Possible benefits are, moreover, potentially infinite, expanding with the availability of money to fund them. The process may result in the virtual or mediated enslavement of productive citizens to those who declare themselves to be in need, without hope of significantly reducing the number of demands.

Another possible justification for large publicly funded programs of enhancement might be built on the intuition of the champions of justice that it is terribly wrong for innocent people to suffer from disability and disease while others no more worthy flourish. This feeling is clearly right, but it can be converted into an argument for social initiatives only if the actions it prescribes could meet with success.

Unfortunately, however, such programs of large-scale amelioration are hopeless. We cannot equalize talents, endow people with will, or undo the ill fortune of those not favored by the natural lottery. But more, the exquisite interplay of the conditions of individuals with their desires and aspirations renders it impossible for us to determine which changes are desirable and which might destroy the delicate balance of a coping life.

This places the advocates of wholesale justice in a precarious position. People of good feeling agree that we must do what we sensibly can to help our fellows. But philosophers in search of closure do not want to leave the limits of such benevolence to be drawn from time to time in the concrete contexts of life by a caring community. They want some sweeping principle on the basis of which we could decide, pretty much once and for all, what everyone has a right to expect. A principle built on human nature would be best, providing a stable foundation for the allocation of publicly funded treatments and function enhancements.

Norman Daniels thinks he can ground such a principle in what he calls "species-typical normal functioning." The range of such functioning is supposed to be ascertainable by the biological sciences in a way that is "relatively objective and non-evaluative."[1] Disease and disability constitute adverse departures from this norm. Those who suffer from them cannot do what others can and hence lack fair equality of opportunity, a condition the community must find ways to overcome.

If Daniels succeeds in establishing the idea that disease must be treated and disability minimized through enhancements of capacities, we will have to find ways to fund a variety of costly new interventions. But on careful reading, it's not clear what exactly Daniels hopes to show. On the one hand, he speaks of disease as a scientifically verifiable objective condition, so that those who once thought that masturbation is an illness were simply wrong. But, on the other, he seems satisfied to present the account of species-typical functioning as political in nature, designed to generate consensus for publicly funded health care initiatives.

What looks like an innocent ambiguity can easily grow into a slippery move in persuasion. Political proposals must be assessed on the basis of their costs and consequences. The appearance that one among them carries the sanction of science confers on it an unfair advantage over its rivals. The advantage is all the more unfair if its claim to scientific objectivity cannot be sustained. So anyone who subscribes to the standard of species-typical normal functioning must be particularly careful not to characterize it to biologists and philosophers as a useful political proposal while presenting it to the public as objective science.

There can be no hope of neat general closure on issues of what treatments and enhancements the public is willing to underwrite, so long as they remain open to political negotiation. For reasons partly sound and partly idiosyncratic, some treatments—such as kidney dialysis—will receive funding and others—such as cosmetic surgery—will not. Philosophers devoted to the rule of principles find such halfway solutions and halting compromises objectionable. But nothing more can be expected in the real world in which any advance can be reversed and grand projects tend to remain unfinished.

So the hope for closure must come from some knockdown moral or scientific argument that would make our obligations unmistakable and hence perhaps unavoidable. Can Daniels's idea of species-typical normal functioning serve as the basis of such a decisive moral or scientific consideration? It could certainly not; in fact it would be difficult to detail all the points on which it falls short. Let me just speak about the most obvious.

It may be possible to describe the species-typical function of oysters, though I suspect our success in doing so may be due at least in part to the distance from which we view the lives of mollusks. With us humans, at any rate, differences of culture and history make it impossible to identify any activity that is uniquely and universally our own. There are, of course, the generalities of biology and anthropology. But what we share biologically, such as the need for food and the activities of metabolism, fails to distinguish us from other animals and especially from other mammals. And such anthropological similarities as cooperation and the search for meaning are too encompassing and hence empty to provide useful insight.

What, then, will count as a species-typical function of humans? One can hardly resist the temptation to select some local characteristics and elevate them to the level of universality or to anoint the statistically normal distribution of traits as the norm. But neither one of these procedures can encompass what everyone does. They also cannot give us an account of what we *ought* to do or what, if we don't or can't do it, will render us ill. Worse, in isolation from local values and practices, they cannot even identify which activities or disabilities put us at a competitive disadvantage.

At first sight epilepsy, for example, looks like an impairment of normal function. But would we consider it that if the vast majority of people experienced epileptic episodes? Under those circumstances, it would be an illness just as little as periodic sleepiness is a disease. Similarly, if the number of those suffering from chronic depression in the United States increased tenfold from the current seventeen million, it would no longer make sense to identify depression as a disease. Generally, what appears as a disability if only some people have it fades into the background conditions of life once its incidence becomes widespread.

Moreover, even when illness appears to be a matter of biological mechanism, involving, for instance, elevated glucose levels in the blood, it is not a simple affair of objective measurements. Such situations frequently involve continua of possible readings, and we have to decide which readings are acceptable and which constitute or betoken disease. How do we know that, in the absence of compensating factors, plasma glucose concentrations in excess of roughly 140 milligrams per deciliter indicate diabetes? This is not a discovery once made about diabetes but a thoughtful decision concerning when intervention is appropriate that continues to be enacted by conscientious physicians.

Since we must *decide* where to draw the line between normal operation and disease, both notions include an element of convention. The construction of diseases and disabilities is, of course, anything but arbitrary. We use extensive observation to put us in touch with the details of people's lives. And we are careful to distinguish illness from acceptable forms or levels of activity by reference to a host of considerations, including the frequency of the problem in the population, our ability to intervene in its course, the undesirability of leaving it untreated, and the way in which it connects to a variety of social practices and religious values.

These considerations suggest that Daniels is wrong not only in thinking that species-typical function is a scientifically objective notion but also in supposing that it is a positive idea by contrast to which we can define disease. More likely, the ideas of illness and disability constitute the foundation of thought in this field, and we construct the notion of normal operation by contrast with such adverse conditions. The unproblematic tends to fall below the level of explicit consciousness; attention is engaged only when things go awry. We note sickness and disability first and seek to bring people back to normal functioning, which we understand as the relatively indeterminate range of activities and conditions that do not display such trouble.

The idea of illness is, at least in our society, not a theoretical or a cleanly cognitive one. In addition to the value judgments and the social and religious significance built into it, the notion of disease is also deeply practical. It serves as a demand for action or at least as a notice and perhaps as a commitment to intervene. This is further indication of the primacy it enjoys over the notion of species-typical function and of its superior specificity to that nebulous idea.

Daniels's account of illness and of its connection to species-typical normal functioning thus appears to be open to disabling objections. But even if it were defensible, the invariable connection he asserts between illness and impaired opportunity could not be demonstrated. The tie between disability and opportunity is not the simple, natural one suggested by the idea that those who have no legs cannot run the marathon. The relation is mediated through social values and practices that may convert what appears as an obstacle into a grand source of achievements. Epilepsy, for example, may come to be viewed as a sacred condition, and those suffering from it can be exalted as priests or rulers. And many societies consider the devastatingly simpleminded as spiritual people free from the constraining rules of everyday life.

Moreover, often though not always, disabilities create opportunities for the development of different, compensating abilities. Many blind persons show exquisite sensitivity to sounds and smells, and those born without arms can attain remarkable skill in operating with their toes. Surprisingly, some who fall far below the average in cognitive capacity may enjoy particularly creative or emotionally rich lives. In these instances and in many others, human ingenuity and perseverance succeed in converting misfortune into victory. So the connection between disability and opportunity is mediated not only by social practices but also by individual values and achievements.

Viewing the situation from a great distance, one can of course intone that it would be better if people did not have to struggle against such misfortunes and obstacles. But this is idle talk that valorizes the common and shows a deep misunderstanding of the role of challenges in life. No one but affected individuals can choose between ordinary and heroic compensatory abilities, and it is by no means clear that, given the chance, they would hasten to embrace the everyday.

There is a deeper way of putting this point. In one sense, fair equality of opportunity must operate in abstraction from the values and the peculiarities of individuals. In another sense, however, such equality remains meaningless and empty unless it takes into account the conceptual frameworks and value structures of affected people. Equality of opportunity for concrete, historically situated persons is very different from how it might operate for bloodless agents of abstract rationality. The critical difference is that the natures of persons with disabilities play a central role in determining what counts as equality of opportunity for them.

A part of the reason for this is that lived disabilities are not accidental afflictions of people whose rational substance remains ever untouched. Chronic disease and permanent disability function as structuring conditions of personhood for those who must live with them. What Alcoholics Anonymous wants to do for its members happens naturally to persons with quadriplegia and even with juvenile-onset diabetes: they come to view themselves as individuals whose choices must and do reflect their conditions.

To choose treatments or enhancements that may provide fair equality of opportunity by bringing them closer to the species-typical norm is, therefore, to opt for selves other than the ones they have become over the years. The difficulties attendant on such courses of action (suppose I choose to become Mother Teresa or Attila the Hun!) are easy to overlook or to understate. Even if people with disabilities embraced such self-changing courses of action and even if the treatments and enhancements worked, it is not at all clear that their lives would be improved. At the very least, they would face periods of painful adjustment and instability.

This train of thought leads inevitably to the conclusion that what we owe humans who suffer from chronic ailments and disabilities may have very little to do with equalizing their opportunities. Nothing is an opportunity unless a person thinks it is both possible and desirable, and opportunities can be equal only if they are commensurable. But the differences among people make it impossible to measure what one values against the commitments of another and hence unthinkable to equalize their chances of pursuing what they want. We are left where people of good feeling have been from time immemorial: we must do what we can to help where we can, both on an individual basis and by social policies that take individual differences seriously.

Whether it is hubris or foolish hope, we wish to fix everything in the world. Nearly daily reports of progress in mapping the human genome assure us that before long we will identify the genes for every desirable and undesirable trait. Then we will obliterate or at least shut down the "bad" genes and enhance the operation of the "good" ones to create human beings who will live long, happy and moral lives. In the meantime, we launch imposing social programs to eliminate injustice by equalizing opportunities and, if not outcomes, then at least income. Nothing but grand schemes suffice, nothing but final solutions attract.

What happened to the recognition of finitude? How can we overlook the fact that we are mired in the details of daily life and that perfection has always been a destructive dream? Is the human race not old enough to recognize the eternal gulf between the ideal and where we are, and to learn to satisfy itself with a little advance here and there in the direction of decency and self-improvement?

Our ignorance is vast and necessary. It is vast because we are not likely to learn everything we need to know and don't really need to know everything we learn. It is necessary because we can never uncover the secret loves burning in the hearts of others or understand their private hopes and satisfactions. But in all our sensible moments we know that it is best to care for individuals in their individuality and to meet needs where we find them, one at a time.

To aim for a little improvement in our children and for some small growth in caring takes the human condition seriously and stands a chance of success. Initiating large social programs and reengineering the genome will fail as surely as every holy war. We can walk and sometimes even run, but flapping arms will never make us fly.

Researchers and Their Subjects
as Neighbors

Uncertainty surrounds everything momentous. The Promethean cave dwellers who first tamed fire had no notion of the long-term results. The genius who invented the wheel was in no position to predict that it would be used in tanks and landing gears. Untutored primitives in the art of genetic modification, we stumble ahead without understanding where our procedures and investigations lead.

To be sure, we try to forecast likely consequences and we concede that the uncertainties surrounding such procedures as egg cell nuclear transfer constitute an important element in assessing their acceptability. But acknowledging uncertainty is often mistaken for dealing with it, and we think we can then yield with good conscience to our desire to explore and experiment at will.

The momentum and the success of science make it impossible for us to draw a line investigators must not transgress. Erecting blanket legal or moral prohibitions is in any case not an auspicious way of handling the varied problems and opportunities that arise out of meeting divergent needs. In a free, multinational world, such restrictions cannot be enforced. Moreover, in banning research we deny ourselves incalculable benefits.

Total freedom in pursuing the goals of science sounds, therefore, like the right policy. It is, if we restrict ourselves to questions about the desirability and effectiveness of bureaucratic regulation. But that is not the best way to conceive the problems arising from the interplay of human needs and scientific advance. To enrich our thinking, we must first remind ourselves that science has no goals, only investigators do. And to understand the purposes that move research scientists, we must examine their relations to their professions, their employers and the patients their discoveries may aid.

Bonnicksen's analysis of the ethical problems and policy options connected with egg cell nuclear transfer is typical of how we think about these matters nowadays.[1] The issue is framed in terms of unchangeable needs and one-dimensional relations. Women with MELAS[2] desire to have children genetically connected to them. Scientists want to learn more about the operations of nature so they may help to fulfill these wishes. Government officials need to develop regulations to protect people from harm. We aver that optimal interaction would maximize satisfaction for patients, funding and freedom for scientists, and safety for future generations.

This way of putting the matter makes it irrelevant from the standpoint of researchers whether the desire for genetically connected children is sensible. It is interpreted as an unchallengeable given, defining a task that, if only money and the patient's "informed" consent can be obtained, demands pursuit. That the desire may be overwhelmingly irrational and that ample alternatives exist to satisfy the yearning for maternity count for nothing and can be safely disregarded.

Is it likely that the desire for genetically connected offspring is so strong that it would carry the day if the patient (experimental subject, in reality) understood the panoply of risks associated with egg cell nuclear transfer? In addition to the heartbreak of early spontaneous abortion, she faces the relatively high likelihood of bearing a child who suffers from birth defects or dies young. Bonnicksen provides but a brief list of potential problems; one of the characteristics of untested experimental procedures is that we can't foresee all the things that may or will go wrong.

A deformed or abnormal child resulting from egg cell nuclear transfer would not be, moreover, the unfortunate but disposable product of an experiment. A living reminder of the mother's stubborn desire, it would have to be loved and shielded in sorrow for years. Is the person eagerly recruited by the research team and ready to undergo the experiment prepared to take on such overwhelming responsibilities? And, given the shortened life expectancy of individuals with MELAS, could she take care of an abnormal child for the rest of its life? Considering the risks of the procedure and the readily available alternatives, the desire for genetically connected children under these circumstances is, though humanly understandable, rationally mad.

The irrationality of the desire is surely no secret to investigators. Would they be willing to see their daughters exposed to such risks? Yet the information that shows the full gravity of participating in the experiment tends not to reach the patient with the clarity and the emotional force that could affect her decision. The reason is the one-dimensional relation between researchers and their subject. They are trading desires: one wants a child, the others want to do an experiment. Talking too much might affect the woman's readiness to participate and ruin the chance of learning something new.

Expecting researchers to take a personal interest in their subjects is to romanticize human relations. The cold world is such that so long as scientists operate by the protocols of distant concern, they can view themselves as being without blame. But even if personal interest is too much to demand, everyone agrees that physicians should act as educators of the public in matters of health. This educational function is cast aside when the desire of a woman with MELAS for a genetically related child is accepted at face value. If researchers viewed themselves as educators as well, they would have to talk to their potential subjects in a way that makes it unlikely they could do their experiment.

There is a good greater than curing diseases or learning about nature. Teaching the human community to live sensibly by making rational decisions admittedly includes offering them options we can provide only through the work of science. But the choices do little good unless they embody the reflective preferences of individuals. Without unconstrained consideration of all the relevant available information, humans cannot act as intelligent adults. The job of persons who know the facts is to make them available in intelligible form to ordinary people.

Professionals with special knowledge and expertise always incur special obligations to contribute to the public discussion of issues in their field and to the education of individuals who come to seek their help. Good lawyers don't let their clients sue everyone in sight. Responsible plastic surgeons question a patient's desire for the third face-lift in five years. Abdicating these duties contributes mightily to making us a society of strangers in which the good of one seems to connect only marginally with the good of anyone else.

Freedom without caring invites the pursuit of dangerous desires and the exploitation of people who think that science offers fulfillment of every wish. If we acquiesce in Bonnicksen's depiction of the moral situation of egg cell nuclear transfer in terms of researchers and women suffering from MELAS having their desires met within the limits imposed by technology and government regulation, we overlook the central complexifying elements of the human context. Bringing the players into a moral relation requires that the desires of each group be adjustable as the good of the other is taken into account.

The government, moreover, is not the sole or the primary agency to put limits on the activities of people. The community stands as a silent and invisible presence in all these life-transforming moral relations. The first and final restriction on people, therefore, is not what the political arm of the society denies them but what, in the name of belonging to the same community, they simply will not do to their neighbors.

The more we shift the responsibility for regulation to the government, the more we feel liberated to pursue our own agenda without self-restraint. The neglected virtue of caring is an indispensable condition of human decency and of community life. Those who enjoy the freedom to investigate must take responsibility for displaying self-control.

The question of what stance we should take to such novel technological possibilities as egg cell nuclear transfer cannot, therefore, be answered in terms of government regulation. As other typical problems of modern industrial society, we need to deal with it through open and intelligent public debate and by demonstrating to all, again and again, the interwoven fabric of our fates.

CHAPTER 14

Dying Old as a Social Problem

We live in times of unprecedented change. Improvements in nutrition, public sanitation and the treatment of disease have enhanced the quality of life and extended its length beyond all but the wildest expectations. We live longer and, in material terms, better by far than any previous generation.

Methuselah was supposed to have lived more than three times three hundred years, but believers who read about him in the twelfth century were glad to make it to thirty. Yet for us, average life expectancy at birth rose from 47.3 years in 1900 to 68.2 in 1950. It has continued to rise since then, topping 75.8 years in 1995, with no indication that a peak has been reached. Optimistic estimates suggest that the human life span can, and will before too long, be extended to 150 or even 200 years.

The elderly population in industrialized nations is increasing far more rapidly than the population as a whole. From 1900 to 1994, the population of the United States tripled, but the number of those over 65 years of age grew elevenfold to 33 million. The number of the oldest old increased even more impressively, growing to 3.5 million persons in 1994, which is 28 times greater than the number of people 85 and over who lived in 1900. Conservative estimates indicate that by 2030, more than 20 percent of the U.S. population will be over 65.[1]

Such advances come at a price. Many of the elderly need personal assistance even with everyday activities. On some occasions, life can be extended only at the loss of many of its satisfactions. On others, the lives saved are such in name only, and families and institutions end up caring for biological organisms whose human potential has been wrecked. Though longer life offers vast benefits, it also protracts the debility of old age and creates a population of elderly people plagued by chronic diseases. Loss of autonomy, successive organ failures and intractable pain suggest that rather than living long, many of these individuals are just slow to die.

The seamy downside of our success in extending life is that a small but significant number of the very sick and the very old want to die, but cannot. Many more people are likely to suffer from a surfeit of life in the coming years. The number of people over 65 in the United States is projected to increase to over 80 million in the next fifty years and the number of those over 85 to possibly 10 million. No matter how fast and how far medical technology will have progressed by then, this will leave hundreds of thousands of people who are tired of battling for life or at least sincerely believe that existence no longer benefits them.

Arguing that one has a right to one's life and can therefore terminate it at will misses the personal dynamics and the social complexities of the situation. This renders attacks on the right to die largely beside the point.[2] Asserting a right may be useful against an intrusive government or as protection from aggressive neighbors, but it has no place in a community structured by the ideal of uniting the values of individuals with the common good. Maintaining, from the other side, that the state has a preeminent interest in the lives of its citizens misses the point no less. The government must be devoted to the good of citizens first, and to their lives only to the extent that they deem them to be conditions of or ingredients in that good.

How, then, should we think about people who no longer wish to live? Clearly, we must think about their plight, because the problem will not go away. But we must not approach complex issues in a simplistic way. Satisfying as it is to take the moral high ground by announcing that all life is sacred, such gestures will not take us very far. No one actually believes this— or, at least, no one believes it, acts on it, and lives long enough to explore all of its merits. Even people who refuse to eat meat kill and dine on broccoli without a moral qualm. Since we cannot survive on stones and mud, it is ineffectual or insincere to pretend that we respect life of every sort.

A look at our practices reveals that we do not even treat human life as sacred. We wash living cells off the face, allow ova to die unfertilized and spread thousands of trillions of sperms around the world without maximizing their chances to grow into new organisms. We remove diseased organs without mercy and kill both healthy and cancerous cells. Would health massage, cosmetology and the tonsorial art—never mind medicine, dentistry and surgery—be possible if we thought all products of the human genome must remain inviolate?

But this, some will insist, is a willful distortion of what earnest people mean: they maintain that only the entire human body need be respected, not its parts. This defense exposes the fundamental and lamentable error to which sanctity-of-life arguments lead. The operation of the entire body is no more an end in itself than is the integrity of its organs; their value derives from the support they provide for a human life. Confusing a human life with the life of a human body is a pernicious mistake, and it remains a baffling irony that religious people who believe in the transcendent destiny of the soul should be the ones most apt to make it.

There must have been a terrible inversion of values in the last fifty or hundred years to focus the attention of deeply believing Christians on the body in its vegetative function. Insisting on the inviolability of intact individuals and protecting the weak, the underprivileged and the disabled are in the best tradition of religious caring. But these are defenses of the body only incidentally; their primary purpose is to honor the wishes, the needs and the ontological status of persons. There is, accordingly, nothing to justify the move from meeting the needs of persons to protecting the presumed rights of the bodies connected to them. Bodies have no rights, and when their sole function is biological, no persons own or inhabit them to give them standing.

Adulation of the body is, moreover, a singularly pagan practice. It shows itself in the heartrending activity of safeguarding the bodies of persons killed by years of coma. Worse, when even biological function ceases, we embalm the body, enhance its look with makeup and put it on display, claiming identity with the departed soul. "Doesn't he look good!" mourners can then exclaim as they walk past the open coffin, feasting their eyes on the simulacrum of a human being, on what is no more than a clump of matter soon to rest underground.

Few seem to reflect on what such practices reveal about our beliefs, and as a result our judgments remain unchallenged and incoherent. We confuse biological activity with human life and assign the value of the person to the body. In this way, we blind ourselves to the sensible and natural line between an intelligently operating organism and that creature reduced to its minimal functions or, in the end, to a gravitating heap.

The principle of the sanctity of all life remains, therefore, an empty slogan, unless those who wish to rely on it as a guide to policy or to morality provide a clear account of what sort of life they have in mind and what manner of beings are to enjoy it at what cost. A more promising approach is to avoid reference to absolute principles altogether, examining each class of cases on its own to see how far it advances or hinders human well-being. Although there may be other values that rightly command our allegiance, we cannot go far wrong in stressing the importance of human flourishing.

The long experience of the race and our personal experiments afford us ample information about the range of human goods. The first and perhaps most remarkable fact that commends itself to our attention is the central, privileged role people play in defining or at least in discovering their good.

Like flowers, humans are scattered to grow in directly self-governing, operationally independent organisms. Although tied to their fellows by bonds of need and love, adult individuals constitute systems that are in some respects complete. They are able to act on their own and, experiencing the outcomes, to make suitable adjustments in their behavior. Though by no means insular, they nevertheless occupy integrated small worlds with an element of privacy unique to each. This is what we normally mean when we say that people live their own lives and die their own deaths, fill out their worlds and close them down, with others grieving or cheering them on but only distantly involved.

This ineluctable element of subjectivity makes individuals specially situated, even if by no means invariably accurate, judges of their own good. Under normal circumstances, they are in a better position than anyone else to know what they wish to accomplish, what pleases them, and what they are prepared to give up to obtain such satisfactions. People find their own private and idiosyncratic value structures familiar and intuitively right; others, by contrast, may not be able to understand how anyone can enjoy or treasure such odd things.

Only under special conditions can others offer us valid insight or useful advice: in times of great stress or passion, for example, we can discount or overlook what caring others plainly perceive. Even psychologists, working from a general knowledge of the range of human goods, have nothing to match the detailed and specific information individuals possess about what is of significance to them. And the best among those who dare to offer advice quickly learn to say only what in the depths of our souls we already know.

The principle that, other things being equal, people are the best judges of what they want out of life provides a sound and sensible basis for dealing with them. If we must remember this principle when our friends seek a better life, we should not forget it when they face death. We should be satisfied to let them chart their own courses, convinced that probably no one knows better what they want than they and that, in any case, they will be first in line when it comes to suffering the consequences of their decisions.

Such decisions are momentous and irreversible, so no one should have to make them without the caring support of the community. But loving concern is one thing, meddling obstruction of the process quite another. Legislation that wrests the decisions from individuals situated in their communities is a blunt and objectionable instrument for the expression of caring.

The vast literature directed against suicide suffers from a very poor argument that has been repeated and judged conclusive even by such sensitive defenders of liberty as John Stuart Mill.[3] Since killing oneself is irreversible, these philosophers maintain, it cannot fall within the autonomous decision-making power of individuals. Consistent thinkers, including Mill, decline extending freedom to any act whose consequences make its reversal impossible, such as selling oneself into slavery and killing not only oneself but anyone. Such consistency is commendable, but it quickly reduces the argument to absurdity. For it is astonishing that murder and slavery are the only irreversible acts these philosophers can find, when we are surrounded by them on all sides.

Actually, since time itself cannot be undone or turned around, all human acts have a sort of finality. Lies and infidelities can be only forgiven, never erased. We can never recapture the squandered opportunities of youth, nor can we atone for occasions on which the time came to act but our hearts froze. Choosing the wrong place to live, the wrong mate or the wrong profession may seem easy to fix by going back to square one and starting again. But though the start may feel fresh, it does not undo the damage of the past; the third spouse may at last be right, but the sadness and pain of the first two always remain.

Something dies in us with every passing day, and though the loss is not of everything at once, as it is with death, it is of almost everything cumulatively over time, leaving little for the final act to take. Being no longer able to do some things is a natural consequence of aging, and it differs only in degree from the inability to do anything consequent upon death. And when death comes at the end of lengthy illness, it stops fewer activities than did the onset of disease. So irreversible loss attends nearly everything we do, and if we don't trust people to make sensible decisions about death, we should not trust their other choices either.

This argument against suicide cuts, therefore, equally against all significant freedom. If the irreversibility of death disqualifies people from choosing it, the irreparable loss that comes of marrying the wrong person renders choice of mate impermissible. If people should not be allowed to choose the time and manner of their exit, they must not be permitted to decide about attending college, buying a house, and having children either. Tyrants can in this way enlist the fundamental structure of reality to justify their rule.

Mill, I suspect, was in the end less bothered about the irreversibility than about the momentousness of the consequences of what we do. This concern is particularly legitimate and understandable in the case of death. Unfortunately, however, assessments of the damage death inflicts tend to be one-dimensional.

Thinkers typically focus on events that are heartrendingly sad instead of examining a broad range of cases. But the value of terminating life, as the value of anything, must be examined in context: each death must be judged individually by reference to the life it ends. Those who take the untimely departure of loved ones or teenage suicide as their model are sure to be misled. The vast loss these represent is a poor guide to assessing the appropriateness of painlessly slipping away at the sick end of a long life. Condemnation of suicide loses its plausibility the moment we consider the daily life and prospects of at least some of the people who seek it.

The fact that individuals are particularly well situated to know what is of value to them does not imply that caring others are always ignorant. Detailed observation of their choices reveals a great deal about what people prize. In the case of healthy teenagers, moreover, it is obvious that the bulk of their life is ahead of them, and the flimsiest knowledge of psychology suffices to convince us that their depressions will lift after a while. Even if Weltschmerz or disappointed love distorts their vision by darkening their days, their otherwise bright prospects justify us in not standing idly by when they propose to take their lives in ill-considered haste.

Similarly, we can have significant knowledge of the condition of old people suffering from a painful terminal disease. Even if we lack what may be in their case exquisitely certain knowledge of what they want, we can understand their situation and assess their prospects. Romanticizing affirmations of the beauty of life are revoltingly out of place here. Their present may consist of drugged stupor and their future of a few more weeks of suffering. Their condition has almost nothing in common with the situation of young people temporarily distressed: it is not subjectively dark but objectively bleak.

Our proper inability to honor the desire of the young for release from life must not blind us to what may well be a sound and sensible wish on the part of people who are both sick and old. Multiple organ failure leaves individuals—like derelict ships at sea—without rudder and destination, marking the days until the final storm floods all compartments. Whoever sees the world from their perspective understands that continued life can do them little good and that the harm quick death would bring is less by far than that caused by life to an unwanted child.

It strikes me as unseemly to try to delegitimate the desire for death by claiming that its source must be depression. Reasonings built on such conveniently loose psychological concepts do little more than confirm one's preexisting judgments. But even if we disregard this obvious point, the argument can be compelling only if depression constitutes an invariably inappropriate response and if it always clouds the faculty of judgment. Both of these conditions, however, are open to doubt.

Depression may well be perverse when its cause is easily removed. If reasonable effort promises to eliminate the external circumstance or personal failure that stands in the way of getting what we want, depression is an irrational response. But when one's condition is genuinely hopeless, it would be strange not to get depressed. Painful and inevitable death is depressing, and the mad response to it is cheerful acceptance, not a crushing sense of impotence. The feeling of being cornered is, moreover, under the circumstances a deeply insightful assessment of one's situation. So, quite apart from the general arguments of such pessimists as Schopenhauer for the view that only the dejected perceive the world the way it truly is, when the prospects for life are dim, depressed people, seeing doom and gloom, render strikingly accurate accounts of their reality.

I conclude that if we honor the ordinary, sensible wishes of people we care for or love, under the right circumstances we must honor their choice of death as well. We must be careful that this choice is not unduly influenced by the desires of others and particularly that it does not originate in what is increasingly talked about as the duty to die.[4] We can understand that the wish not to be a burden to those we love can play a powerful role in the decision to die at an early stage of a debilitating or terminal disease. But it is well worth remembering that we live in a world of relative plenty, so economic considerations should not be allowed primacy in such decisions. And on the psychological side, those who love us may never be satisfied that they have shown their caring unless they have an opportunity to see us through a large portion of our decline.

People who bemoan the tendency of terminally ill people to seek early release from their suffering, attributing it to erroneous beliefs or personal weakness, need to spend more time trying to understand its social causes. In a world busy with work, caring for the sick falls to paid specialists. There is no room in the house for debilitated older people and no time to tend to their wishes. They are shipped to the hospital, to the hospice or, at best, to isolated facilities providing "assisted living"; the place of the nurturing home is taken by the nursing home. Familiar surroundings and routines are replaced by antiseptic rooms that permit no privacy and few activities beyond those needed for physical existence. Tended by indifferent strangers, the old and the ill grow sick at heart and find it pointless to live through days that lack hope and meaning.

In different circumstances, natural, even slow, death could be seen as a wonderful affirmation of the enduring values of family and love. The continuity of life, visibly displayed as responsibility and strength pass from the old to the young, provides a peace words cannot describe. Seeing the energy of children and grandchildren gives hope that all is not lost, that one's life survives in the successes of others. Under such conditions, there is point to living on: a bit of joy and a ray of hope suffice to brighten the day. We see that few of those dying in the midst of their families and feeling their love seek early death or assisted suicide. The nurturing community provides reasons for living and removes the horror of a lonely death.

Our highly mediated society has made different arrangements for taking care of the old, and the problems we face with end-of-life decisions constitute a portion of the price we pay for them.[5] Concentrating the old in special housing developments, isolating the seriously ill from family and friends, and orchestrating the dying process under the supervision of professionals distance vulnerable people from their roots. Many of them cease to want to live even when they are relatively healthy; why live on if the people who matter are beyond reach and the sights and sounds and activities that filled the days with small satisfactions have long disappeared?

No radical change in these social arrangements is likely to occur in the foreseeable future. We shall have to settle instead for modest improvements in how we tend the old and the ill. Those interested in reducing the pressure for legalizing euthanasia and the incidence of suicide among the sick would find greater success by working to make the lives of terminal patients more meaningful than by trying to pass legislation.

Remarkably, retirement home operators have so far shown less than full understanding of the social and spiritual needs of the persons entrusted to their care. Only recently have a few facilities started to invite groups of children to visit and to provide cats and dogs for their residents to love. Such humanizing touches bring the old closer to the sweet energy of life and give them small but potent reasons to get up in the morning. Active people who have shouldered responsibility all their lives cannot be expected to convert themselves into the human equivalents of the potted plants that sit in their still rooms. No one wants to live long without purpose, without some pride in self-reliance and without the sense of being needed.

There are similar signs of promise in how the "management" of death is beginning to change. Economic reasons have led hospitals to discharge the very ill to die, if at all possible, in their own homes. Seeing life and death in the same well-loved or at least familiar surroundings provides comfort and consolation. The ritual of friends coming to visit or to say good-bye confers a sense of touching completion on life. Excruciating pain is easier to bear than abandonment; in any case, so long as one is in the loving care of those one loves, the pain can always be stilled.

Our first concern in dealing with a rapidly aging population must therefore be to provide the support of community to all who face old age and painful death. This support must be more than the anonymous readiness to pay taxes for the treatment of those lacking means. It has to take the form of personal caring, the sort of human relationships that make living worthwhile. Dying people need to feel what we seek throughout our lives: appreciation of the significance of what we have done and who we are. This standing in the eyes of the community, this importance of our passing individuality, is the ultimate recognition we want from our friends and from those who hold jobs in the institutions of the world. Sadly, few ever feel such acknowledgment even at the height of their power. Lacking it near the moment of death kills the soul before the body is ready to go.

To provide this standing in the generous way suffering friends deserve, we must learn to honor the momentousness of dying. Infernal busyness protects us from feeling the nodes of life; we go through the world without savoring the great occasions that make for the pathos and the deep mystery of existence. Religion called these moments sacred, but its decline left us unable to apply such vital concepts. One of the weaknesses of secular society is that it has nothing to offer in their place. As a result, life loses some of its depth and nearly all its articulation: everything happens on a single plane, without the exaltation and the celebration grand events deserve.

At the very least, we must recapture the experience of death for ordinary life. We cannot celebrate the event if it remains hidden from sight in the cancer wards and operating rooms of hospitals. It needs to be a public part of reality, socially fought, bravely faced and openly discussed. It must become a part of the school curriculum as well, so young people can feel its weight and not fear its secrets. If we can appropriate it as a natural event in every person's history, we can rally with sympathy to the sides of those whose time has come. Just as knowing the pain of hunger creates solidarity with those in need of food, expectation of our own death brings us into a special community with those whose expectations are about to be fulfilled.

The second task in dealing with the growing number of old and sick people in our midst is to respect the choices they make about their lives and deaths. They have a special competence to know what they want and an inescapable responsibility for the consequences of their decisions. Accepting their word cannot, of course, mean leaving them alone to sort things out as best they can in the privacy of their souls. What they want affects us as well, and in deciding they need to know that their continued existence and the quality of their daily lives are of vital significance to others. Caring prevents suicide and the need for euthanasia.

We cannot underestimate the human capacity for following the crowd. At times in the history of humankind, suicide was contagiously easy. One lesson of the recent Dutch experience may well be that euthanasia can come to be viewed as a quick solution to multiple problems. We must not let the human tendency for imitation foreshorten the lives of our loved ones. Caring for them conveys the notion that they are wanted, but nothing deters the desire for death more than the thought that one's work is not yet complete. The greatest argument against early death is how much those suffering, in spite of their pain, can still contribute to our lives and how much we can do to enrich theirs. Soon enough we will no longer be able to walk hand in hand, but it matters deeply that we treasure the companionship while we can.

In the teeth of the best efforts of the community, however, sometimes the pain, the bewilderment and the degradation of disease become too much to bear. Alzheimer's patients whose moments of lucidity grow further and further apart, cancer sufferers whose pain can be stilled only by sinking their minds in a pool of haze, those afflicted with amyotrophic lateral sclerosis (ALS) who watch in horror as the paralysis of their bodies approaches the lungs and heart may well judge that it is pointless to hope and struggle on. Respect for them requires that we permit the last word to be theirs.

At such an advanced stage of debility, this is neither abandonment nor lack of caring. We must understand it, rather, as an expression of love. Love wants the other's good as the other defines it. There is no doubt that some people at the distant edge of life decide or recognize that it is better not to be. In condemning their wish to die or failing to give them aid, we allow our own energy and hatred of death to speak. That is the voice we must still, partly to help those we love today and partly to prepare for the time when our own predicaments may reveal the rightness of their stance.

IV

American Philosophers

CHAPTER 15

The Insignificance of Individuals

Scholars generally believe that classical American philosophy is deeply indebted to German idealism. This opinion is generally correct: Peirce, Royce and Dewey acknowledge the influence on their works of Kant and Hegel, and these and other German thinkers are James's and Santayana's favorite foils. We do not yet have a definitive study of all the important connections between Kant, Fichte, Hegel, Schopenhauer and Nietzsche on the one hand, and Peirce, Royce, James, Dewey and Santayana on the other. Such an investigation would trace the influence of the Germans on the Americans, giving a full account both of continuities of conviction and of differences of approach.

I want here to outline one important element of any such future study. However much American naturalists borrowed from German idealists, there is one issue on which their disagreement is complete. Fichte and Hegel announce the insignificance of individuals, holding persons and their happiness in very low esteem. With the possible exception of Peirce, the Americans, by contrast, view individuality as of paramount significance for morality and for social life. This opposition is central: it cuts across the differences between American pragmatists, naturalists and idealists. Understanding it brings us close to seeing the vast gulf between the fully developed forms of American philosophy and its German sources.

First, a word about individuality and the sense in which it is not of ultimate significance. Friends of Hegel can readily, and rightly, argue that the work of spirit is impossible without concrete empirical persons. But that is like maintaining the essentiality of cells for the body. Of course cells are necessary constituents of the organism. Nevertheless, no particular cell is necessary, and hence any cell is dispensable. The peculiarity of individuals is precisely that they occupy the centers of their worlds. From its own standpoint, none of them is dispensable: each lives its own life and experiences thought of its death as the end of everything worthwhile.

Even if individuals and the state constitute an organism in Kant's sense,[1] each serving as means to the welfare of the other, persons do not acquire much significance. Kant's internal teleology may seem to make the relation between state and individuals symmetrical: each has as its end the unconditioned flourishing of the other. But the symmetry is illusory. The relationship is not one-one but one-many, making the welfare of the state the sole object of the devotion of its citizens, while the well-being of any one of them is but a fragment—an insignificantly small fragment—of what the state aims to promote.

The idea that the march of God through the world requires individuals as foot soldiers leaves people understandably cold. What matters from the standpoint of the individual is its own life, integrity and happiness. Hegel was perfectly aware of this, claiming that people act on the basis of self-seeking passions. But every time he writes about ordinary folk, he has in mind the mass of them, the class of individuals, rather than individuals who exist only through their particularity. Individuals, therefore, transcend the category to which they belong; they can be understood only from their own perspectives and never adequately by reference to what they all have in common.

Hegel is aware of this claim also, but famously maintains that the particular attains intelligibility only when raised to the level of the universal. This is part of the war he wages on immediacy and constitutes not so much an argument against particularity as a confession of his inability to adopt and consider as final a centered and limited perspective on reality.

When I speak of individuals, I have in mind persons like ourselves with a finite and peculiar angle of approach to the world. They may be unintelligible from the outside; but from their own perspectives, everything they feel and do seems luminous and for the most part astonishingly right. They are reminiscent of Kierkegaard's Abraham, though without his religious excesses, and Nietzsche's Dionysian, self-creative individual, without an undercurrent of self-absorption. They do what they can to lead as rich a life as they can, focusing on ordinary pursuits executed with personal flair and flavor.

These are the individuals who receive little respect in German idealism. There are two main lines of attack upon them. I have already hinted at Hegel's approach: he thinks that the lives and happiness of individuals are of no ultimate significance and are therefore properly crushed by the juggernaut of history. Fichte, by contrast, argues that finite individuality is a privation to be overcome and announces that it will disappear in the infinitely distant future.

As early as the end of the Preface of *The Phenomenology of Spirit*, Hegel takes aim at individuals. He says:

> [T]he share in the total work of Spirit which falls to the individual can only be very small. Because of this, the individual must all the more forget himself. . . . Of course, he must make of himself and achieve what he can; but less must be demanded of him, just as he in turn can expect less of himself, and may demand less for himself.[2]

The last few words have an especially ominous ring. Individuals have no business making demands on the state; they are to do what little they can for the larger whole. The maxim that since they can do little, they should get little seems right from the standpoint of the totality. Hegel does not consider the possibility of discrepant perspectives: what may appear little to the state is, to individuals, their all.

Later in the same book,[3] Hegel points out that the work of the individual is both consciously and unconsciously universal work, creating a whole (the state) "for which he sacrifices himself." Hegel characterizes this self-sacrifice as "making oneself a Thing" in service to the greater goals of the higher being. He finds it justifiable that history should serve as a "slaughter-bench"[4] that "victimizes" the virtue of individuals. He seems to delight in the fact that the "history of the world is not the theater of happiness": "periods of happiness are blank pages in it, for they are periods of harmony."[5]

Hegel goes on to explain that "[T]he particular is for the most part of too trifling value as compared with the general; individuals are sacrificed and abandoned. The Idea pays the penalty of determinate existence and of corruptibility, not from itself, but from the passions of individuals."[6]

The price is paid in the coin of lost lives and hopes through the depradations of armed conflict. Fortunately, Hegel intones, "[T]here is an ethical element in war."[7] Its "deep meaning" is that "by it the ethical health of the nations is preserved"[8] because their finite aims are uprooted. This is as it should be, because property and life belong in the realm of chance, and "individuals come under the category of means to an ulterior end."[9]

Though no stranger to the glorification of the state, Fichte's contribution to cutting the individual to size is more metaphysical. In the eleventh section of the Second Introduction to the *Science of Knowledge* of 1794,[10] he outlines the moral/metaphysical history of the world in two astonishing paragraphs. That history begins with the self as intellectual intuition, descends into the valley of empirical differentiation, and ends with the self as Idea.

The self as intellectual intuition is an undifferentiated, contentless, impersonal ego or act that is the timeless ground of all. Modeled on Kant's transcendental unity of apperception but reminiscent of the Neoplatonic One, the absolute self serves as the focal unity from which all the necessary conditions of the possibility of knowledge and of moral action may be derived. In its fecundity, it imposes limits on itself and thereby generates the world of experience with all its finite objects and subjects.

Neither the absolute self nor the self as Idea is an individual: in the former, selfhood has "not yet been particularized into individuality," and in the latter, "individuality has vanished through cultivation according to general laws."[11] Individuality occurs only through "sensory restriction"[12] or inadequate rationality and is accordingly something that, as rational beings, we must aim to overcome. To transcend individuality, the self must "exhibit universal reason perfectly within itself" and "fully realize reason outside it in the world."[13] As all Fichtean tasks, this is too great for our finite powers. Since we cannot fully accomplish it, we must strive to "approximate ourselves to this Idea *ad infinitum.*"

The notion of fully embodying reason in oneself and in the world deserves some additional comments. Fichte builds his system on Kantian foundations. One implication of Kant's insistence that morality is simply rationality in act is that if all our actions were moral, individual differences among us would disappear. Everyone acting in accordance with the categorical imperative in relevantly similar situations would do the same thing; differences in action are due to the heteronomous interests of persons.

Differences in character are due, similarly, to sensuous or extramoral influences. Fully moral people would have no tendencies beyond doing duty for duty's sake, and if they did, they would know how to curb them. All the peculiarities of individuals are extraneous to their hard moral core. They are acquired in a lifetime of experience but always remain accidental to what people really are: autonomous agents who act out of respect for the law.

Finally, both Kant and Fichte believe that the operations of the physical world are governed by amoral laws of necessity. When we freely conform our will to the demand for rationality, we replace these laws with the moral law, that is, with the law of human freedom. The task, according to Fichte, is to moralize or humanize the entire world, banishing necessity in pursuit of the final dominance of reason.

We can say some abstract things about a universe in which reason rules agents, their actions and the world, but such generalities are unlikely to prove helpful. What would things be like if desires had no power, bodies did not tempt, doing one's duty was not onerous, accidents never happened and virtue was, always and for everyone, its own reward? Fichte readily admits that such a state of affairs "cannot be determinately conceived."[14]

But no matter. Although the ideal remains inarticulate, it delivers a powerful blow against empirical persons. It declares that individuality is a moral failing relegated to the twilight between first and last things, that is, between the creativity of the absolute self and the perfection of the fully cultivated but unindividuated moral agent. Moreover, it adds that we must strive to overcome our individuality, even though doing so requires unending effort. Instead of being the glory of humankind, the individual is the symbol of our imperfection, demanding that we stamp it out.

A comment on Schopenhauer may be appropriate at this point. Although he does not endorse Hegel's and Fichte's devaluations of individuals and displays the deepest sympathy with personal suffering, he nevertheless refuses to attach lasting significance to persons. The reason is not that individuality must be overcome but that the differentiation it involves is a sort of illusion.

Schopenhauer thinks that the final reality, Kant's "thing-in-itself," is a groundless, ravenous will that sinks its teeth into its own flesh.[15] Finite beings, including human individuals, result from the conversion of this will into appearance. "The person is mere phenomenon,"[16] he declares, created by the principle of individuation which multiplies the unitary will into innumerable appearances by means of space and time. He likens the action of this principle to that of a prism breaking a single beam of light into a momentary play of colors.

Individuals are like the shimmer on the waves of the sea: they are insignificant, dependent and evanescent appearances.[17] Schopenhauer leaves no doubt about his view:

> [I]t is not the individual nature cares for, but only the species . . . nature is always ready to let the individual fall, and the individual is accordingly not only exposed to destruction in a thousand ways from the most insignificant accidents, but is even destined for this and is led towards it by nature herself, from the moment that individual has served the maintenance of the species. In this way, nature quite openly expresses the great truth that only the Ideas, not individuals, have reality proper.[18]

The "Ideas" to which Schopenhauer refers are species essences as we know them from Plato. Even these universals are, of course, dependent on the will and disappear when it is destroyed.

Salvation consists in stopping the cycle of violence the will perpetrates against itself. Humans play a central role in this, grasping in an intuitive way the principle of eternal justice, according to which tormentor and tormented are one. But individuality falls victim to sympathy and the denial of the will to live: the initial illusion of individual separateness disintegrates as the will turns against itself, quiets all desires, and abolishes the phenomenal world.

Attacks on individuality such as Hegel's and Fichte's are almost unheard of in American philosophy. I say "almost" because there is one striking exception. Peirce, whose deep debt to Fichte has never been adequately explored, comes close to adopting the Fichtean attitude to individuality. In the early "Some Consequences of Four Incapacities," he writes: "The individual man, since his separate existence is manifested only by ignorance and error, so far as he is anything apart from his fellows, and what he and they are to be, is only a negation."[19]

Peirce shares with Fichte the Neoplatonic notion of identifying determinateness or differentiation with negation. Fichte connects the differentiation individuality involves with the moral failure of imperfectly rational action. In an unsurprising intellectualization of the same notion, Peirce relates it to the cognitive shortcomings of ignorance and error. The similarity between Fichte and Peirce is clear if we remember that both moral failure and cognitive weakness are due to imperfect rationality. The resemblance is even more striking if we read Peirce as holding that, in the last analysis, moral failure is a sort of cognitive shortfall.

There is reason to believe that Peirce got the idea of infinite progress toward a goal never to be attained from Fichte's notion of what we must but cannot do. In this unending process, individuality shrivels in proportion to the growth of concrete reasonableness. This is so because the emergence of the real at the end of infinite inquiry is the advent at once of truth and knowledge, which eliminate "the ignorance and error" at the heart of individuality.

Perfecting the world requires enhancement of the reach of thirds, or laws and habits, at the expense of chance (firsts) and force (seconds). This happens in part by "the law of continuous spreading"[20] that converts feelings into general ideas. The feelings overflow the confines of individuality, and general ideas cannot, in any case, be imprisoned within the limited perspectives of individuals. As a result, our private worlds are absorbed in a single, continuous stream of inferences or sentience; individuality is submerged as we enter the sea of a universal community.

This is one important respect in which Peirce differs radically from other pragmatists and from the mainstream of American thought. James,

Dewey and Santayana would not dream of entertaining such ideas; even Royce, who is perhaps closest among the classical figures to German idealism, charts a course far from these shallows.[21]

The importance of individuals is celebrated in divergent ways and for different reasons by James, Dewey, Royce and Santayana, but there is striking agreement among them about the preeminent value of individuality. They are not of one mind about the source of this value, identifying it variously as the needy consciousness of persons, the role of individuals in initiating social improvement, the unique self-determining activity of humans, and the fact that individual agents are the center and condition of all values. There is no indication that any of the four considers finite selves dispensable or in the process of being transcended as a part of cosmic evolution.

James, one may fairly say, is in love with the individual. Much of his most eloquent writing concerns the integrity of the private mind.[22] In an article entitled, "The Importance of Individuals," he quotes "an unlearned carpenter" with approval to the effect that "There is very little difference between one man and another; but what little there is, *is very important.*"[23] He believes that the world is as full of discontinuities as of continuities;[24] prominent among discontinuities are those that make it difficult for us to appreciate the possibly glorious inner lives of our fellows. What we choose to believe is also an intensely personal matter: individuals must decide how they relate to the world, to others and especially to God.[25]

The most profoundly important role of individuals, for James, is that they bear upon their shoulders the weight of the entire moral universe. Not only are people the agents who must respond to obligation, they are also the sentient creatures whose needs generate these demands in the first place. James says:

> *Physical facts simply* are *or are* not; *and neither when present or absent, can they be supposed to make demands. If they do, they can only do so by having desires; and then they have ceased to be purely physical facts, and have become facts of conscious sensibility.*[26]

Desires beget demands that must be satisfied. The demands or claims create obligations on anyone in a position to help. So conscious individuals play two central roles in the moral life: through their desires they impose duties, and through their sensitivity they recognize obligations. Our desires and our duties differentiate us, and this differentiation is not lost with time: morality and individuality endure together because "there can be no final truth in ethics . . . until the last man has had his experience and said his say."[27]

Moreover, even the least among us has standing. James shows his sensitivity to the life of the ordinary person when he says: "Take any demand, however slight, which any creature, however weak, may make. Ought it not, for its own sole sake, to be satisfied?"[28] He reaches a level of exceptional eloquence in considering the hypothesis of a world in which "millions [were] kept permanently happy on the one simple condition that a certain lost soul on the far-off edge of things should lead a life of lonely torture."[29] He continues unhesitatingly to assert that we would "immediately feel, even though an impulse arose within us to clutch at the happiness so offered, how hideous a thing would be its enjoyment when deliberately accepted as the fruit of such a bargain."[30]

James's conclusion is clear: neither individuality nor any individuals should be extinguished. War is a horrible thing for which we must find a moral alternative,[31] and people are better employed responding to each other's needs than reducing themselves to the level of things in the service of the state. Without individuals, there is no consciousness, hence no value, hence no morality, hence nothing to make life safe and meaningful.

Dewey may not share James's personal anguish for every lost soul, but his deep belief in the importance of individuals is visible throughout his writings. One could present more than a hundred signal passages from his works dealing with the formation of singular persons, the problems of people in industrial and commercial societies, the social and political conditions that further individuality, and the dangers to individuals represented by developments in the modern world. Nevertheless, none of these passages singly and perhaps no group of them conjointly can explain the reason for the indispensable value of human personality better than does his account of individual minds.

Dewey draws what he characterizes as a "radical" contrast between individuals with minds and individual minds. The former amounts to the idea of a person whose intellect is formed altogether by external forces and includes little that is novel. Such intellectual endowments may appear in individuals, but they simply replicate the "system of belief, recognitions, and ignorances, of acceptances and rejections, of expectancies and appraisals of meanings which have been instituted under the influence of custom and tradition."[32]

Individuals with minds are manufactured by societies to serve the dominant culture: they mouth the certainties of the day, accept the values of their group and enact shared commitments without critical thought. Their desires do not extend to "breaking loose from the weight of tradition and custom, of initiating observations and reflections, forming designs and plans, undertaking experiments on the basis of hypotheses, diverging from accepted doctrines and traditions."[33]

They are satisfied with what is well established, and thus become standardized, virtually interchangeable elements of the social whole. The extirpation of individual differences does not have to wait for the indefinite future, as Fichte believed; these people, cut to the same measure, are essentially indistinguishable in act and thought.

Individual minds, by contrast, are persons who—at least on some salient subjects—think for themselves. Though raised in a tradition, they break down and reconstitute its elements. Their imagination "terminates in a modification of the objective order, in the institution of a new object. . . . [This] involves a dissolution of old objects and a forming of new ones in a medium which, since it is beyond the old objects and not yet in a new one, can properly be termed subjective."[34]

Individuality, therefore, involves a modicum of originality. Those we call individuals reconstruct in large or small ways the social values and common thought with which they were raised. Acting on their particular ideas and desires, they challenge prevailing habits and practices. Such assaults upon the established are the function of subjectivity, which is "a mode of natural existence in which objects undergo directed reconstitution."[35]

Dewey calls this subjectivity "consciousness." He has in mind neither a Cartesian mind ontologically different from everything else nor a Hegelian all-suffusing cognitive urge. Consciousness for him is a reconstructive activity whose privacy is the outcome of its function:

> *When an old essence or meaning is in process of dissolution and a new one has not taken shape even as a hypothetical scheme, the intervening existence is too fluid and formless for publication, even to one's self. Its very existence is ceaseless transformation.*[36]

Subjective reconstructions of tradition that result in the emergence of new objects, habits and practices are essential for social change. Without inquiring persons, we are condemned to stagnation. Individuals are both useful as means to maintaining the vitality of culture and valuable as momentous achievements in the creation of human beings. They are anything but insignificant. We should create conditions that foster their growth rather than hoping for their eventual disappearance.

In spite of the fact that he is deeply indebted to Fichte, Hegel and even Schopenhauer for his ideas, Royce is in sharp disagreement with their attacks on individuality. The central element in Royce's conception of the individual is choice. This is evident throughout his work, though perhaps nowhere more clearly than in *The Philosophy of Loyalty*. The Hegelian, F. H. Bradley, argues that "my station and its duties" are determined for me by my historical and social position.[37] Royce finds commitment to some cause essential for creating the self but, in direct contrast to Bradley, he asserts that: "[H]owever much my cause may seem to be assigned to me by my social station, I must cooperate in the choice of the cause, before the act of loyalty is complete."[38]

Royce readily admits that we are "victims" of our ancestry, which is "a mass of world-old passions and impulses."[39] Yet this past gives scant guidance for the future. We need to chart our own courses: "One of the principal tasks of my life is to learn to have a will of my own. To learn your own will—yes, to create your own will, is one of the largest of human undertakings."[40] This view is surprisingly radical for Royce. It suggests that individuality is not a ruinous condition to which we sink but a grand human achievement. The accomplishment is due altogether to our work; it is something we attain by choosing a cause and faithfully adhering to it. The self-determination is absolute.

In a striking passage, he endorses an idea we shall soon see Santayana defending:[41] "I, and only I, whenever I come to my own, can morally justify to myself my own plan of life. No outer authority can ever give me the true reason for my duty."[42] The causes we choose are both expressive and creative of who we are. Contrary to Kant's view, all moral agents do not perform the same action under similar circumstances; what they do depends on how loyalty to loyalty is best promoted under the circumstances, and that is determined at least in part by the concrete details of the causes they adopt. Individual personalities also vary with the causes embraced; thus it is unavoidable and fitting for differences among individuals never to be erased.

Royce insists on the ultimate value and indestructibility of individuals even more strongly in *The World and the Individual*. Here he depicts conscious persons as elements of the Absolute Individual, God. Any temporal manifestation of an individual may pass from the scene, but the person, consisting of a series of such selves or manifestations, continues. This means that individuals are immortal, seeking fulfillment through endless striving. The fulfillment is impossible to achieve in time but it is eternally granted from the transtemporal perspective of God.

Royce makes essentially the same point by saying that "[I]ndividuality is a category of the satisfied Will."[43] The will can, of course, never be satisfied under conditions of finitude, so individuality must be sought through infinite striving and is attainable only through God. In an astonishing departure from the usual views of merging with the divine, Royce maintains that sinking ourselves into the infinity of God results not in the loss but in the full achievement of our individuated particularity.[44]

The analogy he employs to make this point intelligible shows the full depth of Royce's commitment to human individuality. He pictures God as analogous to the infinite series of whole numbers.[45] Then he proposes that we conceive of each individual as a series consisting of a prime number and its powers. This yields an infinite number of individuals, each an infinite series, and each included within the system of whole numbers that is God.

This makes it beautifully clear how the part can be as infinite as the whole. It also demonstrates that absorption in a greater whole does not obliterate the identity of a series. Most important, however, it attributes unmatched integrity to individuals, showing that no two of them share the same elements. Just as the same number cannot appear in two series consisting of the powers of different prime numbers, so the same experience cannot characterize different individuals. Each individual is an eternal, inviolate unity.

Such high metaphysics has always struck Santayana as "dreaming in words."[46] Nevertheless, he agrees with Royce's belief in the lasting importance of individuality. He cannot take seriously those who attribute causal powers to such abstractions as society and the state. Society, he says, is "not an animal but an institution."[47] As such, it "has a unity and character of its own" only in a "formal" sense,[48] where "formal" is to be contrasted with "dynamic." This means that on the material plane of action, which Santayana thinks is the only realm of agency, institutions can accomplish things only through the efforts of their constituent organisms.

He makes this idea explicit in a subsequent passage: "[S]omebody must feel everything that is felt; somebody must say or do everything that is said or done. It is only by a conspiracy of individuals that society can act, and only by the voice of individuals that it can be judged."[49] The importance of individuals derives, therefore, from their central position in the world of agency. Santayana's view of that position, in turn, is a corollary of the principle that all agency is material. Animals are physical realities that operate in space and time. Societies and states, by contrast, are not additional material entities, but simply the coordinated patterns of activities of their members.

Santayana uses the word "psyche" to refer to the unified agency of individuals. As in its original Greek meaning, "psyche" suggests nothing mental: it is, instead, the sum of the living, purposive actions of the body. The activities involve selections or choices which serve, in turn, as the source of moral discrimination. Impulses to seek and shun thus account for the initial distinction we draw between good and bad, and the specific spatial, temporal, social and historical situation of each psyche creates the unique personal perspectives of which individuality consists. This view of the development of morality from the fertile ground of desires is reminiscent of the position of James, Santayana's teacher and colleague. For both, individuals and their needs are permanently tied to the possibility of the moral life.

A learned scholar may someday show the extent to which, in spite of ultimately divergent commitments, Santayana is indebted to his Harvard colleagues. In addition to adopting a view closely similar to James's concerning the ground of morality, he also agrees with Royce about the volitional integrity of the individual. Royce argues that loyalty and duty require the consent of the individual, so that—in the moral world, at least—alien impositions on the person are impossible. Similarly, Santayana declares: "If anyone, therefore, ever recognises a duty or amiably considers another's pleasure, he does so *necessarily* on his own authority and by obeying some impulse within himself."[50] This makes moral choices outcomes of a "power of synthesis in the will, by which all impulses rooted there are collated."[51] He continues: "Such a synthesis is possible only in an individual mind capable of integrity; so that social bonds have moral authority only if they can justify themselves to the inner man, and subserve a spiritual life."[52] The self-determining unity of the person stands, therefore, as a condition of both individual and social life. Eliminating it robs us of the precious abilities to make choices, act as unified agents, and freely participate in a shared life with our fellows.

But the last passage also speaks of the spiritual life which, in Santayana's view, is an impersonal and, some say, desiccated mode of consciousness. Could one argue that Santayana points, after all, in the direction of overcoming individuality by growth in the spiritual dimension? If so, his thought may be closer to Fichte's than commentators had supposed, even though the disappearance of individuality is connected in the one with improved spirituality and in the other with the perfection of the moral life.

This argument, however, cannot prevail. Individuality does indeed disintegrate in the solvent of pure intuitions. Absorbed in the immediacy of essences, we lose all track of preference and history; the self becomes an object of contemplation rather than a center of concern. Such ingredients of urgent life as past, future, choice, duty, desire and need are converted into appearances without the power to tempt or to compel. Every moment of awareness is luminous and offers peace.[53]

But the state Santayana describes is closer to Schopenhauer's pure will-less knowing than to Fichte's Idea of the self. The former similarity is all the more important because it reveals a central feature of Santayana's spirituality: just like Schopenhauer's absorption in beauty, it is a passing condition of the soul. Moreover, the momentary disappearance of individuality in the realm of consciousness requires the continued operation of the individual psyche in the material world. In this way, rather than being overcome, individuality is simply forgotten for the moment. Only death terminates the individual person.

My argument has shown a remarkable difference concerning individuality between three German and, leaving Peirce aside for the moment, four American philosophers. What accounts for this striking dissimilarity? Along with being an expression and a justification of the values of a culture, philosophy is also a potent force in their construction. We might therefore be tempted to suppose that we are dealing with ultimate national differences here. In that light, the divergence in philosophical views appears as an articulation of the gulf between the German culture of duty and the American veneration of the individual.

But this hypothesis is easily shown to be wrong. Kant and Nietzsche were also Germans. Kant insisted on the supreme importance of the moral individual and declared it immortal.[54] Nietzsche celebrated the individual person no less than did Emerson. Is the explanation to be sought, then, in the contrast between the grand metaphysics popular in Europe and the bounded, empirical thought that America inherited from England? This is closer, but also not correct. Such European master metaphysicians as Leibniz conferred indestructible significance on the individual. And Royce managed to import European metaphysics into the United States without surrendering his commitment to the individual.

I say the second proposed explanation is closer to the truth, because the culprit responsible for denying the significance of individuals is a type of philosophy and not a broad cultural orientation. The philosophy, however, is not metaphysics of the speculative sort, but the idealism of impersonal subjectivity. The hallmark of what we call "German Idealism" is fascination with consciousness or selfhood that is not tied to particular persons. Kant invented the object of the fascination and called it "the transcendental unity of apperception." This, he says, is the purely formal "I think" that accompanies all of our representations.[55]

The peculiarity of the contentless, formal "I" is that it serves as the necessary condition of the possibility of any self, without being the sort of self with which we are familiar in ordinary life. Reference to myself as "I" or uniting all my experiences as mine connects me to the very essence of self-hood, the universal I that touches my particularity but cannot be confined to it. Just as the form of humanity has no eyes and is hence not myopic, so the form of selfhood is not weighted down by personal tendencies and failures. It is consciousness in its purity or selfhood after all its empirical elements have been removed.

Kant had the good sense to resist the temptation to construct a metaphysics around this idea, restricting its application to his epistemology. He saw it as vital to distinguish the purely formal self, the empirical self and the moral self from one another. Difficult as it is in his system to individuate moral selves without reference to sensuous properties, he believed that, at their best, they constituted the glory of humankind.

Fichte removed the careful limits critical philosophy imposed on the metaphysics of the abstract self. He reintroduced the transcendental unity of apperception as the Absolute Self from which all finite subjects and objects could be "deduced." When Hegel noted that his great improvement on Spinoza's system derived from the recognition that substance is subject,[56] he invited us to celebrate impersonal consciousness or the unindividuated self. He must have supposed that as long as he made consciousness the cornerstone of his philosophy, not much of value would be left out.

But this is a grievous error. The stress on faceless consciousness makes it easy to denigrate living individuals; they lack, after all, the momentousness of the history-filling self-development of Spirit. It would be too much to say that the idealists of impersonal consciousness have no appreciation of what humans have accomplished. Actually, they love and admire humanity; it is only human individuals they cannot abide.

CHAPTER 16

Santayana as Pragmatist

Only someone who is not a pragmatist would ask for the marks of pragmatism, for the necessary and sufficient conditions of calling someone a pragmatist. A pragmatist would ask: "What hangs on it?" or "What is your purpose in asking such a question?" Surely it is not to determine Santayana's ideological purity, for being a pragmatist carries no perks. Nor is it to add another foot soldier to the platoon of pragmatists or to justify Santayana's views by showing that a number of philosophers, of whom he did not think well, had similar ideas.

Yet this is not a matter of idle curiosity. There is something pervasively ambivalent, even odd, about Santayana's relation to pragmatism. He subjected his teacher, William James, to withering critique.[1] He attacked Dewey as a "short-winded" naturalist.[2] He appears not to have thought Peirce worthy of direct identification as an antagonist; the few passages that target views similar to his drip with disdain.[3] He was deeply concerned that many viewed *The Life of Reason* as in fundamental agreement with the pragmatists and proposed to write a special introduction to set them right.[4] He repeatedly dissociated himself from pragmatism and rejected, even spoofed, what he took to be its central views.[5] In spite of all of this, however, it is difficult to read much Santayana without running into ideas that bear remarkable resemblance to what one finds in Dewey and in James. The complexion of his thought and his ultimate positions on certain central issues are, moreover, strikingly pragmatic. In spite of obvious differences in style and temperament, even Santayana's mature ontology appears much closer to pragmatism than he himself thought or admitted.

I have no interest in addressing the issue of whether or not Santayana *is* a pragmatist. Such questions presuppose belief in an odd sort of essentialism or in something like natural kinds among philosophical positions. By stressing the element of choice in our categories and in the range of their application, Dewey and other pragmatists reject such commitments. Santayana's view that the realm of essence is infinite and that our favorite generic essences enjoy no special privilege within it leads him to agree with this rejection. My aim, accordingly, is not to reveal such hidden truths as that Santayana is or is not a pragmatist, but to see how much viewing him as a pragmatist contributes to our understanding, assessment and appreciation of his philosophy.

This may be a sensible approach but it is not enough to get us off to a good start. For what does one have to hold to be a pragmatist? No one specific view, nor a precise collection of theses. Sandra Rosenthal is correct in saying that pragmatism has an "elusive spirit."[6] H. S. Thayer speaks of it as a "broad philosophic attitude toward our conceptualization of experience"[7] and wisely characterizes it only in very general terms. Nothing can be gained from seeking precision where it is neither necessary nor possible, so I will refrain from using most of the rest of this paper to polish a fragile and irrelevant definition. The general stock of our knowledge enables us to make sense of such statements as that the intruder was a large man, even if we are not given his precise measurements. Similarly, it should be enough for me to say that pragmatism is a complex set of views concerning knowledge and its role in experience, the nature of the ultimately real, meaning, truth, human satisfaction and our relation to the future. I shall characterize these ideas in general terms in the process of relating them to Santayana's philosophical positions.

Let me begin by focusing on a collection of beliefs about the nature, functions, prospects, limits, justification and context of knowledge. A strand of philosophy that began with Plato and achieved dominance with the work of Descartes has devoted special attention to the cognitive life. Thinkers in this tradition typically believed that knowledge enjoys a five-fold primacy. 1) It is, they thought, our primary mode of contact with the rest of reality. As a result, 2) it demands pride of place in philosophy: we must give an account of its nature and possibility before we can proceed to any other subject. Since anything else that has a place in our lives enters through the portals of cognition, 3) knowledge (or mind or consciousness or discourse) provides the first and ultimate context of reality. This means that instead of being viewed as a function of natural organisms, knowledge came to be conceived as the universal medium in which the perception of natural creatures and the idea of a world would have to find their place. Since it is our most significant attribute, 4) knowledge for its own sake plays a central role in human fulfillment. A nonreligious version of this claim derives from Aristotle, who thought that contemplation was the highest virtue. The religious version, that after death those saved would know God face-to-face, stresses the role of cognition in blessedness no less. Consequently, these thinkers maintained, 5) the pursuit of disinterested knowledge is or ought to be our first and central aim.

The notion of the fivefold primacy of knowledge was accompanied in this tradition by a particularly exalted conception of it. Proper understanding was thought to be certain and infallible—an unfailing grasp of reality by the mind. At first, the mind was supposed to have been made for the task of knowing the real; as the claims of knowledge became exaggerated, the belief that reality exists to make knowledge possible took its place. This infallible grasp of unchanging being, or of changing beings governed by unchanging laws, was to be achieved starting from the subjective viewpoint proper to mind. Finite subjects were credited, in this way, with cognitive possession of infinite objectivity; such achievement transmutes the insecurity of animal life into divine certainty about what really counts.

Pragmatists typically reject this entire complex of beliefs. They do not think that our primary mode of contact with reality is cognitive and that the world exists in or for consciousness alone. They are fallibilists, dispense with the solitary subject, and remain resolute in the attempt to situate knowledge as an incident of animal life. As a result, they are prepared to view cognitive efforts as directed upon ordinary objects, as falling short of comprehensiveness and as never achieving certitude. They think of the human good as more robust than to include only understanding and of disinterested knowledge as a contradiction or a worthless ornament.

Viewed in this perspective, Santayana is in complete agreement with the pragmatist. The first part of *Scepticism and Animal Faith* constitutes his version of the futility of the quest for certainty. Its message is that the skeptic can undermine all attempts at cognition so long as the criterion of knowledge is absolute certainty and its starting point is an isolated self. Reflection thus cannot begin with an account of knowledge; Santayana's new philosophy of animal faith starts with the animal in action and proceeds to revise the traditional idea of cognition. Knowledge as we live it, he thinks, is assurance in action expressed in symbolic terms. The function of knowledge is to advance animal life, its objects are limited to physical existents, and its ultimate test is successful action in space and time.[8]

We find in Santayana, moreover, an exact parallel to Dewey's attack on the spectator theory of knowledge. This theory or lurking assumption conceives the mind as a disinterested organ whose primary activity is to render itself passive and thus accurately receptive of external facts. Knowledge, for it, consists of a dispassionate vision of reality, of an accurate, immediate picture of what exists. Dewey's attempt to discredit this idea was a part of his project of uncovering the role of purposes and values in cognition and thus of placing knowledge in the context of animal life. The language of Santayana's version of this critique is different, but the underlying project is the same. Dewey uses the metaphor of the spectator; Santayana, the image of the mirror. The mirror gives an immediate and accurate picture of what is placed before it: this is the ideal of intuition which promises direct possession of its object. Intuitions occur in mental life or discourse, but discourse, Santayana says, "is a language not a mirror."[9] Knowledge, therefore, is symbolic rendering of the absent, rather than sure possession of the present. Though intuitions capture essences, the immediate never amounts to knowledge: it is not the object of knowledge, nor is it, without intent, knowledge of an object. Consciousness that lacks the transitive force of animal faith remains only contemplation of essence. The idea that knowledge is intuition is identical with the notion that in knowing we dispassionately inspect present objects; Santayana and the pragmatists agree that this assumption leads to a radically misguided epistemology.

I said before that, for the pragmatist, disinterested knowledge is an impossibility. On this point at least, one could object, Santayana differs from Dewey and from James. He views intuition of essence as detached from the cares of animal life, constituting the liberation brought by spirituality. Such disinterested contemplation or enjoyment of the immediate is surely not impossible; although systematic achievement of it requires discipline, Santayana is clear that occasional moments of it are open to all of us. This reading of Santayana is correct. But though pure intuition is both disinterested and possible, it is not knowledge. Knowledge as the conscious transcript of the life of the psyche is laden with animal concerns. Intent is driven by hope and fear; the interests of the living creature motivate cognition, fix its objects and direct its development. Disinterested intuition, therefore, yields spirituality, not knowledge; disinterested knowledge, for Santayana as much as for the pragmatists, is a contradiction in terms.

Commitment to universal process and a naturalistic, evolutionary view of human beings unite Santayana and the pragmatists in their assessment of the centrality of action. By such centrality, pragmatists do not mean that action is the aim or purpose of life. It is, however, an essential element in it. Dewey goes so far as to say that thought is a sort of action or the manner in which actions are performed. Intelligence is a means that renders what we do effective; our actions, in turn, are means to making life better. If we want to understand the function of thought and the bulk of life, we must focus on the activities in which we engage. Accordingly, the analysis of action, of its conditions and of its consequences, must constitute the starting point and the heart of philosophy.

Although Santayana's language is, once again, different, the core of his beliefs closely resembles these pragmatist tenets. His use of the term "substance" hides the similarity by misleadingly suggesting that changeless, enduring beings constitute the ultimate elements of the world. This is not, however, what "substance" means for him. He professes to use the term in its "etymological sense" of "a thing or event subsisting on its own plane."[10] Even when he speaks of "material substance," he means only the world, which consists of embodied essences. The embodiment of an essence constitutes a natural moment.[11] The ultimate units of existence are, therefore, passing occurrences rather than enduring things.

This transitoriness pervades animal life. The precarious existence of the psyche demands that it devote its energies to maintaining itself. Self-maintenance, growth, striving for a better life all require action; accordingly, the psyche is a center of habitual, adaptive and intelligent activity. Only by understanding this activity can we give a sensible account of animal life, and only by understanding animal life can we sketch an honest and defensible picture of reality. For the world is a field of action continuous with our bodies; space and time serve as the media of continuity, and the reciprocity of action as its ultimate measure.

The centrality of action in animal life must be reflected in our theories. Accordingly, Santayana's philosophy of animal faith proposes that we begin with the unquestionable reality of action and limit our beliefs to those implicated in such activity. One could sensibly suppose that this approach to philosophy makes Santayana's thought more pragmatic than that of the pragmatists. For it amounts to the commitment to believe nothing for which action fails to yield evidence, nothing, in other words, but what the conditions and consequences of action sanction. The tenets of animal faith end up, in this way, not only identical with what pragmatists believe but also justified by a process pragmatists can adopt.

The massive agreement I have shown in epistemology is replicated concerning vital issues in ethics. On the negative side, Santayana and the pragmatists are at one in rejecting the notion that knowledge is an end-in-itself. Santayana's devotion to spirituality may seem to run counter to this agreement, but the appearance dissipates the moment we remember that pure intuition is neither knowledge nor a value. Both cognition and valuation involve relations, typically to the absent, and the hallmark of spirituality is nonrelational absorption in the immediate. Admittedly, the spiritual life is reminiscent of Aristotle's view of contemplation as the highest perfection of humans. But in Santayana's hands, traditional ideas undergo wrenching transformation; though spirituality is a phase of consciousness, it is not properly cognitive, and though it is a sort of perfection, it has no value, offering as it does an escape from the endless cycle of animal goods and evils.

On the positive side, both the pragmatists and Santayana ground the good in the needs and desires of living creatures. An unmistakable family resemblance connects James's account of the source of obligation in "The Moral Philosopher and the Moral Life," Dewey's discussion of the construction of good in *The Quest for Certainty*, and Santayana's comments on animal nature and the good relative to it in "Hypostatic Ethics." The similarity is due to the fact that here, too, James, Dewey and Santayana are engaged in the same general enterprise. The naturalization of knowledge and the naturalization of value are of one piece: both must be situated in the life cycle of animals making their way in a difficult, sometimes even hostile, environment. Moreover, no pragmatist extols the value of intelligence in maximizing satisfaction any more than Santayana. The rhetoric differs, of course. Pragmatists speak of intelligence and rationality in the language of the trades, as tools or instruments. Santayana prefers the language of the fine arts, especially music, and conceives of reason as a harmony or an impulse for the harmony of impulses. The idea, however, is the same: humans have no alternative to reason in their efforts to achieve the good. Individually and socially, intelligent action can improve life and, within limits, maximize our satisfactions. These satisfactions can be and frequently are divergent: a tolerant pluralism is therefore particularly appropriate to accommodate nondestructive differences in needs and wants and tastes.

Those who love Santayana or pragmatism but not both may, by now, find my silence on two topics and what may appear as unwillingness to engage the issue on a third vexing. Many believe that the heart of pragmatism is a theory of meaning or a theory of truth. They can object that I have said nothing on either of these issues and have therefore not really addressed the question of Santayana's relation to pragmatism. They or others can also point out that although I have touched on Santayana's notion of spiritual life, I have not undertaken to assess the compatibility of that idea with the general orientation of pragmatists. Do the relations to which I have called attention so far amount to more than chance similarities if these three central points of potential disagreement remain unexplored?

These points must, of course, be dealt with, but whatever conclusions we draw about them should not be allowed to obscure the remarkable resemblances we have already seen. The comparison with respect to theories of meaning is the simplest to accomplish. Pragmatists tend to subscribe to some version of a theory that identifies the meaning of ideas with their sensible outcomes or the meaning of beliefs with the consequences of acting on them. We have no systematic way of determining where Santayana stands on this matter because he has no developed theory of meaning. If one cannot be a pragmatist unless one subscribes to a theory of meaning, and in particular to some version of the one I have just identified, then Santayana's pragmatist credentials stand impugned. But I find such attempts at identifying a single necessary and sufficient condition for pragmatism both inappropriate and implausible. And, in any case, we do not hesitate to call C. I. Lewis and Richard Rorty pragmatists, even though neither embraces such a theory of meaning. Finally, there is ample evidence in Santayana that he is not unsympathetic to at least some forms of this thesis. In the last chapter of *The Realm of Matter*,[12] for example, he argues that the verbal differences between idealists and materialists capture no significant difference so long as their actions with respect to the realities involved remain the same.

Things are more complicated with respect to the so-called pragmatic theory of truth. Santayana is clearly on record as endorsing a sort of correspondence theory. The truth about a fact is its standard comprehensive description.[13] The fact is an existent; its "description" consists of essences. Our judgments are true whenever we capture some of these essences—in other words, when the essence that appears in consciousness is identical with what is or what has been embodied in the world. This sounds simple and elegant, but it leads to problems. It may well be the case that of the forms appearing in the mind, some are also embodied by matter and some are not. Unfortunately, however, we have no sure way of knowing which essences (if any) are exemplified: we lack direct access to the material world. Which essences belong to the realm of truth is, therefore, always conjectural. None is so marked; we have to try to establish membership on the basis of circumstantial evidence.

The radiation of truth makes the issue even more involved. The truth about any fact includes both the perspective of the world that may be had by taking it as center and the perspectives that may be taken of it from the standpoint of every other center. This makes the truth about any fact infinitely extended.[14] It includes every distorted perception and every misinterpretation of it—all of these are true of it if we take into account the distance from which it is viewed and the obstacles in the way of clear vision.

The problem here is the opposite of what we faced in trying to determine which essences belong in the realm of truth. There we had difficulty in finding truth, here we have trouble escaping it. The radiation of truth makes every essence referred to a fact true of it. This means that honest people who report their ideas accurately cannot be wrong: whatever they think of any topic is true of it, at least from their perspective.[15] Santayana is clear that each consciousness is central in and to itself, so we cannot hope to reach truths that are nonperspectival. How, then, can we identify essences that belong to the realm of truth and how can we distinguish more adequate renderings of the way things are from less adequate accounts?

Santayana's answer brings him very close to pragmatism. We encounter the "substantial nature" of objects and events only through action. Our knowledge of the truth increases as we strip off "the sensuous and rhetorical vesture" of these events and lay bare their dynamic relations.[16] The closer we keep our ideas to animal faith and the more we learn of the dynamic relations between events, the more successful our actions will likely be. So prosperous activities lead us to truth or to more adequate truths and, conversely, those ideas or essences are true that lead to successful action. We can hear in this formulation overtones of James's definition of the truth of an idea as its property of leading fruitfully to where we want to go.[17] Of course, Santayana does not wish to say that such truth is exclusive; depending on what we wish to accomplish, the goddess Diana may be a better symbol for the moon than the dull terms of astronomers.[18] Diana makes for better poetry; the scientific description, for better "material exploration." Which of the two we want is a matter of choice, which brings to mind Dewey's insistence on the importance of purposes in our pursuit of the truth. The true comes, on this view, very close to what serves in a context defined by choice and circumstance as an instrument of successful operation.

The significance of this movement by Santayana in the direction of the pragmatic theory of truth should not be overstated. He could attempt to minimize it by reminding us of the distinction between the nature and the test of truth and claiming that successful action serves only in the latter capacity. And he is, indeed, uncompromising in affirming the independent reality of truth, which he always associates with the precise character of the world of flux. The source of this steadfast commitment to a truth that is neither an opinion nor a property of beliefs is his ultimate, metaphysical realism, which represents, as I shall try to show, the watershed that separates him from pragmatism. Nevertheless, it is important to note that when the realm of truth as the ideally complete record of all existence presents Santayana with severe philosophical difficulties, he is quick to apply a pragmatic remedy. The turn is so swift that pragmatists, declaring his ideal of infinite truth ineffectual, could well maintain that the view of truth he effectively embraces is not very different from theirs.

The spiritual life of which Santayana speaks consists of a string of pure intuitions. Each of these is a causal blind alley in the operation of the world, yielding no extraneous results. Each presents an essence enjoyable for its own sake, without regard to spirit's impotence. The psyche does the work of the organism; mind, in the form of immediate consciousness, only plays. Pure intuition liberates us from animal care about the absent and the yet-to-come; it constitutes the only unadulterated joy open to sentient creatures in a cruel life.

Formulated in terms of an ontological category of causally inefficacious actualities, this view appears to be a far cry from anything a pragmatist would believe. Yet Dewey showed important sensitivity to what can be enjoyed for its own sake, to the celebratory or consummatory aspects of conscious life. Santayana himself knew this and said: "Spirit has in my view the status that Dewey assigns to 'consummation.'"[19] Dewey effected a compromise with his pragmatism, however, by declaring that what is enjoyed in being had is also, in another of its offices, the cause of further consequences. Means and ends thus form, for him, an unbroken chain: everything can be embraced for its intrinsic features, yet everything leads usefully to something else.

There is no reason to believe that either Santayana's or Dewey's view captures the reality of spiritual and aesthetic enjoyment any better than the other. To be sure, there are differences between them: the generative model of Dewey's conception is continuity, while Santayana's idea derives from the cool, spectatorial capacity of consciousness. Since Santayana does not think spirituality adds to our true beliefs, however, he does not run afoul of Dewey's critique of the spectator theory of knowledge. It is not far-fetched, therefore, to suppose that whatever differences there may be between the two concerning consummation are mainly technical or verbal, or at most, the expression of personal predilections. For enjoyment of the immediate is a relatively rare occurrence, wedged between the useful and necessary processes of life. Santayana does not deny the efficacy of those total natural events that we experience as such enjoyments, he only lodges it on the side of the psyche as its work. Neither he nor Dewey doubts that such moments of spirituality can revitalize the reformer and make the poet more dreamy or morose. Their only disagreement is that Dewey assigns these effects to the experience in one of its roles and Santayana to its psychic ground.

I conclude that though Santayana's theory of the spiritual life is not in any obvious sense a pragmatist idea, it is more easily reconcilable with pragmatism than it at first appears. The primary stumbling block to reconciliation is not, as some might think, Santayana's epiphenomenalism, commitment to which is motivated by his notion of the spiritual life, rather than the other way round. It is, instead, the sharp ontological line drawn between psyche and spirit, a line Dewey conceived not in terms of ontological distinctions but of differences of function.

It would be a grave error to conclude from this discussion that there are no irreconcilable differences between Santayana and the pragmatists. I shall focus on two, one of profound contemporary philosophical significance and the other a theoretical difference based on factors of temperament.

I have noted that both Santayana and the pragmatists take an interest in naturalizing knowledge, in situating it as an incident of animal life in a contingent world. This commits them to the view that the object of knowledge, or that which is to become the object of knowledge, exists independently of our explorations. Though Dewey thinks that the objects we know are constituted in the process of inquiry, even he maintains that this activity is directed upon preexisting material and so amounts to a reconstruction rather than a creation out of the resources of the subject. This epistemological realism, the commitment to seconds in Peirce's terms, is adequate to avoid the most absurd versions of constructivist idealism.

Santayana wants, however, to go a long step beyond this. He affirms the independent and fully formed existence of a nature in which human experience is an insignificant and relatively isolated reality. Such experience comes to no more than the cognitively harnessed sentience generated in individual, highly developed organisms. The dark flux of matter sustains this consciousness and outruns it on all sides. Although spirit is a natural product, its luminous nature is in a fundamental way discontinuous with or different from its source. It cannot, therefore, know matter firsthand and cannot capture the unintelligible surd of existence in its net of eternal forms. Accordingly, we live as forlorn strangers in a world that "is indefinitely, perhaps infinitely, deep and inhuman."[20] No advance in knowledge can pierce the ultimate mystery of this great whirlwind of existence. It surrounds us and provides our sustenance, and then engulfs and annihilates us.

We might refer to this view as "metaphysical realism," though I prefer the name "inhuman realism" because it calls attention both to the independent existence of the material world and to its discontinuity with our cognitive life. Affirmation of the independent reality of matter has distrust of the ultimate adequacy of human experience as its epistemic counterpart. Santayana is, of course, no rationalist: he is satisfied that we can learn about the world only by coming in sensory contact with it. Our senses, however, suffer the defects of their status. They are midsized existents out of scale with the minute ultimate constituents of nature. Accordingly, they can give us no direct or accurate account of vast reaches of existence. The suspicion that experience is not the medium of the disclosure of all realities is supported by Santayana's analysis of consciousness. If nothing given exists, the immediate objects of our awareness must be summary symbols or essences that provide but hints of the substantial realities behind. This does not mean that experience resembles a veil that obstructs our vision; it is closer to a glove through which we feel the distant pulse of being. Inhuman realism is in this way naturally connected to critical realism. If the world is different from anything that appears in consciousness, our perception of it cannot be direct. Intuited forms mediate our cognitive contact with the inaccessible depths of matter.

Pragmatists reject this inhuman realism and the attendant concerns about cognitive adequacy when they start their philosophy with human experience. Such a departure implies the belief that experience is homogeneous with nature, that in some important sense "the trail of the human serpent," as James said, "is over everything."[21] The trouble, Santayana points out, is the naïve empiricism inherited by pragmatists and converted into the view that everything is real when, as and where experienced.[22] Such radical empiricism leaves the pragmatist with an exploration of the objects of experience alone and without a sense of the dark inhumanity and mysterious generative power of the material world. This is why Santayana charged Dewey with being a "half-hearted and short-winded" naturalist and a philosopher of the foreground,[23] where "foreground" means the luminous, accessible perceptual world that is stretched like a thin mask over the horrible, inhuman face of existence. If Santayana were alive today, he would see philosophies even further removed from real life. These thinkers deal only with the foreword to the foreground, insisting that words, concepts, symbols or discourse constitute the backbone or even the totality of being. One can only conjecture what images of contempt Santayana would create to convey the shallowness, the sad absurdity, of such views.

The ultimate difference between Santayana and pragmatism, then, is one of metaphysical starting point. But this theoretical disagreement or difference of vision is at once a deep moral rift. For if experience and nature are all of one piece, we have reason to be sanguine about human prospects in the world. The pragmatic stress on progress has its source and justification in the conviction that existence is intrinsically receptive to human initiative. James did not want to call this optimism, for that suggested to him that things would turn out well irrespective of our efforts.[24] The special moral flavor of pragmatism is distilled in the belief that perseverance furthers, that earnest commitment, keen intelligence and hard work suffice to improve the human condition. This faith in the possibility of amelioration is closely connected with the American temperament and it constitutes the second major difference between Santayana and the pragmatists.

A keen observer of human events, Santayana did not overlook the great advances made possible by the Industrial Revolution. He understood that a rational approach to the problems we face may help to resolve them. But he placed all this progress in broad historical perspective and in dwarfing cosmic context. Consequently, he came to see our advances as local, reversible and insignificant incidents in the natural world. He viewed human prospects from the standpoint of the individual and saw that the moral difficulties of life, the problems of ambition and achievement, of attaining happiness and making peace with death, are not resolved by material improvements. As a result, he could not share the pragmatists' commitment to amelioration and their fascination with the future. Although he was not European enough to glorify the past, he was not American enough to look to the future for the solution of our ills. With mystics and stoics and disillusioned Indian sages, he held that only the present, the now that gives access to eternity, yields escape from pain or a small measure of fulfillment.

The remarkable similarities between Santayana's thought and pragmatism demonstrate that even though he subjected America to withering criticism and left it as soon as he could, its culture and its intellectual milieu made a profound contribution to his cast of mind. The deep metaphysical and temperamental differences between his philosophy and those of James and Dewey testify to the fact that whatever he learned from America, he could not embrace its sunny and perhaps innocent optimism. However much he stressed the importance of reason and the significance of action, in the end he always felt like the Ionians he once described, who stood with horror and fascination on the shores of the boundless sea.

CHAPTER 17

Neoplatonic Elements in the Spiritual Life

At a time when the history of philosophy receives less than respectful and conscientious attention from those who consider themselves constructive philosophers, it is good to remember that some of the great thinkers of the past were also masters of the great thoughts or systems of others. George Santayana, in particular, spent countless hours studying the classical works of philosophy.

He studied Plato in exquisite detail and was an avid reader of Aristotle, all of course in Greek. The story has it that, late in his life, an earnest priest tried to bring him back to the Catholic faith of his youth. The priest attempted to quote St. Thomas to show Santayana the error of his ways, but did not quite get the passage right. Santayana helped him out by giving a precise rendition of the text in Latin.

Santayana was no less familiar with the works of the moderns. He read everyone from Descartes to Hegel in the original language of the author, and his library contained annotated copies of the works of Bergson, Heidegger and Bertrand Russell, among many others.[1] He read Plotinus and was thoroughly familiar with both major and minor figures in the Neoplatonic tradition. Similarities between his thought and selected elements of Neoplatonism are due not to historical accident but to elective affinity on his part.

I must add at once that, though it is important to see Santayana as in some central respects a Neoplatonic thinker, we cannot rightly say that his complex philosophical views come simply to a repetition of some prior position. In *Platonism and the Spiritual Life*, his most explicit discussion of Plotinus and Plotinian themes in contemporary thought, he specifically

limits the scope of his agreement with Neoplatonism. He has two fundamental quarrels with the tradition. He is deeply suspicious of metaphysics,
particularly a metaphysics that operates with such dialectical ideas as those
of Being, the One, and Mind. And he charges that the Neoplatonic conception of spirituality is not spiritual enough. I shall discuss the first disagreement immediately, the second only near the end of this essay.

In one sense, of course, Santayana has a metaphysics, or at least an ontology, himself. But his is a characteristically modern, almost postmodern,
ironic metaphysics—one that does not claim access to the hidden structures of reality. He thinks that metaphysics of the traditional sort cannot
yield results. The nature of reality is best explored by science; philosophy
has no alternative to offer to careful empirical investigation. Instead of engaging in metaphysical speculations, he wishes to concentrate on explicat-
ing the view of the world tacitly contained in the active life, in the undeniable fact that we act in a multicentered cosmos deployed in space and time.

He views his ontology as nothing more than a systematic account of the
beliefs implicated in what he calls "animal faith," the confidence of the
human animal in the independent existence of enduring but manipulable
objects. Philosophy can do no more, he thinks, than follow the outlines of
common sense. Speculations beyond that amount to "dialectical physics,"
which is the attempt to gain insight into the real or into what matters by
means of the play of words. I wish more of our postmodern colleagues
shared his caution about such an enterprise.

Here is the way he puts it himself. "Metaphysics, in the proper sense of
the word, is dialectical physics, or an attempt to determine matters of fact
by means of logical or moral or rhetorical constructions."[2] Such an enterprise is "neither physical speculation nor pure logic nor honest literature,
but . . . a hybrid of the three, materialising ideal entities, turning harmonies
into forces, and dissolving natural things into terms of discourse."[3]

By contrast, Santayana views his own ontology as consisting of categories that capture the features of the world he finds "conspicuously different and worth distinguishing." The ontology is modest, constituting his attempt "to think straight in such terms as are offered to me," in order "to
obviate occasions for sophistry by giving to everyday beliefs a more accurate and circumspect form."[4] It is, therefore, nothing new: as "a feast of
what everybody knows,"[5] it expresses "a certain shrewd orthodoxy which
the sentiment and practice of laymen maintain everywhere."[6]

This means that in adopting and adapting the insights of the Neoplatonic tradition, Santayana strips them of their straightforward metaphysical bearing. He takes Plotinus' account of cascading emanations to be a

story pointing to potential salvation for humans, rather than a description of the structure of existence. But even if the story reveals no facts, it discloses profoundly significant aspects of the human condition, especially the condition of the human spirit or consciousness in a moving and dying world.

In *Platonism and the Spiritual Life*,[7] he criticizes the Neoplatonist William Ralph Inge, dean of St. Paul's, by arguing that, if we take it literally, Plotinus' view of our distance from the source is severely misleading. Yet he also demonstrates that the same idea, used as a symbol, offers deep insights into our spiritual condition. The rejection of literal and the embrace of symbolic truth is typical of Santayana's approach to the work of philosophy.

We need to distinguish two distinct moments in the development of Santayana's aesthetics. His reflections on the technical problems of aesthetics are contained in his first book, entitled *The Sense of Beauty*.[8] Although Hobbes and other British empiricists lurk in the background, the primary influence on this work is German philosophy. Santayana draws on Schopenhauer's aesthetics and responds to Kant's view of the nature of beauty. A thorough search of the text could perhaps reveal some connections to Neoplatonic sources, but it would be difficult to see these as more than incidental.

His later, ontologically explicit work, which began to see the light of day in 1923 with the publication of *Scepticism and Animal Faith* and continued to develop until the appearance of the fourth volume of *Realms of Being* in 1941,[9] presents an altogether different picture of aesthetics. *The Sense of Beauty* dealt with aesthetics as a set of philosophical problems; the system articulated in *Realms of Being*, by contrast, incorporates the disinterested intuition of beauty as a structuring feature of ultimately satisfying human lives.

That system depicts aesthetic immediacy as the central character of what Santayana calls "the spiritual life" and establishes spirituality as the only way of escaping the concerns, pains and tragedies of the world of change. At this stage of Santayana's work, Neoplatonic influence is ubiquitous. This is the aesthetics I shall discuss.

There is no better place to begin the study of anything Neoplatonic than the contrast between the temporal and the eternal. Santayana finds himself in wholehearted agreement with drawing a sharp distinction between the two and assigns important prerogatives to the eternal. The temporal world, of course, is our home as human animals. Santayana is uncompromising in viewing biological existence as the foundation of all life, including the spirituality that in a special and limited sense takes us beyond it.

Existence as an animal, however, is fraught with frustration and danger; not even momentary victory lifts fear and worry from organisms that must fight to survive. The insecurity of existence permeates all aspects of life, and the imperfection of time, doling out only passing moments of satisfaction, makes it impossible for us to rest. No animal can thus elude disappointment, aging and eventual death. None of us, as he puts it, is "too good for extinction,"[10] and in the meantime, none can experience more than momentary joy.

Morality cannot help us overcome the structural inadequacy of the processes of life. Good and evil are categories attaching to things and actions as a result of the interest our living psyches, which are physical organisms, take in them. Such assessments are the outcome of caring, and caring is an expression of the vulnerability of animals: "The whole psyche is a burden to herself, a terrible inner compulsion to care, to watch, to pursue, and to possess."[11] Frustration and death are the certain fate of a creature as much in need as this.

So no repose or ultimate satisfaction can come from the tortured life of pursuing the good. Our only hope is to transcend the world of means, of unmeaning processes, and embrace something timeless and perfect. Yet actual transcendence, implying departure from our ambushed bodies, is impossible. Since taking leave of our spatial and temporal stations would mean instant death, not eternal life, we must find the moment of peace within the one life we have been granted.

Transcendence of animal life within the confines of that life is made possible by Santayana's Platonism. Organisms fighting one another in a treacherous world are endowed with consciousness. This sentience, "the total inner difference between being asleep and awake,"[12] serves as an indispensable condition of knowledge.

Santayana adopts Plato's idea that the objects of mind are eternal forms; these forms, which he calls "essences," constitute the realm that appears to consciousness. Each moment of awareness reveals an essence or set of essences and thereby opens immediate access to the eternal. The eternal thus surrounds us, or at least stretches in all directions before the mind, in such a fashion that we can partake of it without effort. We sink into the eternal simply by waking up or by focusing our minds.

Santayana's view of universals differs in three centrally important ways from Plato's. First, although they are objects of thought, essences do not function, for Santayana, as objects of knowledge. Cognition connects the animal to its world, making it possible for it to identify the forces that affect its life.

Knowledge, therefore, is discovery of realities that bear hidden potential, that is, true belief about what exists in the flux. It is "belief in a world of events, and especially of those parts of it which are near the self, tempting or threatening it."[13] Awareness, by contrast, presents crystalline pictures of eternal actualities that lack potential. The object of knowledge is the dynamic substance of the world, the object of mind is essence in its lifeless and hence indestructible eternity. Santayana summarizes this point by his oft-repeated motto that "nothing given exists," which amounts to the claim that only inexistent forms can be present to consciousness.

Second, essences are, for Santayana, forms of definiteness unlimited in number. Plato found it difficult to decide whether or not hair and dirt had forms corresponding to them. Santayana, by contrast, maintains that every identifiable specificity is an essence. He holds that numbers, the generic forms that define natural kinds, such moral ideas as goodness and justice, all colors and relationships, and even the forms of events are essences.[14] This makes the realm of essence a nested infinity, that is, an infinity consisting of such infinities as the number of numbers and the number and diversity of motions that have, will have, and could have taken place during the unending history of the world.

The infinity of essences strips them of power. In its native element, no form has sufficient claim on existence to instantiate itself. In the great Western tradition, the ontological proof of God's reality was supposed to have identified the one and only essence that required or entailed its own existence. As usual, Spinoza held a stronger view, maintaining that all essences containing no contradiction automatically exist.

Santayana rejects the ontological proof and notes that Spinoza can sustain his belief only by refusing to allow the distinction between essence and existence or by denying that in the final analysis anything touched by time is real at all. In sharp contrast, Santayana thinks that the temporal world is the only existent reality; the realm of essence serves only as an infinite reservoir of passive forms or, as he puts it in a striking image, a costumer's gallery of the clothes in which existence may garb itself.[15]

Third, the infinity of essences removes their moral prerogatives. No essence is better than another, and hence the realm does not constitute a hierarchy cascading down from the Good or the One. The value of essences is extraneous to them, as is their meaning. They are characterized by the principle of self-identity and consist of all and only the features they display.[16]

The essence of a black Labrador that includes the character of friendliness or trustworthiness is not a better, only a different, essence from that of the same dog characterized by viciousness. Since we can focus on them, there are such essences as Being, the Good, and the One, but there is nothing special about them, except perhaps their excessive emptiness or generality. Trees create their own structure and animals generate other animals, but generic essences do not construct themselves or beget specific beings. In Santayana's language, they do not belong to "the generative order" of nature.

A consciousness confronted with an infinity of essences has no basis on which to choose among them. Choice is a hallmark of animal life: love and revulsion express the values of organisms. This leads to the shocking, and redeeming, realization that selectivity is of no significance to essence or to pure consciousness. Since essences are inactive, eternal forms, nothing matters to them. And consciousness, or "spirit" as Santayana calls it, is "an impartial readiness"[17] to intuit any universal; it is as happy to contemplate one form as another.

This consideration reveals that inexistent essence and spirit in its purity are for each other; they constitute a natural pair. When essence is instantiated, it becomes a part of the physical world and acquires significance to the struggling animal. And as long as spirit is harnessed to the service of the organism, it cannot take joy in all that comes its way; it suffers the loves and pains of the organic psyche that gives it birth. But spirit set free from servitude to the demands of the body can delight in whatever form it finds. When spirit is permitted to be spiritual and intuition to be pure intuition, the concerns of animality fall away and we taste the peace that passes all understanding. The reward is eternal joy.

This joy is eternal but not everlasting.[18] Animal life is limited: the moment passes and soon we are no more. But eternity is not a quantity to measure. It is activity *(energeia)* in Aristotle's sense, requiring no duration in time.[19] How long the bliss lasts is thus irrelevant. Only its quality matters, and that is unsullied as long as consciousness remains unperturbed by care and retains a clear view of its object. What counts is the moment in which, as Santayana puts it, the ultimate becomes immediate,[20] and we rest, if not in the bosom of Abraham, at least in the Elysian fields of transcendent delight.

Spirituality becomes, in this way, the aesthetics of blessedness. The relation between spirit and its objects is clearly aesthetic. It is immediate apprehension that carries joy in the beautiful. The mind leaves its cares behind as it focuses attention on the play of forms. The joy experienced is, as Kant correctly believed, disinterested; as means to nothing further, contemplation and enjoyment constitute an ethereal song.

Since consciousness is involved and forms are apprehended, such moments display a cognitive or what Santayana sometimes calls a "synthetic" element. But they do not constitute knowledge in the full sense of the word. They have no external objects and they are not intelligently adaptive to surrounding substances or facts. On the contrary, what makes them special is that they are freed from the demand to adapt to anything—they are unconnected or superfluous to the needs of animal life.

Pure intuitions or moments of liberated, unconcerned consciousness move in this way beyond all preference and valuation. The distinction between good and evil and the drive for perfection express "the subterranean" activities of the animal psyche,[21] its desperate need to distinguish what fosters from what inhibits its life. There is, therefore, nothing spiritual about moral judgments. The latter constitute testimony of the work of selectivity essential for continued life; the former is the selfless—and, dare I say, indiscriminate—embrace of whatever essence may come our way. The latter wants victory over time; the former is content to disappear into the eternal.

This is the source of the second major criticism Santayana levels against the Neoplatonic tradition. In *Platonism and the Spiritual Life,* he repeatedly characterizes the Neoplatonic adherence to exalted values, including the value of spirituality, as "political." He says, for example:

> *The friends of spirit, in their political capacity, will of course defend those forms of society in which, given their particular race and traditions, spirit may best exist: they will protect it in whatever organs and instruments it may already have appeared, and will take care that it pursues its contemplative life undisturbed in its ancient sanctuaries.*[22]

This is an understandable interest in safeguarding what are normally seen as the conditions of spirituality. They are, however, moral and not spiritual concerns about the human good; they express the desires of our psyches to live long and to live well. Such "political zeal, even in the true friends of spirit is not spiritual,"[23] for much as the life of the spirit in us presupposes a flourishing or at least a relatively intact organism, it cannot adopt the aims of that animal without losing its soul.

Santayana's critique of the Neoplatonic tradition comes, then, to the claim that it presents an impure conception of spirituality, mixing true devotion to the eternal with the moral or political desire to protect its sources and to extend its dominion indefinitely into the future. The lesson Santayana wants to teach instead is that "spiritual life is not a worship of 'values'" but "a disintoxication from their influence."[24] This means that the pure intuitions constituting spirituality take no interest even in their own continuance; they are absorbed in a satisfaction that is "free from care, selfless, wholly actual and, in that inward sense, eternal."[25]

Evidently Santayana does not wish to deny that, as living creatures, *we* can have a legitimate desire to extend our moments of spirituality for as long as possible. But from the standpoint of the spiritual life, such desires have no standing. Considered from the outside of such experiences, we may well wish for the moments of rapturous union to continue. But from the inside, that is, in those moments when we find ourselves absorbed in a landscape of eternal forms, no desire for anything temporal is possible or proper. If a desire arises, the magic of eternity is shattered; if, amazingly, the magic is sustained, the desire loses its urgency and becomes but another eternal object to contemplate.

We may characterize such all-encompassing absorption in the immediate in a variety of ways. We can speak of it in secular terms as joy in the beauty of all things. But we can also say that it involves the concentration of mind that constitutes the heart of prayer. Santayana refers to it as liberation as well:[26] it gives us the feeling that we have been set free of the incubus of material existence so we may dwell in eternity.

In *Realm of Spirit,* Santayana also uses the language of union with God, with the One, with the Absolute and with Brahma.[27] Phenomenologically, absorption in the object feels like return to the source or reunification with primordial reality. The outcome is a profound sense of selflessness or a oneness whose vibrant reality cannot be expressed in words.

That the experience Santayana calls to our attention can be captured in the language of metaphysics, aesthetics, religion and poetry suggests that these disciplines converge on key elements in the life of spirit. For Santayana, at least, none of these discourses can be taken as literally true, though all of them constitute useful languages in which we can express vital insights, and remarkably the same ones, into the human condition.

Spirituality does not constitute a life that can serve as an alternative to the one requiring food and air. It does not liberate us in any permanent way from the burdens of existence, nor does it return us to Being or its Source. The experience may feel as though that were happening, and the languages we use to convey or explicate it are marvelous symbolic tools for fixating it. But when all is said and done, what happens is simply that in these moments of calm consciousness the mind touches the eternal. It does not embrace the One or achieve union with God, though saying so can be a splendid poetic way of describing the event.

These last few comments can be used to measure the true distance between Santayana and Neoplatonists. Although he is in full agreement with the great tradition of Neoplatonism concerning the central significance of eternity for achieving the measure of perfection possible for our finite frame, he cannot accept the metaphysics of Neoplatonism at face value.

Emanation schemes, talk of a unitary source of Being, hierarchical conceptions of reality and the idea that determination is negation strike him as dialectical moves out of touch with the physical reality in which we operate. When it comes to existence, he says again and again, all substance is material, meaning that it is "the physical substance . . . found in things or between them."[28] If we ever discover the structure of the real world, we will have physics and not metaphysics to thank.

This means that in Santayana's view, Neoplatonism as a philosophy of existence or nature will always be wide of the mark. As a philosophy that points the way to salvation, however, it is right on the money. "The Greek naturalists," he says in one place, and in others specifically adds Plotinus,[29] "have been right on the chief issue, the relation of man and of his spirit to the universe."[30] And when we look past the heat of desire and the fierce partialities of animal life, that alone is what truly matters.

Accordingly, it is no small achievement to have developed an understanding of our relation to eternity. None but Plato and his followers were able to do this in the West. Even if we reject their metaphysics, we must accept its spiritual significance for the human race. The enduring worth of Neoplatonism resides not in what it says about the world, but in how it shows us the boundless play of eternity in our lives.

CHAPTER 18

Peirce: Inquiry as Social Life

At a time when science is one of our largest institutions and teams of re-searchers explore nearly every corner of the world, what does Peirce add to our understanding of these practices by reminding us that they are social? The person who does not know that scientific endeavor is cooperative must have been unconscious longer than Rip van Winkle was; the spectacular success of our investigations of the physical universe over the past several hundred years has been due in large measure to the cumulative efforts and the free flow of information among millions of investigators. We have now reached the stage, in fact, where research is *globally* social, involving the work of multiple teams located in a number of countries. Scientific break-throughs are unthinkable without the devoted work of nameless members of these teams and without large-scale financial support from the broader community. The claim that inquiry is social appears today as the blandest platitude.

Noting the social nature of research, however, is not the same as under-standing it and its implications. As a practicing scientist, Peirce was fully aware of the centrality of cooperation in inquiry. In discussing the "causes of the triumph of modern science," he remarked that:

> [T]he considerable number of workers, and the singleness of heart with which . . . they cast their whole being into the service of sci-ence lead, of course, to their unreserved discussions with one an-other, to each being fully informed about the work of his neighbor, and availing himself of that neighbor's results; and thus in storm-ing the stronghold of truth one mounts upon the shoulders of an-other who has to ordinary apprehension failed, but has in truth succeeded by virtue of the lessons of his failure. (CP 6.51)[1]

The full meaning of these well-known facts, however, cannot be appreciated without a grasp of the nature of inquiry and of the reasonably expectable consequences of its vigorous pursuit. What is novel and interesting when Peirce speaks of the sociality of inquiry is not that he notes it but that he places it in the broader context of an account of truth, reality, scientific method, the moral life and even the eventual fate of individuality.

One pervasively attractive feature of Peirce's work is the way in which he combines intellectual devotion to the pursuit of truth with a robust sense of the practical. His theory of inquiry is a good example of this reconciliation. He wishes to give an account of inquiry as it actually operates in the lives of people rather than as an abstract process that can be started at will and that must meet fanciful standards of certainty. His philosophical target is, among others, Descartes, who thought that sound investigation
• begins with a pretense of universal doubt and ends in demonstrable certainty. Peirce maintains, by contrast, that inquiry presupposes a living, actual doubt and concludes as soon as a stable belief takes its place.

Although this may sound cynical, long observation of human behavior convinced Peirce that, typically, people think only when all else fails. Without a problem that disrupts routine, we are happy to operate in our customary way. The function of thought is to solve problems; as long as things go our way, there is no need for reflection and we are disinclined to worry our heads with it.

Peirce thinks of doubt and belief as similar to biological functions. Drawing on a long tradition of philosophers who maintain that belief and action are organically connected, Peirce declares that to believe something is largely to be disposed to act in certain ways. My conviction that there is food in the refrigerator, for example, is, among other things, my tendency to go to it when I am hungry, to tell others to check it out when they are ravenous, and to open it when it is time to feed the dog. Peirce calls such complex tendencies "habits" and declares that: "The essence of belief is the establishment of a habit, and different beliefs are distinguished by the different modes of action to which they give rise" (W 3.263–264).[2]

When a belief proves wrong, that is, when a habit is shattered, doubt fills the mind. Peirce thinks of doubt as an "irritant" that evokes thought. Inquiry, for him, begins with some such doubt and ends when a new belief takes the place of the old. Thinking in Darwinian terms, he declares inquiry to be not just a process but a struggle (W 3.264) whose aim is to "settle" or reestablish belief. Peirce's image is of an operational equilibrium that is first disrupted by some untoward event and then restored. Thought ceases when stability returns and the organism's habits become, once again, adequate to meet its needs.

All this seems supremely practical and displays thought as an instrument of adjustment. The central concern is the successful operation of the organism, not truth for its own sake. In fact, Peirce goes out of his way to stress that the inquiry to resolve doubt may start from any premise that is itself free from doubt and end in any conclusion that is stable and satisfying. Moreover, the satisfactoriness of an opinion or habit results from its stability and success, not from its objective truth.

For those who think that this is a crude application of evolutionary biology to the sphere of mind, however, Peirce has a stunning surprise. He says that inquiry in just the sense discussed, if conducted properly and long enough, inevitably leads us to the truth. "The opinion which is fated to be ultimately agreed to by all who investigate, is what we mean by the truth," he says, "and the object represented in this opinion is the real" (W 3.247).

This may sound, on first hearing, as a subjectivist reduction of the truth to what is or will be believed. But the initial impression is misleading, as is the appearance of mindless optimism suggested by the claim that our opinions are destined to converge on the truth. A full understanding of what Peirce has in mind will have to wait for later. Suffice it to say, for now, that this is the first hint of the way in which Peirce sees inquiry as social: truth, reality and the conduct of inquiry are all connected to the intellectual development of the community. Peirce goes so far as to refer to the view of actuality that grows out of this line of thought as "my social theory of reality" (CP 6.610).

Once the irritation of doubt has unsettled belief, we have a choice concerning how to "fixate" or stabilize it. In an argument somewhat reminiscent of Bentham's attempt to prove hedonism,[3] Peirce introduces four methods of developing beliefs. The first, which he calls the method of tenacity, consists in believing whatever we wish and doing so with all our power of concentration. To accomplish this, we must disregard all contrary evidence and overlook other plausible views. Conspiracy theorists tend to arrive at their opinions in this fashion: they begin by discarding other views without examination and then discredit evidence against their claims as having been planted by conspirators.

Peirce thinks that this way of settling opinion fails because it is not social. What fuels belief on this procedure is private conviction, not public fact. Worse, the "social impulse" (W 3.250), which makes us take the views of others into serious account, bears against it. Maintaining one's ideas when everyone else disagrees is psychologically difficult, and sooner or later even tenacious believers must confront the devastating thought that the opinions of others are no worse than their own.

The second method, that of authority, establishes and enforces opinions on the basis of power alone. This is a vastly successful enterprise giving people the comfort of believing the official view, embracing religions' dogmas or following the party line. The fact that it renders us "intellectual slaves" has not served as a major deterrent to its popularity. Human beings are always ready to have others tell them what to think and when.

The method of authority proves inadequate for at least three reasons. Although orthodoxy can demand compliance with many edicts, no power or authority can prescribe opinions concerning everything. Moreover, because the ruling institution may be insufficiently aware of relevant facts, its imposed beliefs may be disastrous for its followers. Hitler's and Rev. Jim Jones's opinions rendered their communities, along with their beliefs, self-liquidating. Most important, humans who "possess a wider sort of social feeling" (W 3.251) realize the contingency, even the arbitrariness, of the official view by comparing it with what other cultures and other ages have believed.

The *a priori* method proposes to substitute the pronouncements of reason for tenacity and authority as the determinant of belief. But what reason declares varies from individual to individual. Rational investigation convinced Spinoza that there is one substance, Descartes that there are two sorts, Leibniz that there is an infinite number, and Hume that there is none. Agreement is impossible on this basis, and the formation of belief is quickly reduced to a matter of individual propensity or taste. Where the rational is determined socially without any external constraints, it is subject to the same arbitrary cultural variations as we saw in the case of authority. Although it may give personal satisfaction, the *a priori* method is not a reliable public avenue to stable beliefs.

This leaves Peirce with inquiry proper or scientific method. The central notion this introduces is that of an "external permanency" (W 3.253). The ultimate weakness of the other methods consists in their having no extrahuman factor to control belief. We cannot expect self-control in what we believe without acknowledging the external control of independent facts. Once we combine the two sorts of control, inquiry not only stabilizes belief but also leads us to the truth.

Inquiry always begins with a surprising fact. This is what shatters our habit and requires to be accommodated in a revised system of beliefs. The first of the three stages (CP 6.469ff)[4] that constitute inquiry is forming a hypothesis, which Peirce calls "abduction" or "retroduction." Intriguingly, he thinks that this is an inferential procedure in which we articulate some law or general state of affairs that, if it obtained, would make the surprising fact part of the common run of nature. The second stage, deduction, is the attempt to identify consequences of the hypothesis that may be open to observation. If we are unable to find any sensible differences that the truth of the hypothesis entails, Peirce's pragmatic criterion declares it to be meaningless. Since the sum of the practical consequences of a concept or group of concepts constitutes its meaning, the search for the possible perceptible outcomes of the theory is simply the investigation of its significance.

Having developed the "conditional experiential consequences" of the claim, we can proceed to the stage of testing, which Peirce calls "induction." This requires checking whether the predicted observations can be made. In the process, we must repeatedly assess the probable truth of the hypothesis by determining the ratio of successful observations. The result in every case is a judgment of probability. Human knowledge consists solely of such judgments, which means that we can know nothing with certainty and exactitude, and that even our most dearly held beliefs may with time turn out to be false.

This fallibilism hits exactly the right note today. The expansion of our knowledge has gone hand in hand with the growth of modesty concerning its epistemic claims. Thoughtful people now agree that, in spite of our vast investment of social energy in the scientific enterprise, we cannot hope to know anything with absolute certainty. Peirce does not think that this fact is lamentable. Fallible knowledge has practical consequences no less than the infallibilities other thinkers fancied themselves to have found. Moreover, he believes that the pervasiveness of uncertainty and inexactitude itself reveals important facts about the world, especially the universal presence of continuity.

Most important, however, is that knowledge of our fallibility establishes our cognitive task. Uncertainty in the world and the uncertainty of our inferences are inseparably connected, so investigation can never stop. Although Peirce frequently speaks of his own love of truth, he does not suppose that social inquiry is fueled by a purely intellectual drive. It develops in the wake of the worry and doubt that go with shattered habits, and habits break when they encounter the uncontrolled, unpredictable, chance element in nature.

Infinite inquiry, therefore, is the life-sustaining response of any intelligent race to the contingencies of life. But such investigation is not only of biological use. It is also a demand of logic: whoever is not committed to it violates the principles of inference. With this surprising and magnificent move, Peirce establishes a bridge between logic and social life, ethics, and even religion. The connection may at first appear as a stretch, but on closer scrutiny it turns out to be as good a try as has ever been made to derive concrete moral obligations from austere epistemic principles.

The types of inference we employ in our cognitive practice differ from one another in their degree of probability. This "real and sensible" difference consists in the varied rates at which they yield true conclusions. How long must we test each sort of inference to determine its probability? Any limit is arbitrary. In a world that contains chance events and faces an open-ended future, questions of probability can be settled only on the basis of infinite or at least indefinitely protracted trials.

All who wish to add to the sum of human knowledge—that is, all who inquire—are therefore tacitly committed to the indefinitely sustained pursuit of investigation. This comes to the requirements that they see their work as continuous with the labors of past and future inquirers and that they identify their interests with the good of this "unlimited community" (W 3.285). Individual thinkers become in this way members of a community of inquiry that transcends nations and ages. It is not only transgenerational and universally human, however; Peirce goes so far as to extend it to all forms of life devoted to intellectual pursuits.

The ultimate purpose of this imaginative expansion of the boundaries of the community is the breakdown of the walls of the self. "To be logical, men should not be selfish," Peirce writes, for logic "is rooted in the social principle" (W 3.284). In his metaphysics, he is explicit in showing that the self is social in its constitution and that it is continuous with the environing world of minds. In discussing the implications of logic, he stresses the moral significance of devotion to the boundless community of inquirers, of making this commitment supreme in our lives, and of hoping for "the unlimited continuance of intellectual activity." By a characteristic leap of insight, he identifies these three sentiments or activities with the traditional Christian virtues of charity, faith and hope. Although he does not expand on the idea, it is clear that he thinks intellectual, moral and religious values are connected to the point of identity. That he believes this is reinforced by what he says about the "hypothesis of God" (CP 6.452ff), an abductive idea that plays not only a religious but also a cognitive and a moral role in our lives.

The boldness of the argument from logic that takes us beyond selfishness pales by comparison with the reasoning from semeiotics, the study of the nature of signs and symbols, which promises the obliteration of individuality itself. A clear and simple version of this latter argument begins with the premise that as inquiry progresses, our minds get filled with more truths and fewer errors. The more truths we know in common, the more like each other we become; in fact, if we were omniscient, differences between us would be limited to such relatively insignificant matters as the current focus of our attention (W 3.57). This suggests what Peirce explicitly declares elsewhere—that individuality is a negation grounded in ignorance and error (CP 5.317) or at least that our minds tend to lose their distinctness and their differences as our ideas spread and acquire generality (CP 6.104). The progressive improvement of our understanding is, therefore, also movement toward social union through uniformity.

The semeiotic version of the argument sets out from Peirce's views that all mental action is of the form of inference and that the entirety of the world is a flow of signs. These signs carry richer meaning in proportion to the community's progress in inquiry: the closer we get to the final fixation of belief, the more truth and the less ignorance and error they comprise. Since human beings are themselves vastly complex signs (CP 5.314), the growth of shared truth in them goes hand in hand with the reduction of the unlawlike element of error that makes for difference or individuality. Full rationality eliminates what separates us; the similarity of what we believe, and thus do and are, "welds" us into social unity.

The identification of individuality with negation or imperfection goes back to Plato. But Peirce's immediate inspiration for his view is likely to have been Kant, for whom moral rationality consists in being determined by a universal law. This leaves no room for individuality in the ethical sphere; we can differ from one another only by the way we violate autonomy or fall short of the demand for universal self-determination. Peirce may also have been thinking of Fichte, in whom total moral self-possession becomes a historical task. Fichte, although much less interested in science and far less empirically minded, is in any case one of the great overlooked influences on Peirce; there is reason to suppose that he was the inspiration for Peirce's bittersweet idea of an infinite (read, never to be completed) progress toward truth. As early as 1797, Fichte spoke of the Idea of the rational being as one who, by embodying reason in both self and world, loses its individuality.[5] His account of the source of individuality in "sensory restriction" also bears a close resemblance to Peirce's idea that individuality is due to error and ignorance.

The power of such ideals of social unanimity to the point of identity tends to be lost on us today. We have become suspicious of agreement because we have seen how easily it can be created by appealing to our baser instincts and by machineries of propaganda. We also find little reason to be enthralled with the uniformities brought about by a global industrial culture. With this backdrop in mind, it is especially important to stress that Peirce's idea is nothing like these worrisome tendencies. If anything, he would be more distraught about these developments than most of us, for his ideal is a social unity based on intellectual harmony, which in turn is the outcome of free, extensive and competent inquiry. Uniformities achieved in this way signal the loss only of individual peculiarities built on our favorite illusions.

We have noted before that Peirce thinks of the truth as what the community of investigators will eventually embrace, and of inquiry as the process that inevitably conducts us to this final opinion. But the claim that truth is that on which we will all agree in the end is ambiguous. It may be read in line with a realism that sees truth as the independent and fully formed objective of inquiry; its discovery is the reward of our labors. It may, however, also be seen as conveying an alarmingly subjectivist, or intersubjectivist, message: whatever we agree on in the long run is to be anointed as the truth. There is evidence in Peirce's writings for both interpretations, and accordingly, commentators tend to line up praising him or attacking him for being a scientific realist or a historicist.

Neither interpretation is complete or accurate, however, if it is developed independently of Peirce's beliefs about evolution. For inquiry is first and foremost an evolutionary process: it consists of the conversion of seconds or resistant forces into thirds or lawlike and intelligible realities. The "external permanencies" that the scientific fixation of belief requires are the surprising, shocking powers that surround us. By being taken up into the abductive, deductive and inductive activities of minds, their brute existential status is upgraded and they emerge as fully interpreted elements of a rational system. Admittedly, this process of interpretation takes infinite time. But evolution cannot take less time than that—it cannot stop—and inquiry is the prime factor in the growth of "concrete reasonableness" and in the ultimate emergence of a fully crystallized system of thirds.

Viewed in this light, the differences between the realist and the intersubjectivist interpretations of truth simply disappear. Truth and reality, which is its object, are sets of thirds that reach their completeness only at the end of infinite inquiry. In that perfected world, truth will exist in glorious objectivity, independent of what anyone thinks. But of course, since all opinions will have converged on it, minds will be filled with nothing but the truth. This renders such questions as "Is 'There have been n (substitute the correct number) generations of humans in the history of the universe' true for objective reasons or only because we all believe it?" both misleading and inappropriate. Prior to the end of infinite inquiry, such propositions are not true at all; on the final fixation of belief, they are both objectively true and universally believed. At the infinitely distant, never-to-be-reached end of investigation, truth and belief are indissolubly wedded, and in such a relation neither party enjoys priority.

Of the four methods of settling belief, only scientific inquiry distinguishes between "a right and a wrong way" (W 3.254). It can do so because it acknowledges public realities that serve as an external check on our cognitive endeavors and because groups of investigators can freely replicate or criticize one another's results. This is what makes the scientific enterprise self-correcting and what in the end justifies Peirce in thinking that it will surely conduct us to the truth. Self-criticizing inquiry is like a negative feedback loop that by stages approximates a final resting point. That point, not surprisingly, is one in which the flowering of reality is matched by fullness of knowledge. Peirce conveys how high the stakes are by his repeated warning: "Do not block the way of inquiry" (CP 1.135).

Although abductive (hypothesis forming) originality resides in individuals, everything else about inquiry is social. We need large teams of investigators because the world we wish to explore is vast. We must support the transgenerational continuance of scientific effort because all knowledge is fallible and rests on probabilities. Social feeling is perhaps the strongest motive and a prime outcome of cooperative investigation. Little by little, we will realize that because ideas spread and the lines between selves are fluid, even individual selves are social in their contents and in their architecture (CP 6.104ff). Finally, the tacit objective and ultimate result of inquiry coincide in the development of a society of intelligent, harmonious and fully informed minds.

What of interest can Peirce add to our grasp of the social nature of scientific investigation? In two simple words: context and vision. His message is that without a clear view of the metaphysical underpinnings of our efforts, we cannot succeed in defining our purposes. Without ideals extrapolated from our practices, moreover, we have no basis for criticism of our blinding and all-consuming day-to-day activities. Peirce calls our attention to the ways in which the community and the individual are made for each other, along with the ways in which they continually remake one another. The historical context of our struggles for knowledge and the vision of a magnificent future provide essential materials for our self-understanding.

We can say of all humankind what Peirce says of the individual: "It is what the man is destined to do, what of the future is wrapped up in him, that makes him what he is" (CP 7.666).

There is a related lesson here for inquirers working in the humanities. The great growth of cooperative research in the physical and more recently in the social sciences has left philosophy, literature and connected fields largely untouched. Researchers in the humanities continue to engage in private reflection and look to other, equally solitary thinkers only for a response to their completed labors. This is worse than wrestling giants with a hand tied behind one's back; it brings to mind those unfortunate artists who, lacking hands and feet, paint with brushes held in their clenched teeth. Without cooperative effort at every stage of thought, we can make no systematic progress in solving the central value problems we face. Without such progress, our society will not learn to replace stumbling experimentations with intelligent experiments. Philosophers, in particular must heed the call for cooperative inquiry so that they may at last make their unique and obligatory contribution to the improvement of human life.

CHAPTER 19

Peirce and Santayana on Purposes

Evidence of purposiveness surrounds us on all sides. I don't want to swallow the cherry stone, so I spit it out. In order to sell shoes, the merchant creates an attractive display. For decades, thousands of scientists coordinate their activities to find a cure for cancer.

One might think that philosophers cannot deny these facts without exposing their enterprise to derision. Yet many do, employing a simple strategy whose effectiveness in certain contexts is reinforced by the findings of science. To see that the sun sets, we need to simply look westward on a cloudless late afternoon. But what we see, or seem to see, deceives: *we* turn from the sun, not the sun from us. What appears as an obvious fact, therefore, may be all appearance and not a fact at all.

This is how it may be with purposiveness, as well. It may only *seem* to us that processes seek certain end-conditions or that conscious intentions and our assessment of the good are effective forces in the world. In their case no less perhaps than in the case of the setting sun, we need to distinguish how things seem from how they truly are. Just as a sophisticated astronomy teaches us not to trust what we think we see in the afternoon sky, a thorough understanding of nature may convince us that its mechanisms seek nothing and an advanced neurophysiology may instruct us not to believe that it is our purposes that yield results.

Processes may just end in certain states of affairs without those having been their objectives or ends. Actions and their outcomes, moreover, may well be the effects of some current impulse in the organism, with the experience of intention serving simply as the index that certain physical processes are going on. Such analyses do not deny the obvious, observable fact that organized and controlled human effort engages and changes portions of the world. Instead, they offer a novel and presumably better account of how this happens. And they also do not deny that our purposes seem effective. Instead, they seek to explain why this appearance, which fails to capture the truth, arises in the first place.

Something like this is clearly the approach Santayana takes to the everyday evidence for teleology. He accepts the observable facts of purposiveness but denies both that natural processes aim at anything and that conscious purposes are efficacious. After dismissing the teleology of nature, he makes this striking claim about human purposes:

> Final causes certainly exist in the conduct of human beings, yet they are always inadequate to describe the events in which they are manifested, since such events always presuppose a natural occasion and a mechanical impulse; and these cannot flow from the purpose or choice which they make possible and pertinent. The whole operation of final causes therefore requires, beneath and within it, a deeper flow of natural forces which we may darkly assign to fate or matter. . . .[1]

Behavior that displays the intelligent adaptation of means to ends is, therefore, a reality. Its source, however, is not the intentions or purposes of mind but the impulses of the psyche, which is the dynamic, material agency in living things.

In this and in other passages, Santayana embraces a stronger thesis than that final causation requires the operation of efficient causes. Aristotle and Peirce agree in endorsing that view,[2] which is a ringing affirmation of the reality of purposiveness. Santayana, by contrast, maintains that in an important sense our experience of final causation is illusory and our beliefs about it are parts, in the language of current debates, of a scientifically inadequate folk psychology.[3] Causation is a matter solely of the "deeper flow of natural forces"; it is material or "mechanical," leaving neither need nor room for the agency of mind.

To cast the question of teleology in these terms is helpful because it brings out the central role mind plays in any full-fledged view of final causation. When purposes operate, the absent, the possible, the future and the good exert an influence on the course of affairs. This can occur only through the work of mind: only thought can make the nonexistent appear and distinguish what is from what ought to be. Consciousness is, therefore, indispensable for teleology in both of its major traditional forms. Without it, individuals could not frame purposes and act them out. And without organizing intelligence, in the form of a single designer or dispersed throughout the cosmos, the world could presumably not display the rational structure, the evolutionary advance and the exquisite adaptation of part to part that we observe. The teleological proof of the existence of God derives from one version of the idea that purposiveness without mind is impossible.

The moment we see effective intellect as a condition of final causation, it becomes clear why Santayana could and would have none of it. He viewed the mind, after all, as an impotent by-product of physical changes. It becomes equally clear, on the other side, why Peirce thought of final causation as fundamental and ubiquitous. He believed that minds constitute the ultimate ingredients of the universe, that matter itself is but effete,[4] degraded, undeveloped[5] or partially deadened[6] mind. Purposiveness is the characteristic mode of mental action, and hence "final causation alone is primary."[7] Peirce is so deeply devoted to purposiveness that he conceives even personal life as involving a "developmental teleology."[8] To be a person is not only to carry out purposes but also purposively to seek new purposes to pursue. Persons, therefore, are self-directing, self-developing and self-controlling units in a growing world.

The universe itself is, for Peirce, in process of evolution, and this development is purposive to the core. Its agapastic drive is love, which is "a positive sympathy among the created springing from continuity of mind."[9] Its ultimate aim is the emergence, at the end of infinite inquiry, of the fully structured real, which is mind crystallized, a world governed by rational laws or a system of exquisitely interconnected thirds. The evolutionary process reveals in this way that "bare existence by . . . its destiny betrays an intrinsic affinity for the good."[10]

Peirce hints that such an evolutionary philosophy "is so far from being antagonistic to the idea of a personal creator that it is really inseparable from that idea."[11] Unfortunately, however, he never honored this vague promise of orthodoxy with a set of developed ideas. Nevertheless, it is worth remarking that Peirce does not need a personal God to complete his system and might, in any case, not be able to accommodate one. His Hegelian inspiration makes him see the world as carrying its own internal teleology. As a system, it resembles a seed much more closely than it resembles a mind-designed machine: it is a self-developing whole. And if the universe undergoes "a continuous growth from non-existence to existence,"[12] there is neither need nor room for a Creator to interfere with this natural process.

Even for an idealist, Peirce's devotion to purposiveness is extraordinary. He thinks that it is ubiquitous and world-structuring. He rejects Kant's hesitation in affirming it; our knowledge of it is positive and not a matter of merely subjective necessity. The contrast with Santayana could not be sharper and it is made more poignant by the fact that both of them belong to the now rapidly diminishing group of philosophers who believe in the irreducible reality of mind. If the difference in their views of teleology is a result of the difference in their ideas about the causal power of mind, how can we account for their sharp divergence of opinion about what mind can do?

There is a ready explanation at hand, and Peirce's categories are well adapted to expressing it. Peirce thinks of mind primarily as thirds,[13] whereas Santayana believes that it consists exclusively of firsts. As thirds, ideas are mediating signs that "spread continuously,"[14] influencing the stream of inferences of which our lives consist. They affect the world, to be sure not by brute causal power but by the force of reason, sympathy and love. Their hold on the course of events at any given time may be tenuous, yet in the long run their power is irresistible. Through them, the best part of the universe issues its civilizing call to heed the demands of law and reason. Yet thirds do more than simply carry this call. They are effective agencies on its behalf, seeds of reason in an improving world.

Santayana, by contrast, limits mind to the immediacy of firsts. The foundational mental act is intuition, which is direct acquaintance with essences. Even when other forms of mentality, such as belief, supervene upon intuition, the mind remains ineffectual. Its ultimate perfection, the spiritual life, reveals its innermost nature: it is the necessary condition of simple presence, the space in which immediate qualities and feels gain manifestation.[15] Obviously, we do not lack the semeiotic and intellectual powers with which Peirce credits us. But even among these processes, nothing is mental but their immediacy or their presence in consciousness. In Peirce's language, Santayana thinks that only the firsts of thirds are mental, thirds themselves are not.

If we put the matter in Santayana's terms, the view is that mind consists exclusively of consciousness. This is a theory Peirce believed he had to deal with and he spent some time discussing it. His argument depends, however, on the now dubious work of von Hartmann. Peirce thinks that von Hartmann "has proved" the existence of unconscious mind "conclusively."[16] As a result, Peirce feels free to assert that final causation is the hallmark of the mental and the "essential subject" of psychology.[17]

The problem, of course, is that such an approach yields no results. Identifying phenomena below the level of consciousness that mimic purposiveness does not help us decide their nature: they can as readily turn out to be biological as mental. In fact, a significant portion of the history of psychology has consisted in finding physical causes, correlates or explanations for functions at first supposed irreducibly mental. Santayana recognized this trend and assumed its indefinite continuance. He believed that only by tying putatively mental functions to physical or neurophysiological processes can science progress. This was precisely what led him to limit mind to its final residue, the immediate feel or consciousness of life. He thought that this at least, though physically grounded, was ultimately irreducible. For the rest, he declared his "deliberate refusal to admit the possibility of any mental machinery."[18]

The vast difference between Peirce's and Santayana's views of purposiveness is the outcome of their divergent ideas about the efficacy of mind. Their disagreement about that is the result of conflicting commitments concerning the nature of the mental. And those incompatible commitments express in turn the variance in their assessments of the proper direction and likely outcome of scientific investigation. This last point leads to a bitter irony.

Peirce was a man of science who claimed to have spent forty years in the study of the methods of inquiry and to have made "positive contributions" in "mathematics, gravitation, optics, chemistry, astronomy, etc."[19] Santayana, by contrast, did not hesitate to characterize himself as "an ignorant man, almost a poet."[20] It seems that when it comes to forecasting the direction in which science was likely to progress, the poet did much better than the scientist. Santayana is thoroughly contemporary in his perception of where science is going and has to go in order to enhance our knowledge of the human will and intellect. Peirce, by contrast, clung to nineteenth-century ideas about universal purposiveness and world-constitutive mind. There is no doubt that if Peirce had believed less of Hegel, we could believe more of Peirce.

Metaphysics and the Social Construction of Human Nature

The historian looking over philosophical developments in the last fifty years will not be impressed by their novelty or boldness. Judged by the number of those whose academic title includes the word "philosophy" or by the tidal wave of books and articles published each year, our field enjoys unprecedented prosperity. Yet we suffer from a loss of spirit that calls itself caution. We satisfy ourselves with small points of clarification or retreat to the study of the great thinkers of the past. We skirmish over how best to do our job, a job that in these skirmishes we never get to do. We hear more and more from thinkers who announce the end of philosophy, though they are unwilling to end their own. Those who don't philosophize keep telling us that we can't.

Lost in the love of texts and subtexts, lost in the controversies about language and thought is the great traditional task of philosophy. In the last fifty years, few have had the daring of Paul Weiss to attempt to see things and to see them whole, to settle for nothing less than an integrated vision of life and the cosmos. To be sure, such an ambitious enterprise is fraught with danger. But it is the danger of high adventure, of a grand challenge embraced, of doing what our calling demands. Even if, in the ultimate sense of learning the truth, such efforts are almost certain to fail, we must respect them as expressions of our insatiable drive to know. They probe the limits of understanding and show the power of creative mind. They grapple with the deepest questions of life, with the problems we can neither answer nor forget.

I do not share the qualms of positivists, sceptics and postmodern souls about the sort of enterprise Weiss undertakes, and have nothing but admiration for his boldness. "The problem of the nature of man is one of our most neglected problems,"[1] he says, and proceeds to develop a full account of that nature. Targeting human life as the ultimate object of investigation and thinking, as he does, that moral concern is at the center of that life seem to me clearly on the right track. I am not bothered in the least by the generality of Weiss's statements about our frame. My objection is only that he makes the wrong ones. In particular, he underestimates the extent to which human nature is a social product, and as a result, he falls prey to the age-old error of supposing that it is universal and uniform.

Both in his written work[2] and in his classes, Weiss showed a fascination with the Thomist view that there is something metaphysically unique about human beings. Aquinas thought that, at some point after conception, God substitutes a human soul for the animal form of the embryo. Although each such soul is a singular individual, all of them belong to the same species. They distinguish humans from perishable beasts and establish our everlasting moral self-identity.

Weiss raises a variety of objections to this view, but in the end adopts one not very different from it. To be sure, he rejects both the need for divine intervention in human reproduction and the idea that the embryo becomes human only after a while. He maintains, however, that we have selves, or "fixed cores,"[3] which differentiate us from animals. Each human has such a self from conception; without it, we could not affirm the "undeniable truth" that "it is the same man who is adult and who was embryo or child."[4]

The self makes it possible for us to be identical through time and thus to be responsible for our acts. By means of it, we can evaluate ourselves and, when needed, exert self-control, criticize and even discipline ourselves. This nonbodily power, which is "essential and constant," serves as the source of our uniquely human abilities.[5] Regardless of their achievements, all humans have such a self or power and all animals lack it.[6]

Each self is connected to a body, though only to the sort of body we usually identify as human. Its presence is, therefore, in the end a matter of biology: as soon as sperm and egg unite, an unduplicable self attaches itself to the resultant organism. The breakthrough to full humanity cannot occur "through mere growth," he writes, "but requires a radical change in the composition of an entity, and . . . this is achieved at conception."[7] Although he says that the appearance of a self is not due to the physiological character of the sperm and egg, Weiss does not discuss what other features of such blobs of matter may be responsible for attracting selves and why selves do not inhabit the bodies of apes and porpoises.

Weiss struggles with how his view of a fundamental difference between humans and animals comports with the theory of evolution. He avers that the self emerges as a result of developments in the animal psyche. Such psyches are presumably self-centered; when they become concerned with the good of others or the good everywhere, they turn into selves.[8] Weiss gives no hint of why, when and how this change occurs or once occurred. The current absolute distinction between animals and humans suggests that it must have taken place long in the past and cannot be replicated now. We can easily teach chimpanzees to care about what happens not only to them and other apes, but also to all manner of beings that surround them. I doubt, however, that Weiss would think this gives them selves and thereby makes them human.

From time to time, Weiss speaks of selves as concerned not so much with the good of others as with the universal good.[9] This turns our attention away from moral concern as definitive of humans and toward abstract conceptual skills, making his position less satisfactory. A concrete moral being may be interested in the welfare of this or that or any number of needy individuals. Such devotion is quite different, however, from commitment to the universal good, which requires the ability to think in extremely general terms. We have little knowledge of how far animals are capable of totalizing thought, but it is clear that, even among humans, it is a late and difficult achievement.

The Indian tribes that lived by the shores of the Gulf of Mexico, for example, had names for the water adjoining their homes but none for the Gulf as a whole. It fell to mapmaking Europeans to make an abstract totality of all the bays and of the vast stretches of open water that connect the three Americas. If some humans have trouble thinking of the totality of a body of water part of which is before their eyes, we have little reason to suppose that they can be devoted to the sum of good in the world. Such sophisticated abstract conceptions must not be imputed to the embryo and can therefore not serve as the distinguishing feature of the human self.

This issue aside, the central problem Weiss faces is how humans can reproduce themselves. In our sexually liberated culture, this might seem unproblematic to anyone out of kindergarten. Nevertheless, Weiss's premises make the phenomenon difficult to explain. The union of sperm and egg is adequate to reproduce our physical nature. Our bodies, however, are not fully human without the presence in them of a self. How can such nonphysical, uniquely human selves be produced?

The problem arises because Weiss wants to maintain both that humans emerge as a result of evolutionary advance and that they are different not only in degree but in kind from animals. Our physical continuity with animals is undeniable; Weiss postulates the self to account for the discontinuity. Unfortunately, his tendency to ontologize makes him dismiss an obvious and well-explored explanation of the generation of selves. Thinkers as diverse as Mill and Hegel maintain that human nature is a social product, that nothing but the forces of socialization can convert our biological potential into the complex actuality of a human life. Related to Weiss's view, this means that if what renders us human is indeed the presence in each of us of a self, then that self is developed over time through the processes of child-rearing and social interaction.

The argument Weiss presents against this view is less than convincing. "Man has a nature before he attains the status of a social being," he says, and thinks this implies that we "can be human and still exist apart from any society."[10] The context of these statements makes it clear that he has in mind fully developed human beings ("men," in his language); he speaks of retreating from society "many times during the day" and of remaining outside it indefinitely. This is perfectly possible for adults, though only in a superficial, primarily spatial way. Those in the early stages of development, however, cannot even do this; infants denied a nurturing social environment fail to survive. And though adults can leave society, society never leaves them. The skills, habits, value systems, thought patterns and emotions that structure our lives are all products of socialization. They are the indelible marks the social world leaves on the soul—marks that define who we are and what will satisfy.

Instead of accepting the view that we are humanized in the process of social life, Weiss insists on an explanation that combines biological facts with metaphysical speculation. He realizes that the problem consists of two parts. One demands an answer to the question of how the first human emerged from nonhuman animal life. The other requires an account of the continued production of humans with selves through the physical means that is the only method open to human bodies.

There is an important difference between the two cases, according to Weiss. The second is easy, he thinks, because it requires only "a peculiar egg and sperm."[11] The initial emergence of humans is more difficult to explain and is likely to involve a multitude of circumstances. In a conjectural mood, Weiss asks if it occurred as a result of "the meeting of some animal sperm and egg" or after birth on account of "the acquisition of tools or speech." He replies uncertainly: "Perhaps both conditions are needed. Perhaps only in some unusual state of the world can the new kind of unity appear, be carried to term, and then live somewhat like a public man?"[12]

The language of the above quote reveals that Weiss thinks both of being human and consequently of the emergence of the human as all-or-nothing affairs. He sees evolution not as a gradual process of change in which something we may with hesitation call human appears over many thousands of years. He supposes, instead, that there was a specific time in the past when the first human being was conceived and then "carried to term." No being prior to this had been human, and this creature was human through and through. Such is precisely the view he must take if he is to remain consistent with his idea that we are rendered human by the self that attaches itself, in some mysterious way, to the zygote at fertilization. Weiss must have Adam in mind, though he situates the abrupt emergence of the fully human in a historical time and a biological matrix.

Once the first few humans are on the scene, explaining the rest of them presents little problem. An evolutionary achievement of this magnitude "cannot be undone." Accordingly, once "human beings are produced, only human beings are produced."[13] The "quantum leap" to humanity occurs at the radical event of conception. But such events are not unique to the human race, and Weiss maintains that the physiological character of the sperm and egg are inadequate to assure the humanity of the offspring. What, then, accounts for it? Without a pause, he offers the following speculation: our humanity is due to the manner in which the sperm's and the egg's "lived-through beings as at once inward and acceptive of what is outwardly conditioned, are combined."[14]

I must admit to not being able to make much of this suggestion. I am bothered, of course, by the thought that there is no conceivable way for us to know about the inwardness of sperms. As to their acceptiveness, they strike me as pesky little things that are rather more aggressive than agreeable toward external conditions. But these epistemic qualms aside, how are inwardness and acceptiveness as necessary conditions of humanity themselves passed on from generation to generation? If as inheritable features of organic objects they are carried in the genes, then everything about the descent of humans can be explained by reference to physical facts alone. And why should we suppose that the proposed description is accurate about human sperms and eggs but somehow misses the mark concerning the genetic instruments of other species? Perhaps the sperms and eggs of whales are just as inward and acceptive as those of your neighbor down the street. And what if my wife's second cousin's eggs are not very acceptive? Does this mean that whales are more likely to produce human offspring than Ann is?

What generates these problems is Weiss's notion that our humanity is an objective condition grounded in the possession of a self that accrues to us at conception. Each element of this notion is open to question, and the idea as a whole is sufficiently improbable to justify doubt. The development of humans from apelike ancestors was too gradual to enable us to say that the creatures at any point in the continuum were simply either human or not. Each group of forebears we have been able to identify were more or less human, or human in certain respects but not in others. Whether or not they were sufficiently like us to warrant being called human is a matter of judgment.

Such judgment seems never to drop out in issues as important as determining who is human and, therefore, who has obligations and rights. The history of civilization may, in fact, be viewed as the story of the development of an inclusive notion of humanity or, what comes to the same thing, the story of the gradual expansion of our sympathies. For many years, strangers, enemies, those of a different race or religion, people of divergent tastes or habits, cripples, idiots and the mentally ill were not regarded as human. The fact that, by and large, now they are establishes neither that that is not a matter of judgment nor that the inclusive opinion is right rather than just more satisfying or better.

Weiss might, of course, respond by saying that exclusivist judgments are simply wrong. To make this plausible, he must show either that we are in possession of a standard of humanity independent of what we can derive from observing ourselves and neighboring others or that our recognition of humans is intuitive. The first of these strikes me as completely hopeless. Our access to essences or abstract concepts is unavoidably mediated by sensory experience. Since our experience is severely circumscribed, one cannot avoid asking how good a sample my friends and I make as paradigms of the human frame. All standards we derive will be as partial, regional and fallible as the experience that undergirds them.

The second alternative may seem to hold more promise, and accordingly, Weiss embraces it. He asks why we take autistic children, idiots and the senile to be humans. After reviewing some rival opinions, he says, "Our acknowledgement of them as human is too immediate, too ungrounded in experience, reflection, or knowledge, to make it possible to account for their acceptance as humans in these suggested ways." Our feelings are evoked by these beings directly; we sympathize with them and respond to them in a way that appears to come without reflection or tutoring, from the depths of our soul.

Here again, Weiss forgets the formative experiences of children. Intuitions are deeply ingrained responses, flowers growing from the compost of habits. We learn to recognize humans in the crib: they are the loving shapes who minister to our needs. Thieving birds learn to identify humans no less breathlessly; the scarecrow does not even have to look much like a person for the flight to be unreflective and immediate. Without a history of interaction with many resembling and reliable people, we could not enjoy intuition of our kinship with humans. A child growing up among wolves would learn to view itself as similar to them and them, instinctively, as family. Our intuitions are not native recognitions of essence but the residue of regional observations.

Weiss arrives at his account of human nature by ontologizing social processes. Humans acquire selves, that is, characteristic patterns of feeling and operation, through lengthy exposure to social attempts at handing on culture. Weiss attends only to the product of these efforts, a product which is itself always in process of change, converts it into a stable, enduring being, and projects it to the moment of conception to serve as the element that renders us human from the start. The moves this involves appear suspect, if not transparently unacceptable, as soon as they are properly brought to critical attention. A philosopher as discerning as Weiss would have noticed them and would have had his suspicions aroused had he not thought that the postulation of such a self is necessary to account for self-evaluation, self-control and self-identity.

Everyone who has dealt with children knows that teaching them the skills of evaluating, controlling and disciplining themselves are central goals in raising them. We do not need to suppose that young people have a nonphysical self in order to explain how such education is possible. We see ample analogues to it in the way animals can be socialized. Extensive exposure to the way I affirm values in the yard has made my dogs act in ways that suggest a conscience: they try to control themselves, and when they cannot, they append bad feelings to self-indulgence. Sometimes they act in ways so human that I have to remind myself that they are only beasts. We have little reason to suppose that children learn in a different way or that they learn much better.

Self-identity is a different matter: instead of a skill taught, it is a condition determined by reference to socially developed standards. The demand for it is primarily moral and political, not metaphysical. We need to be sure, for example, that the people brought to justice are the same ones as those who committed the crimes. In other cases, we may have to find the rightful heirs to land and fortune, that is, let us say, the grown individuals identical with the children who drifted away from home. The problem may also be personal and psychological: victims of amnesia or those suffering from Alzheimer's disease may have to be identified and helped to recover their memories or their feelings that they know who they are. In all these situations, we operate with public standards of varying stringency, none of which refers and none of which needs to be supplemented with reference to an enduring, nonphysical self.

The postulation of a hypostatized self, therefore, is neither necessary nor useful. The social practices that involve questions of identity can proceed happily without supposing that such things exist. And maintaining that they do adds nothing to our grasp of the world. They fail to offer criteria of identity independent of the ones we use, and because they are an odd sort of existents, their relations to the ordinary objects of our experience become vexed problems. Attending to the contexts of life in which questions of self-identity acquire function and significance makes it less tempting to invent a set of ontological structures that shadow social processes. This is particularly important because philosophy cannot focus its efforts on understanding and enriching life as long as it occupies itself with such coinage.

Weiss's tendency to ontologize social processes shows itself in another way, as well. He thinks that humans are different in kind from animals, that the human race is rigidly separated from all other species, and that human nature is invariant through time and space. All of us, therefore, manifest a single essence, which defines a fixed and uniform human nature objectively embodied in the world. Since who we are determines what we ought to do, this enables Weiss to hold all human beings to the same standard of behavior: all of us must pursue the universal good.

Why should we suppose that species are anything but collections of variously resembling individuals? The similarities must, of course, be adequate to justify lumping the creatures together, but what is adequate in any given case depends on the purposes we have and the decision we make on the basis of them. If we look only at ourselves and our friends, the similarities among humans may seem overwhelming. This, however, indicates not the uniformity of human nature, only a biased sample. The natural tendency on the part of those who establish absolute standards of humanity by such partial observations is to use the measure by which others fall short of it as a mark of their deficiency.

To see what is involved in classification, we must expand the sample to include all the individuals that constitute our apelike ancestors—the Neanderthals, China Man, Java Man, and the near-humans who resided in Africa—along with the full variety of people who lived in roughly the past 100,000 years. Among the last of these, we must take into account not only the shining exemplars of civilized intelligence, but also catatonic schizophrenics, congenital idiots, hydranencephalics, the borderline deranged, perverts, cannibals, those crippled or distorted in body, mind or will, mass murderers, necrophiliacs and persons duller and less sensitive than sheep. Is there any essence we can detect that all these beings share? Many of them will seem far closer to animals of one sort or another than to humans, just as many domesticated animals will seem like our sisters and brothers when compared to them. Nothing physical, mental, emotional or spiritual, no skills, desires or activities are common to them all. Even their genetic material differs: the average divergence among contemporary humans is 3,000 nucleotides.[15]

To order this vast continuum of individuals, we must pick out traits we think particularly important and decide how similar they must be to justify assigning those who display them to the same group. The choice of traits and the decision about adequate similarity constitute a double judgment, both of which involve our values and our purposes. Sorting by reference to the time at which the creatures lived may appear natural but expresses, in fact, an interest in tracing genetic heritage and developmental patterns. Viewed in this light, the last Neanderthal expired perhaps 25,000 years ago. If we group people by intellectual endowment and emotional propensities, however, a number who live today must be classed with the Neanderthals. To ask which is the correct way to classify is to miss the central role choice plays in the process. No way is *the* way, though some ways are clearly better for certain purposes. It all depends on what we want to do and what we are prepared to give up or overlook to accomplish it.

Simple ontological realists, such as Weiss, live in an austere world. Reality for them is like a heap of bones, each clearly articulated, sparingly endowed with properties, barely touching at the joints. A single thought captures what they are; their other properties can be derived from this, their essence, or else constitute an accumulation of irrelevance. I understand how one can think of the world in this fashion, but the image bears only the faintest resemblance to the rich reality that washes over us. The properties and relations surrounding us constitute a web indefinitely deep. Our minds can create neat, human order out of this luxuriance in any number of ways; the point is not to get to the ontological rock bottom or to uncover the intellectual structure that explains it all, but to organize it in a way that will make life more satisfactory. This in the end is the meaning of Weiss's correct insistence that our ultimate concern is always with the good. Lordly intellectuals may find it a sad lesson that knowledge is a subordinate instrument, but in their candid moments even they admit that none can live only the life of mind.

What, then, makes for the humanity of human beings? Different collections of features at different times. Picking properties that make the class exclusive may be unfortunate, unproductive or lamentable, but it is not intellectually wrong. Within limits,[16] there are many ways of carving groups out of the continuum of individuals and, since each stresses existing similarities, none is more accurate than the others. Morally, of course, some classifications are simply abominable. Excluding persons from the human race on account of their height, their gender, their religion, their income, their political persuasion, the color of their skin or the length of their hair strikes us as unacceptable and perhaps even wicked. All of these (and more) have at one time or another been used to distinguish humans from those who do not count, and we want to be ready to argue against them when people say they are markers adequate to strip others of rights. We cannot do so on purely epistemic grounds but we can on the basis of our broader purposes.

An inclusive notion of human nature has, in fact, gained such dominance in the last hundred years that it may be time to insist on important differences between human natures. A single nature suggests a single perfection: if human nature is universal, the human good should in broad outlines be uniform. Intolerance used to live by excluding groups from right-bearing status; it can flourish now by forcing its standards on all admitted to the human race. Weiss appears to recognize this and accordingly raises the possibility that gender and color, perhaps even musculature, make for divergent human natures. He sees that there are important differences among us and thinks it is "imperative that we do not minimize the bearing of gender, color, and age on individuals."[17]

Although this is a promising start, Weiss quickly reverts to his ontological schema and asks how such bodily features relate to the unchanging self that, after all, constitutes our nature. He replies that, in the end, the differences among us change only the efforts we must make. The fundamental task remains the same for all: to render ourselves "representative of mankind" and to make our exertions advance the universal "value intrinsic to the self."[18] Our differences are not, therefore, of the essence; as variations in our circumstances introduced by the body, they change only the details of how we pursue the good.

Such an approach acknowledges neither the role social life plays in creating the self nor the fact that who counts as human involves a social (and sometimes political) decision. Without such recognition, it is impossible to develop an adequate theory of human nature or even to understand the functions of such theories. Postulating a changeless self as the core of each human being misleadingly shifts emphasis from the realities of empirical life to the intangible characteristics of the hypothetical. Declaring that all selves share a concern for the universal good flies in the face of experience and throws the door open to the intolerant imposition of standards and to the widespread condemnation of those whose nature resists them.

It takes courage to do metaphysics in the old, time-honored way by setting sail for deep, uncharted waters. In matters of such profound impact on our lives as our conception of who we are, however, it may be better to steer closer to the shoreline of facts.

Notes

Chapter 1

1. George Santayana, *Reason in Common Sense,* Scribner's: New York, 1905, p. 284.

Chapter 5

1. Mary T. Clark, "An Inquiry into Personhood," *The Review of Metaphysics* 46 (1992), p. 28.
2. Ibid., p. 23.

Chapter 6

1. See D. L. Hull, "The Effect of Essentialism on Taxonomy: 2000 Years of Stasis," *British Journal for Philosophy of Science* (1965) 15:314–326, 16:1–18.
2. R. C. Lewontin, *Biology as Ideology* (New York: HarperCollins, 1993), p. 68.
3. Contrast Peirce on secondness (*Collected Papers of Charles Sanders Peirce,* C. Hartshorne and P. Weiss, eds. [Cambridge, MA: Harvard University Press, 1931], vol. 1, *passim*) with Nelson Goodman on creating worlds by the manipulation of symbols (*Ways of Worldmaking* [Indianapolis: Hackett Publishers, 1978]).
4. James J. Sheehan, "Coda," in *The Boundaries of Humanity: Humans, Animals, Machines,* James J. Sheehan and Morton Sosna, eds. (Berkeley: University of California Press, 1991), p. 259.
5. Arnold I. Davidson, "The Horror of Monsters," in *The Boundaries of Humanity,* p. 36.
6. Ibid., pp. 53–64.
7. Elsewhere, I have called the outcome of such judgments "choice-inclusive facts." See John Lachs, *The Relevance of Philosophy to Life* (Nashville, TN: Vanderbilt University Press, 1995), pp. 229ff.
8. John Dupre, "Reflections on Biology and Culture," in *The Boundaries of Humanity,* p. 130.
9. John Dupre, "Human Kinds," in *The Latest on the Best: Essays on Evolution and Optimality,* John Dupre, ed. (Cambridge, MA: MIT Press, 1987), p. 337.
10. Ibid.
11. Ibid.

12. Ibid., p. 341.

13. Ibid., p. 342.

14. William James, "The Moral Equivalent of War," in *The Writings of William James*, J. J. McDermott, ed. (Chicago: University of Chicago Press, 1977), pp. 660–671.

15. William James, "On a Certain Blindness in Human Beings," ibid., pp. 629–645.

Chapter 7

1. Harry Frankfurt, "On the Usefulness of Final Ends," *Iyyun* 41 (January, 1992), p. 4.

2. Ibid., p. 15.

3. John Lachs, "Aristotle and Dewey on the Rat Race," *Philosophy and the Reconstruction of Culture: Pragmatic Essays after Dewey*, John J. Stuhr, ed. Albany, N.Y.: SUNY Press, 1993, pp. 97–109. "Rat Race" hereafter.

4. John Dewey, *Art as Experience*, in *The Later Works*, 1925–1953, vol. 10, Jo Ann Boydston, ed. Carbondale & Edwardsville, Ill.: Southern Illinois University Press, 1987, p. 202.

5. Ibid., p. 201.

6. See my "Rat Race."

7. G. W. F. Hegel, *Phenomenology of Spirit*, A.V. Miller trans. Oxford: Oxford University Press, 1977, pp. 111–119.

8. Ibid., p. 116.

9. Epictetus, *The Handbook*, Indianapolis: Hackett, 1983, p. 13.

10. Aristotle, *Nicomachean Ethics*, Terence Irwin, trans., Indianapolis: Hackett, 1985, pp. 273–275.

11. Immanuel Kant, *Foundations of the Metaphysics of Morals*, in *Critique of Practical Reason and Other Writings in Moral Philosophy*, by Lewis White Beck, trans., Chicago: University of Chicago Press, 1949, p. 82.

12. Kant, *Critique of Practical Reason*, pp. 225–234.

13. A good example of Dewey's critique of modern institutional life may be found in John Dewey, *Experience and Nature*, *The Later Works*, vol. 1, Carbondale, Ill.: Southern Illinois University Press, 1988, pp. 271–277.

14. Ibid., p. 66.

15. Dewey presents a good discussion of his idea of natural histories in *Experience and Nature*, pp. 69–99.

16. Ibid., pp. 275–276.

17. Dewey, *Art as Experience*, p. 201.

18. Dewey, *Experience and Nature*, p. 275.

19. Dewey, *Art as Experience*, p. 201.

20. Dewey, *Experience and Nature*, p. 277.

21. Ibid., p. 272.

22. Aristotle, *Nicomachean Ethics*, p. 275.

23. I discuss chains of mediation and the resultant alienation in *Intermediate Man* (Indianapolis, IN: Hackett, 1981).

24. Dewey, *Experience and Nature*, pp. 275–276.

25. See my "Rat Race."

Chapter 8

1. Immanuel Kant, *Critique of Pure Reason*, B 307, trans. Norman Kemp Smith (London: Macmillan, 1953), p. 268.

2. Immanuel Kant, *Critique of Judgment*, Section 22 and elsewhere, trans. J. H. Bernard (London: Hafner, 1968), p. 78.

3. Arthur Schopenhauer, *The World as Will and Representation*, trans. E. F. J. Payne (New York: Dover, 1969), vol. I, pp. 146–147. This account of life recurs throughout the book and structures Schopenhauer's recommendations for dealing with it.

4. Nowhere is this clearer than in what he says about the possibility of happiness. See *World*, vol. I, pp. 196, 319 and elsewhere.

5. Schopenhauer, *The World*, vol. I, pp. 411–412.

6. Ibid., vol. I, p. 185.

7. Ibid., vol. I, p. 129.

8. George Santayana, *Realms of Being* (New York: Cooper Square, 1972), p. 30.

9. Santayana, *Realms of Being*, pp. 812, 823.

10. The literature of *ennui* from Flaubert to Schopenhauer is, perhaps paradoxically, fascinating. Schopenhauer says that next to striving for survival, our most powerful drive is "the effort to get rid of the burden of existence, to make it no longer felt, 'to kill time,' in other words, to escape from boredom. Accordingly, we see that almost all men, secure from want and cares, are now a burden to themselves. . . . In middle-class life boredom is represented by the Sunday, just as want is represented by the six weekdays." *World*, vol. I, p. 313.

11. Oscar Wilde, *The Picture of Dorian Gray* (Baltimore: Penguin Books, 1959).

12. This may be the solution to the conflict such commentators as Irwin Edman thought to have discovered between the life of reason and the spiritual life in Santayana. A complete and fulfilling life of reason may well need to leave room for moments of spiritual joy.

Chapter 9

1. Thomas Hobbes, *Leviathan*, in *Selections*, ed. F. J. E. Woodbridge (New York: Scribner's, 1930), chap. 14.

2. See Rene Descartes, *Meditations on First Philosophy*, John Cottingham, trans. (Cambridge: Cambridge University Press, 1996), pp. 37–43.

Chapter 10

1. John Stuart Mill, *On Liberty*, in *Essential Works of John Stuart Mill*, Max Lerner, ed. (New York: Bantam, 1961), p. 264.

2. See Section III of *On Liberty*.

3. Immanuel Kant, *Critique of Practical Reason*, Lewis White Beck, ed. and trans. (Chicago: University of Chicago Press, 1949), pp. 227ff.

4. Martin Heidegger, "Being, Dwelling, Thinking," in *Poetry, Language, Thought*, Albert Hofstader, trans. (New York: Harper and Row, 1971), pp. 160ff.

5. Friedrich Nietzsche, *Thus Spoke Zarathustra*, in *The Portable Nietzsche*, Walter Kaufman, trans. (New York: Viking, 1954), p. 130.

6. Thomas Hobbes, *Leviathan*, in *Selections*, ed. F. J. E. Woodbridge (New York: Scribner's, 1930), chap. 13.

7. Benjamin Constant, "The Liberty of the Ancients Compared with that of the Moderns," *Political Writings*, trans. and ed. Biancamaria Fontana (Cambridge: Cambridge University Press, 1988), p. 313.

8. Plutarch, *The Lives of the Noble Grecians and Romans*, trans. John Dryden (New York: Random House, 1932), p. 431.

Chapter 12

1. Norman Daniels, "Normal Functioning and the Treatment-enhancement Distinction," *Cambridge Quarterly of Bioethics* 3 (2000):309–322.

Chapter 13

1. Andrea L. Bonnicksen, "Transplanting Nuclei between Human Eggs: Implications for Germ-Like Genetics," *Politics and the Life Sciences* 17, no. 1, (March 1998): 3–10.

2. MELAS is short for mitochondrial encephalomyopathy with lactic acidosis and stroke-like episodes. It results in neuromuscular degeneration, seizures, heart failure and death, usually before the age of 40. The disorder is generated by mutations in mitochondrial DNA; the mutations are passed on to offspring. Some scientists think that it may be possible to extract the nucleus of a woman's unfertilized egg, discard its diseased mitochondrial DNA, fuse the nucleus to a donor egg, fertilize it and implant it for pregnancy. If this as yet untested procedure of egg cell nuclear transfer worked, it would enable a woman with MELAS to bear a genetically related child free of the disease.

Chapter 14

1. U.S. Bureau of the Census, Jennifer Cheeseman Day, *Population Projections of the United States, by Age, Sex, Race, and Hispanic Origin: 1993–2050*, Current Population Reports, P25-1104, U.S. Government Printing Office, 1993.

2. I have in mind such attacks as Leon R. Kass mounts in *Is There a Right to Die?* Hastings Center Report 23, no. 1 (1993), pp. 34–43.

3. John Stuart Mill, *On Liberty, in Essential Works of John Stuart Mill*, Max Lerner, ed. (New York: Bantam Books, 1965).

4. See John Hardwig, *Is There a Duty to Die?* Hastings Center Report 27, no. 2 (1997), pp. 34–42.

5. For an extended treatment of the consequences of mediation, see my *Intermediate Man* (Indianapolis, IN, and London: Hackett, 1981).

Chapter 15

1. Immanual Kant, *Critique of Judgment,* J. H. Bernard, trans. (New York: Hafner, 1968), pp. 216–222.

2. G. W. F. Hegel, *Phenomenology of Spirit,* A. V. Miller trans. (Oxford, Oxford University Press, 1977), p. 45.

3. Ibid., p. 213.

4. G. W. F. Hegel, *Introduction to the Philosophy of History,* in *Hegel Selections,* J. Loewenberg, ed. (New York, Scribner's, 1929), p. 365.

5. Ibid., p. 372.

6. Ibid., p. 380.

7. G. W. F. Hegel, *Elements of the Philosophy of Right,* Allen W. Wood ed. (Cambridge: Cambridge University Press, 1991), p. 361.

8. Ibid.

9. Hegel, *Philosophy of History,* p. 380.

10. Fichte, *The Science of Knowledge,* P. Heath and J. Lachs, ed. & trans. (Cambridge University Press, 1982), pp. 83–84.

11. Ibid., p. 84.

12. Ibid., p. 83.

13. Ibid.

14. Ibid., p. 84.

15. Arthur Schopenhauer, *The World as Will and Representations,* E. F. J. Payne, trans. (New York: Dover, 1969) p. 354.

16. Ibid., p. 353.

17. Ibid., p. 206.

18. Ibid., p. 276.

19. C. S. Peirce, "Some Consequences of Four Incapacities," in *Collected Papers of Charles Sanders Peirce,* Charles Hartshorne and Paul Weiss eds. (Cambridge, MA: Harvard University Press, 1963), p. 5.317. Nathan Houser has been kind enough to call my attention to two variants of this idea which show Peirce's connection to Fichte even more clearly. The first (*Writings,* vol. 2, p. 162) reads: "we can discover ourselves by those limitations which distinguish us from the absolute Ego." The second (*Writings,* vol. 2, p. 169) declares: "Error and ignorance, I may remark, are all that distinguish our private selves from the absolute ego."

20. C. S. Peirce, "The Law of Mind," 6.143.

21. The tone of American philosophers is remarkably uniform concerning individually. Emerson exalts individuals to the point of ascribing impossible powers to them. Personalists from Bowne to Brightman see permanent and indestructible value in finite persons. The standpoint from which W. E. B. DuBois, Alain

Locke and Jane Addams, to mention but a few, examine social problems is always that of suffering individuals.

22. See especially such essays as "On a Certain Blindness in Human Beings," in *Talks to Teachers on Psychology* (Cambridge, MA: Harvard University Press), pp. 132–149.

23. William James, *The Will to Believe and Other Essays in Popular Philosophy*, (Cambridge, MA: Harvard University Press, 1979), p. 191.

24. William James, *Pragmatism*, (Cambridge, MA: Harvard University Press, 1975), Lecture IV, pp. 63–79.

25. William James, "The Will to Believe," in *The Will to Believe*, pp. 13–33.

26. William James, "The Moral Philosopher and the Moral Life," in *The Will to Believe*, p. 145.

27. Ibid., p. 141.

28. Ibid., p. 149.

29. Ibid., p. 144.

30. Ibid.

31. William James, "The Moral Alternative to War," *Essays in Religion and Morality*, (Cambridge, MA: Harvard University Press, 1982), pp. 162–173.

32. John Dewey, *Experience and Nature, The Later Works, 1925–1953*, Volume I, Jo Ann Boydston, ed. (Carbondale: Southern Illinois University Press, 1988), p. 170.

33. Ibid., p. 169.

34. Ibid., p. 171.

35. Ibid.

36. Ibid.

37. F. H. Bradley, "My Station and Its Duties," in *Ethical Studies* (Indianapolis: Bobbs-Merrill, 1951), pp. 98–147.

38. Josiah Royce, *The Philosophy of Loyalty* (Nashville, Vanderbilt University Press, 1995), p. 57.

39. Ibid., p. 16.

40. Ibid.

41. Ibid.

42. See footnote #48.

43. Ibid., p. 16.

44. Josiah Royce, *The World and the Individual* (New York: Dover, 1959), Second Series, p. 432.

45. Ibid., pp. 434–435.

46. Ibid., pp. 449–50.

47. George Santayana, *Scepticism and Annual Faith* (New York, Dover, 1955), p. 7.

48. George Santayana, "The Unit of Ethics is the Person," in *Physical Order and Moral Liberty*, John and Shirley Lachs, eds. (Nashville: Vanderbilt University Press, 1969), p. 196.

49. Ibid.

50. Ibid.

51. Ibid.

52. Ibid., p. 197.

53. Santayana gives powerful descriptions of the spiritual life in *Plantonism and the Spiritual Life* and in chapters 5–9 of *The Realm of Spirit.*

54. Immanuel Kant, *Critique of Practical Reason and Other Writings in Moral Philosophy,* L. W. Beck, trans. (Chicago: University of Chicago Press, 1949), pp. 225–227.

55. Kant, *Critique of Pure Reason,* p. 152.

56. Hegel, *Phenomenology of Spirit,* p. 10.

Chapter 16

1. George Santayana, *Character and Opinion in the United States* (Garden City, NY: Doubleday, 1956), pp. 39–60, and elsewhere.

2. "Dewey's Naturalistic Metaphysics," in *The Philosophy of John Dewey,* P. A. Schilpp, ed. (New York: Tudor, 1951), pp. 245–261.

3. A good example is in *Character and Opinion,* p. 8.

4. John McCormick, *George Santayana* (New York: Knopf, 1987), p. 186.

5. Ibid., pp. 186, 446. Also, *Character and Opinion,* p. 53, "Dewey's Naturalistic," p. 252, and elsewhere.

6. Sandra Rosenthal, *Speculative Pragmatism* (Amherst, MA: University of Massachusetts Press, 1986), p. 3.

7. H. S. Thayer, *Meaning and Action* (Indianapolis, IN: Bobbs-Merrill, 1973), p. 227.

8. George Santayana, *Scepticism and Animal Faith* (New York: Scribner, 1937), Triton Edition, vol. 13, pp. 149–167. Hereafter, SAF.

9. SAF, p. 161.

10. Ibid., p. 163.

11. George Santayana, *Realms of Being* (New York: Cooper Square, 1972), p. 280.

12. Ibid., pp. 382–398.

13. SAF, p. 237.

14. Ibid., p. 238.

15. "An animal vision of the universe is, in one sense, never false." *Realms,* p. 456.

16. SAF, p. 160.

17. William James, *Pragmatism* (Indianapolis, IN: Hackett, 1981), pp. 92–93.

18. SAF, p. 160.

19. George Santayana, "Apologia Pro Mente Sua," *The Philosophy of George Santayana,* P. A. Schilpp, ed. (LaSalle, IL: Open Court, 1940), p. 541.

20. Santayana, *Realms,* p. 207.

21. Rosenthal, *Pragmatism,* p. 33.

22. Santayana, *Character and Opinion,* p. 49.

23. Santayana, "Dewey's Naturalistic," pp. 251, 253.

24. Rosenthal, *Pragmatism,* p. 128.

Chapter 17

1. Daniel Cory, his literary executor, sold portions of Santayana's library to interested universities. A significant collection of his books may be found in Austin at the University of Texas Library.
2. George Santayana, *Scepticism and Animal Faith* (New York: Dover, 1955), p. vii.
3. Ibid.
4. Ibid., pp. v, vi.
5. Ibid., p. ix.
6. Ibid., p. v.
7. George Santayana, *Platonism and the Spiritual Life*, in *Winds of Doctrine and Platonism and the Spiritual Life* (New York: Harper, 1957).
8. George Santayana, *The Sense of Beauty* (New York: Scribner's, 1986).
9. George Santayana, *Realms of Being* (New York: Cooper Square, 1972).
10. John Lachs, ed. *Animal Faith and Spiritual Life: Previously Unpublished and Uncollected Writings by George Santayana with Critical Essays on His Thoughts* (New York: Appleton-Century Crofts, 1967), p. 368.
11. *Realms of Being*, p. 341.
12. *Realms of Being*, p. 572.
13. *Scepticism*, p. 179.
14. Ibid., p. 293.
15. *Scepticism*, pp. 70–71.
16. George Santayana, "Some Meanings of the Word 'Is,'" in *Obiter Scripta*, J. Buchler and Schwarz, eds. (New York: Scribner's, 1936).
17. *Scepticism*, p. 284.
18. Santayana presents a marvelous discussion of these and related terms on pp. 270–271 of *Scepticism*.
19. Ibid., p. 217. See also *Realms of Being*, p. 816.
20. *Platonism*, p. 301.
21. *Realms of Being*, pp. 335ff.
22. *Platonism*, p. 256.
23. Ibid., p. 257.
24. Ibid., p. 248.
25. Ibid., p. 247.
26. *Realms*, pp. 736ff.
27. Ibid., p. 769.
28. *Scepticism*, p. 209.
29. *Platonism*, p. 288 and elsewhere.
30. Ibid., p. viii.

Chapter 18

1. *Collected Papers of Charles Sanders Peirce*, 8 vols, Charles Hartshorne and Paul Weiss, eds. (Cambridge, MA: Harvard University Press, 1931–1958). Hereafter

CP in text. References are followed by volume and parapraph numbers (i.e., vol. 6, paragraph 51).

2. *Writings of Charles S. Peirce: A Chronological Edition,* 5 vols, Max H. Fisch et al. eds. (Bloomington: Indiana University Press, 1982–. Hereafter W in text. References are followed by volume and paragraph numbers.

3. Jeremy Bentham, *Introduction to the Principles of Morals and Legislation,* J. Lafleur, ed. (New York: Hafner, 1970), chap. 2.

4. This is by no means the only account Peirce gives of scientific method, but it is the clearest and most systematic.

5. J. G. Fichte, *The Science of Knowledge,* P. Heath and J. Lachs, trans. (Cambridge: Cambridge University Press, 1982), p. 83.

Chapter 19

1. George Santayana, *Realms of Being* (New York: Cooper Square Publishers, 1972), p. 319. RB hereafter.

2. T. L. Short makes this point nicely in his "Peirce's Concept of Final Causation," *Transactions of the Charles S. Peirce Society* XVII (1981), 370.

3. He disagrees with those who think that mental acts *exist* only in the view of folk psychology. For Santayana, the error or illusion relates not to the existence of consciousness but to its own view of what it can accomplish.

4. *Collected Papers of Charles Sanders Peirce,* Charles Hartshorne and Paul Weiss, eds. (Cambridge: Harvard University Press, 1931–5), 6.25. CP hereafter.

5. CP 6.264.

6. CP 6.102.

7. CP 6.101.

8. CP 6.156.

9. CP 6.304.

10. CP 6.305.

11. CP 6.157.

12. CP 1.175.

13. From time to time, Peirce hints that he views simple consciousness as mental or at least as a psychological phenomenon, as well. But it is clear that he associates mind primarily and predominantly with thirds.

14. CP 6.104.

15. George Santayana, *Scepticism and Animal Faith* (New York: Dover, 1951), pp. 284ff.

16. CP 7.364.

17. CP 7.366.

18. RB 332.

19. CP 1.3.

20. RB 829.

Chapter 20

1. Paul Weiss, *Nature and Man* (New York: Henry Holt, 1947), p. 134.

2. See, for example, *Nature and Man,* pp. 130–132.

3. Ibid., p. 267.

4. *Nature and Man,* p. 134.

5. Ibid., p. 127.

6. Ibid., p. 128.

7. Paul Weiss, *Philosophy in Process,* vol. 7 (Carbondale, IL: Southern Illinois University Press, 1978), p. 498.

8. Ibid., p. 138.

9. *Man's Freedom* (New Haven, CT: Yale University Press, 1950), p. 201; *Modes of Being* (Carbondale, Ill.: Southern Illinois University Press, 1958), p. 49.

10. *Man's Freedom,* pp. 37–38.

11. *Philosophy in Process,* vol. 7, p. 499.

12. Ibid.

13. Ibid., p. 498.

14. Ibid.

15. R. C. Lewontin, *Biology as Ideology* (New York: Harper Perennial, 1992), p. 68.

16. I discuss these limits in "Human Natures," *Proceedings and Addresses of the American Philosophical Association* 63 (1990): pp. 29–39.

17. *Philosophy in Process,* vol. 7, p. 123.

18. Ibid., p. 124.

Bibliography

Aristotle, *Nicomachean Ethics*, Terence Irwin, trans., Indianapolis: Hackett, 1985.

Bentham, Jeremy, *Introduction to the Principles of Morals and Legislation*, J. Lafleur, ed., New York: Haffner, 1970.

Bradley, F. H., *Ethical Studies*, Indianapolis: Bobbs-Merrill, 1951.

Constant, Bejamin, *Political Writings*, trans. and ed. Biancamaria Fontana, Cambridge: Cambridge University Press, 1988.

Descartes, Rene, *Meditations on First Philosophy*, John Cottingham, trans., Cambridge: Cambridge University Press, 1996.

Dewey, John, *Art as Experience*, in *The Later Works*, vol. 10, Jo Ann Boydston, ed., Carbondale & Edwardsville, Ill.: Southern Illinois University Press, 1987.

———*Experience and Nature*, in *The Later Works*, vol. 1, Jo Ann Boydston, ed., Carbondale & Edwardsville, Ill.: Southern Illinois University Press, 1988.

———*The Philosophy of John Dewey*, P. A. Schilpp, ed., New York: Tudor, 1951.

Dupre, John, ed., *The Latest on the Best: Essays on Evolution and Optimality*, Cambridge, MA: MIT Press, 1987.

Epictetus, *The Handbook*, Indianapolis: Hackett, 1983.

Fichte, J. G., *The Science of Knowledge*, P. Heath and J. Lachs, trans., Cambridge: Cambridge University Press, 1982.

Goodman, Nelson, *Ways of World Making*, Indianapolis: Hackett Publishers, 1978.

Hegel, G. W. F., *Elements of the Philosophy of Right*, Allen W. Wood ed, Cambridge: Cambridge University Press, 1991.

———*Introduction to the Philosophy of History*, in Hegel Selections, J. Loewenberg, ed., New York: Scribner's, 1929.

———*Phenomenology of Spirit*, A. V. Miller trans. Oxford: Oxford University Press, 1977.

Heidegger, Martin, *Poetry, Language, Thought*, Albert Hofstader, trans., New York: Harper and Row, 1971.

Hobbs, Thomas, *Leviathan*, in *Selections*, ed. F. J. E. Woodbridge, New York: Scribner's, 1930.

James, William, *Essays in Religion and Morality*, Cambridge, MA: Harvard University Press, 1982.

————*Pragmatism,* Cambridge, MA: Harvard University Press, 1975.

————*The Will to Believe and Other Essays in Popular Philosophy,* Cambridge, MA: Harvard University Press, 1979.

————*The Writings of William James,* J. J. McDermott, ed., Chicago: University of Chicago Press, 1977.

Kant, Immanuel, *Critique of Judgment,* J. H. Bernard, trans., New York: Haffner, 1968.

————*Critique of Practical Reason and Other Writings in Moral Philosophy,* Lewis White Beck, trans., Chicago: University of Chicago Press, 1949.

————*Critique of Pure Reason,* trans. Norman Kemp Smith, London: Macmillan, 1953.

Lachs, John, ed., *Animal Faith and Spiritual Life: Previously Unpublished and Uncollected Writings by George Santayana with Critical Essays on His Thoughts,* New York: Appleton-Century Corfts, 1967.

————*Intermediate Man,* Indianapolis, IN, and London: Hackett, 1981.

————*The Relevance of Philosophy to Life,* Nashville, TN: Vanderbilt University Press, 1995.

Lewontin, R.C., *Biology as Ideology,* New York: Harper Collins, 1993.

McCormick, John, *George Santayana,* New York: Knopf, 1987.

Mill, John Stuart, *On Liberty,* in *Essential Works of John Stuart Mill,* Max Lerner, ed., New York: Bantam, 1961.

Nietzsche, Friedrich, *Thus Spoke Zarathustra,* in *The Portable Nietzsche,* Walter Kaufman, trans., New York: Viking, 1954.

Peirce, Charles Sanders, *Collected Papers of Charles Sanders Peirce,* C. Hartshorne and P. Weiss, eds., Cambridge, MA: Harvard University Press, 1931, vol. 1.

————*Writings of Charles S. Peirce: A Chronological Edition,* 5 vols, Max H. Fisch et al. eds., Bloomington: Indiana University Press, 1982.

Plutarch, *The Lives of the Noble Grecians and Romans,* trans. John Dryden, New York: Random House, 1932.

Rosenthal, Sandra, *Speculative Pragmatism,* Amherst, MA: University of Massachusetts Press, 1986.

Royce, Josiah, *The Philosophy of Loyalty,* Nashville, Vanderbilt University Press, 1995.

————*The World and the Individual,* New York: Dover, 1959.

Santayana, George, *Character and Opinion in the United States,* Garden City, NY: Doubleday, 1956.

————*Obiter Scripta,* J. Buchler and Schwarz, eds., New York: Scribner's, 1936.

————*The Philosophy of George Santayana,* P. A. Schilpp, ed., LaSalle, IL: Open Court, 1940.

————*Physical Order and Moral Liberty,* John and Shirley Lachs, eds., Nashville: Vanderbilt University Press, 1969.

————*Platonism and the Spiritual Life,* in *Winds of Doctrine and Platonism and the Spiritual Life,* New York: Harper, 1957.

————*Realms of Being,* New York: Cooper Square, 1972.

————*Reason in Common Sense,* New York: Scribner's, 1905.

————*Scepticism and Animal Faith,* New York: Scribner's, 1937.

————*The Sense of Beauty,* New York: Scribner's, 1896.

Schopenhauer, Arthur, *The World as Will and Representation,* trans. E. F. J. Payne, New York: Dover, 1969. vol. 1.

Sheehan, James J. and Morton Sosna, eds., *The Boundaries of Humanity: Humans, Animals, Machines,* Berkeley: University of California Press, 1991.

Stuhr, John J., ed., *Philosophy and the Reconstruction of Culture: Pragmatic Essays after Dewey,* Albany, New York: SUNY Press, 1993.

Thayer, H. S., *Meaning and Action,* Indianapolis, IN: Bobbs-Merrill, 1973.

Weiss, Paul, *Nature and Man,* New York: Henry Holt, 1947.

————*Philosophy in Process,* vol. 7, Carbondale, IL: Southern Illinois University Press, 1978.

————*Man's Freedom,* New Haven, CT: Yale University Press, 1950.

————*Modes of Being,* Carbondale, Ill.: Southern Illinois University Press, 1958.

Wilde, Oscar, *The Picture of Dorian Gray,* Baltimore: Penguin Books, 1959.

Index